The Symbolic Language of Religion

An Introductory Study

THOMAS FAWCETT

The Symbolic Language of Religion

An Introductory Study

SCM PRESS LTD

334 01566 9

First published 1970
by SCM Press Ltd
56 Bloomsbury Street London WIC1B 3QX

© SCM Press Ltd 1970

Printed in Great Britain by
Billing & Sons Limited, Guildford and London

Contents

Preface

THE STUDY which forms the basis of this book was first undertaken as preparation for a course of lectures delivered for the Extramural Department of the University of Liverpool and as part of the Divinity course at Chester College of Education.

It attempts to provide a broad survey of the nature of religious language, to clarify the meaning of the terms used and to outline its development. While particular attention is paid to the Hebraic–Christian tradition, this is set within the larger context of world religion and seen against the background of mythology. It seeks, therefore, to be a guide to a vast subject and will have achieved its purpose if a basis is given on which further study can be undertaken.

My debt to a large number of scholars in various fields of research will be apparent from the notes. To some of these I owe the transformation which has taken place in my own understanding of the subject while writing this book and for this I am profoundly grateful. I should also like to express my gratitude to the SCM Press for making the publication of my work possible, to my colleagues for their encouragement, and especially to my wife who has given freely of her time, assisting with the preparation and typing the manuscript.

PART ONE

Forms of Symbolic Language

I Sign-Language

THE PREVALENCE AND SIMPLICITY OF THE
LANGUAGE OF SIGNS

WE BEGIN our study of the nature of symbolic language in
religion with a consideration of sign-language. There are two
fundamental reasons for starting our exploration at this point:
signs are one of the commonest forms of symbolic langue in
both the secular and the religious life, and they are a comparatively simple and direct form of faith-language.

Sign-language abounds in the art and architecture of
Christianity. It finds its place in stained-glass windows, in
the carvings of lecterns, pulpits, choir stalls and screens, in the
banners which drape the walls or stand proudly in a corner,
and even in the tiling of the floor. A church building is able
in this way to spell out the faith of those who use it in a simple
and direct manner, making use of signs which are recognizable
throughout the Christian world. These signs constitute, therefore, a kind of language which transcends national and de-
nominational barriers. They enshrine the heritage of Christian
faith in a way that goes back to its earliest days.

The use of sign-language varies greatly in its extent in the
various churches of Christendom, appearing most abundantly
in those churches whose roots are oldest. The reason for this is
not hard to find. In the Middle Ages, sign-language flourished
because it was the easiest means of providing a basic statement
of the content of the faith to men and women who were largely
illiterate. In churches, the windows, walls, screens and pews
formed a visual statement of Christian faith, a kind of picture-

13

book story of Christian history. The Reformation coincided with the emergence of printed books, diminishing the need for such visual material, and its protest against the dangers of idolatry led to a number of the churches abandoning all visual portrayals whatsoever. Those churches which have their roots in a puritanical, post-Reformation era are thus largely devoid of sign-language. This also has its dangers, for the worshipper is provided with little aid to contemplation, and in the starkness of a bare-walled church is thrown entirely on his own interior resources and his ability to conceptualize.

THE CHARACTERISTICS OF SIGNS

The simplicity of sign-language derives from its basic nature. Signs are denotative; they stand for or point to a specific object, event or person. They are therefore a clear means of recognition. The work of the sign-writer is that of one who enables the public to locate the merchant or service required by providing signs which are generally and immediately recognizable. For this purpose it is essential that the signs should not be ambiguous in any way, but indicate precisely and specifically. In order to achieve its purpose, a sign must not be able to represent a number of different trades or professions, but must have a clear one-to-one relationship with that which is signified. The sign-language of much Christian art is unambiguous in precisely this way, enabling the viewer of a religious painting, a stained-glass window or a piece of sculpture to identify both the historical event being portrayed and its significance for faith.

If signs are to be read, however, their language must be learnt, for signs are only meaningful by convention. Signs are not intrinsic symbols; they have no built-in resemblance with that which they signify, and so they cannot be read off by anyone who has not learnt their language. Sign-language is not in this respect in any way different from ordinary language in which each word is a sign for a particular idea, object, person or action. English makes sense to the Englishman because he has grown up to associate particular words with their referents.

The English-speaking foreigner has achieved the same end by a more laborious learning process in which English words have been associated with words in his native tongue and both together with those entities signified by the words. In so far as religious sign-language is largely made up of hieroglyphs, i.e. of certain shapes, ideograms or basic pictures, it resembles more obviously the sign-language of the sciences, of mathematics, chemistry, astronomy and physics. Any of these sign-systems must be learnt to be understood; for the connection between sign and referent is entirely a matter of convention.

Signs are, in fact, characteristic of the scientific method in so far as they operate entirely on the level of object-thinking. They refer to entities considered as objects, as entities whose characteristics are known by observation. They do not attempt to 'get inside' that which they signify. The colour blue enables us to identify the Virgin Mary in a painting, but it in no way enables us to achieve any knowledge of the subjectivity of the mother of Jesus and it is not in itself capable of speaking to our subjectivity, i.e. of being existential. It is important to note that signs signify that which is known or believed to be known. A sign simply designates something for our convenience, but it does not of itself have the ability to open up new areas of knowledge or experience.

We begin to see now that sign-language is the product of a group of people who share a common heritage or a common interest which is pursued by the use of conventions which everyone in the group holds. Signs are a social phenomenon, arising out of the life and work of a society and having validity only within that society. It is, of course, true that certain sign-languages have become almost universal, as in the case of mathematics, but this has arisen solely because men and women have universally agreed to adopt the same conventions. An example of the way in which a particular sign-system can move towards universality is afforded by the steady change towards a decimal system, a system whose sign-language is arbitrary, but a common allegiance to which will afford greater facility on the international scene. In so far as the development of modern technology has broken down many of the barriers between peoples, there is an increasing tendency for sign-language to become universal.

We are not yet, however, at the stage of a universal sign-system, and the social origin of signs is still much in evidence. The significance of the colour white varies dramatically, for example, in that in the west it is the sign of purity and chastity while in the far east it often signifies death. There are numerous examples of the creation of sign-systems with the avowed object of erecting a communication system restricted to a particular group of people. Societies have been created throughout history of people who wished to employ a secret sign-language. In some cases this was necessitated by circumstances of persecution and danger. It was in this way that the cryptograms of the early Christian church came into being, for while it was essential to be able to recognize a fellow Christian, it was equally necessary that such recognition should not be possible for informers and hostile authorities. These cryptograms have survived and found their way into the common stock of Christian sign-language. The use of the fish as a sign of Christian allegiance in the early church is well known. Similarly, abbreviations for the name or titles of Jesus were employed and are a common feature in Christian churches to the present day.

While signs can function perfectly well when they are merely arbitrary devices, as in the case where letters of the Greek or Hebrew alphabets are used to signify specific manuscripts, they are not always void of all logical relationship with that which is signified. It is necessary, therefore, to distinguish two kinds of sign-language, an arbitrary and a logical one. Purely arbitrary sign-language is employed, for example, in algebra and astronomy. In these cases the choice of the sign is neither determined by any intrinsic characteristic nor by any historical or other relationship. In a vast area of sign-language, however, there is this logical connection. The choice of tradesmen's signs and of numerous heraldic devices was determined by some sort of logic. In religious sign-language there is almost always some vital connection between a religious sign and its referent.

We must now see what kind of logic determined the choice of religious signs in Christianity.

THE CREATION OF LOGICAL SIGNS

The Bible provided an important quarry for Christian sign-making, although Scripture itself does not normally use the word sign in the sense adopted here.[1] By deriving signs from its sacred literature, the Christian community embodied the substance of sacred history into its life and worship. The simplest way of creating a sign out of scripture was to translate a text into a visual sign statement. The clearest example of this procedure is seen in the use of the Greek letters alpha and omega. This derives, of course, from the book of Revelation,[2] and the portrayal of these letters in Christian churches was a simple way in which the Christian could express his allegiance to Christ as the dominating influence in his life and the context in which life and history received its meaning. The cryptogram of the fish already referred to was similarly derived from scripture. Not only did the Greek word for fish spell out in letters a short form of the Christian creed – Jesus Christ, Son of God, Saviour – but it was also associated with a number of incidents in the biblical narrative, so that it was capable of representing such concepts as the divine eucharistic feeding and the resurrection.

The signs which were created to indicate biblical characters were almost always taken from some outstanding characteristic belonging to the story of the person concerned. The combination of a javelin and crown easily suggested the career of king Saul to those familiar with the narrative. Similarly, a harp represented king David and scales of justice stood for king Solomon. The obviousness of these devices was such that they could still be used in the twentieth century on stamps issued by the state of Israel. The heraldic devices of apostles and saints were usually obtained from biblical narratives substantially supplemented from legendary material. They invariably make use of the instrument of a saint's death as a sign, for in this way not merely his identity was indicated but also his character as witness, martyr, for the faith. In this way sign-makers were led to make some statement as to the character and theological importance of the person portrayed. The use of keys to represent St Peter recalled both the biblical incident narrated in Matthew and the theological importance of Christ's pronouncement. The simple device of leaving the shield of Judas Iscariot empty, on the other hand, was capable of evoking a direct and substantial theological insight.[3] At this point we can see that signs have the capacity to assume symbolic power.

THE POWER OF SIGNS

The type of sign which we have just been considering is closely related to the way in which ideograms or ideographs are formed. Ideograms are non-phonetic visual symbols representing an idea, for example the use of a triangle to represent the Trinity. The triangle is at once an indicating symbol which can merely replace the word Trinity, and also embodies a fundamental theological concept, namely that of three in one unity. The pictorial representation in this case is therefore something more than a mere sign. In a rather simple manner it participates in the reality it attempts to indicate, which (as we shall see) is one of the chief characteristics of symbols. The circle of eternity functions in the same way. Here we have a sign which is universal in usage, an indication of its symbolic power, which also mirrors the reality towards which it points. This is just one of the ways in which signs take to themselves the character of symbols and become charged with power.

Another common way in which signs increase their power is by the simple expedient of being used together in a systematic relationship which may be called a sign-complex. We need, however, to distinguish two types of such sign-complexes, for they operate at quite different levels, the one being void of symbolic power and remaining essentially within the limitations of signs while the other begins to possess power to such a degree that it virtually becomes symbolic.

The first type of sign-complex operates at the level of one-for-one correspondence, the fundamental characteristic of signs. As a means of communication the isolated sign is of very little importance or value, but when signs are connected together in a logical way, their power of expression is increased to far more than the total of the signs employed. For example, a series of signs devised for those who are deaf and dumb is capable when used of functioning as a language with all the expressiveness of which a spoken or written language is capable. The economy of sign-language is capable of making statements of universal truths when used in the ordered structure provided by mathematics or formal logic. In each of these cases we do not have merely a collection of signs: in addition to a vocabulary (the signs) there is also a grammar (the ordered structure in which they can function).

We are dealing here with forms of communication, with a language. In order for the language to function, the signs embodied within it must be related to one another in a coherent way. When this is achieved, the possibilities of statement are increased and further, the sign-language can become the medium of investigation and discovery. Reflection upon the extent to which the sign-complex of mathematics has been the means for the furtherance of knowledge in the sciences is sufficient to spell out the power that is inherent in the use of signs when they are used within an ordered structure or system of relationships. Hypotheses can be set up in the sign-language of mathematics and validated or invalidated logically and experientially. The progress of science would have been impossible without this tool. It is not, of course, accidental that the supreme example of this first type of sign-complex should be associated with the sciences, for the sign in its primary or non-symbolic form has been found most appropriate to scientific thinking. The associations of the sign are with objective, empirical thinking, whereas the symbol (again, as we shall see) is associated with the emotional and existential levels of human operation.

The second type of sign-complex tends to transcend the level of the sign. Musical signs are in themselves trite yet capable in combination of making expressive emotional and conceptual statements. Similarly, artistic devices can be used in a total structure of pictorial statement in such a way that the signs cease to constitute a mere code but come to possess evocative power at both the emotional and intellectual levels. We need here think only of the impressive sign-complexes set forth in the iconographic murals of Byzantine art at Ravenna and elsewhere to appreciate how a number of formalized devices or signs have been used in such a way as to possess tremendous symbolic power.

SIGNS AND SIGNALS

The association of signs with specific experiences can transform them into signals. A signal is a physical stimulus which is operated through physical, chemical or biological messages, etc. We are constantly played upon by such signals which tell us that we are hungry, tired or cold. We share these signals with the animal world, for all organisms participate in this signal world, all are exposed to such messages. They are not created by man, but are built into the physical structure of which we are a part. A sign becomes charged with such evocative power when it has been associated with a meaningful, existential experience. We are all familiar with the way in which a song, a street, a name can become important to us emotionally because reference to it recalls experiences of importance to us. Sometimes these associations are pleasant, and we experience a good deal of pleasure as the sign brings back nostalgic memories. On the other hand, the sign may evoke memories which are painful, leading us to avoid sight or mention of the associated sign.

One of the commonest ways in which signs operate as signals is provided by our system of traffic lights. These are purely arbitrary devices or signs to which we have learnt to respond. They are not a part of nature, for at first we have to be taught to recognize these man-made signs and the appropriate responses to them. After some continued experience of them, however, the signs begin to act as though they were true signals. The practised driver does not think through his instruction when suddenly faced with a red light, for he has allowed himself to be conditioned to respond instinctively to it so that his foot moves almost unconsciously on to the brake pedal. A sign has become a signal.

Signs may be created for the specific purpose of operating as a signal for a particular community, powerful enough to overcome the natural signals which are likely to emerge on a field of battle. A regimental standard is in itself a purely arbitrary sign which has no emotive power for the recruit. In the course of time, by a process of association deliberately and constantly maintained, the standard can come to represent the regiment and carry in itself the power of a signal. The standard or regimental sign thenceforth has the power to evoke the sensations of pride and loyalty, respect and obedience. When such standards were carried into battle they were capable of providing a focus for the emotions of the troops, the sign being preserved even at the cost of life. Flags of one kind or another are probably the commonest example of this kind of sign, performing the function of a signal to a community despite their originally arbitrary character. The importance of such devices is clear from the fact that each new movement which wishes to gain the loyalty of its members to the greatest possible extent, inevitably resorts to the creation of signs of some kind which it seeks to charge with emotive power by the creation of a tradition, a sequence of events with which the sign is seen to be intimately associated.[4]

THE SIGN OF THE CROSS

Up to this point we have ignored the sign which came to have the greatest power in the context of Christianity, the cross. The history and nature of this sign is an extremely complex one and includes within its history many of the features of signs which we have already noted. These we shall now examine briefly and in doing so we shall observe yet another feature of signs, that they possess a life-span in the course of which their significance can vary greatly in intensity and radically change in orientation.

The cross has become a common means of recognition. It appears lifted high above Christian churches, it marks the location of a church upon ordnance survey maps and is embodied in all sorts of devices which by the inclusion of this item are immediately known to be Christian. It possesses, therefore, the primary characteristic of a sign, the ability to identify (in these instances) a building, a person or a book as Christian.

The choice of the cross as the Christian emblem was not, of course, an arbitrary one. It was chosen for the same reason that many of the signs of the saints were chosen, because it re-presented an event in the career of Jesus which expressed his character and the nature of his mission. The adoption of the sign was a momentous event. In the Roman empire at large the cross was an instrument of degradation and pain, of foreign occupation and tyranny. The use made of the cross in the Roman empire charged it with great emotive power for the subject races of the Mediterranean.

When it was adopted by the Christian community, it appeared strange and unacceptable. To the men and women who had witnessed mass crucifixion, the glorying of St Paul in the cross of Jesus appeared inexplicable. In fact the im-portance attached to the crucifixion by the early Christians was a subject of ridicule by their contemporaries. What made the cross acceptable to the Christian community, however, was the resurrection, and the form of the sign which they adopted was that of the empty cross which pointed beyond the crucifixion to the victory over death in the rising from the dead. The Christians took a common sign of defeat and death, turning it into a sign of triumph and life. Even as late as the sixth century the portrayal of the crucifixion, of Christ suffering on the cross, was offensive to Christian eyes, for the only cross which was really acceptable in the early centuries was that which signified everlasting life.

Once accepted, the ideographic possibilities of the sign could be related to the resurrection event. The sign of the cross was a common one in the ancient world and appears in many diverse places in civilization. The significance of these signs appears to have been largely ideographic. The Latin form of the cross was, however, the distinctive Christian form. Ideographically it could represent the resurrection because its combination of the vertical and the horizontal expressed the meeting place of history and eternity. In this way the early Christian Church charged a potentially powerful ideogram with supreme evocative power by bringing it into association with the historical event of Christ's death and resurrection. It is this process of finding the significance of an ideological sign embodied in an historical event that was characteristic of Christian faith.

Within the Christian community the symbolic possibilities of the sign of the cross were discovered to be diverse. It began its life as a sign of the resurrection, a usage which was perhaps helped by the fact that it had been used as a sign for immortality in ancient Egypt, but later its association with the suffering and death of Christ became paramount. This development took place particularly in the thirteenth century, when the sign tended to become a crucifix in order to stress the death element in the cross. Such a form of the cross became a favourite with ascetics, contemplatives and mystics. Their type of Christian piety centred upon meditation on the sufferings of Christ and is exemplified most obviously in the life of St Francis of Assisi, whose meditation on the suffering element in the sign of the cross enabled him to participate in the experience of Christ to such a degree that he developed the stigmata or wounds in his own person.

On the other hand, other forms of the cross stressed the idea of Christ as Lord, and in this case the figure on the cross is not portrayed as a sufferer but as a king adorned in his glory and power. This form of the sign was a favourite of those who were concerned with social reform and with the spreading of the Christian message of freedom throughout the world. These men took it as the sign under which they would create the kingdom of God upon earth. Unfortunately, a train of events was sometimes set in motion which created a very different association for the sign than that of freedom and spiritual victory. The ancient Byzantine empire and its ideological successor the Tsarist church of Russia undoubtedly intended to create a Christian world, but the adoption of the programme by the state brought the sign into association with power which was not always used according to the spirit of Christ. The form was easier to maintain than the spirit of the cross, and ultimately it was perhaps inevitable that the sign of the cross should sometimes be identified not with the servant Lord but with the autocratic power wielded pretentiously in his name. Such a process created a new symbolic factor for the cross: it came to stand for despotism and cruelty which had to be destroyed in the name of freedom and humanity.

In the various examples which have been cited it is clear that the cross achieved its power as a sign by its association with true symbols such as the shedding of blood, resurrection and kingship. Its power as a sign was constituted by the fact that it stood for real symbols, while of itself it could be nothing but a conventional designatory shape which might be used at will as a mere device, as on the shields and standards of the crusaders. At the present time the cross has become a mere sign again for a large number of people. The figure which has been such a powerful one in the course of Christian history, often correctly called the story of the cross, has now become problematic. When it is not anchored clearly in an associated symbol, it ceases to have meaning at any depth or to be charged with any emotive power. In this way signs can experience a kind of death, although they may linger as a carcase which waits to be revivified.[5]

NOTES

1 An exception is found in Acts 28.11, where reference is made to the emblem of Castor and Pollux, twin heroes of Greek myth. The frequent allusion to signs in scripture is usually of the type dealt with in ch. 10.

2 Rev. 1.8; 21.6; 22.13.

3 For comprehensive treatments of Christian emblems see L. H. Appleton and S. Bridges, *Symbolism in Liturgical Art*, Charles Scribner's Sons 1959; G. Cope, *Symbolism in the Bible and in the Church*, SCM Press 1959; G. Ferguson, *Signs and Symbols in Christian Art*, Oxford University Press 1961.

4 For a most useful discussion of symbolic language from the perspective of psychology see J. Havens (ed.), *Psychology and Religion*, Van Nostrand 1968.

5 For a detailed study of the development of the sign of the cross see C. E. Pocknee, *Cross and Crucifix*, Mowbray 1962; N. Laliberté and E. N. West, *The History of the Cross*, Macmillan 1960.

2 Symbols

IN OUR DISCUSSION of the nature of signs we have had occasion
to make use also of the word symbol. It is necessary now to
attempt to clarify the current use of this term in the consideration of religious language. In popular usage the word
symbol is used to cover both the figures we are to examine in
this chapter and those we have designated as signs. Until
recently this was the usage also in academic circles, and a
nineteenth century book on Christian symbolism would almost
certainly turn out to be a delineation of the signs, figures,
monuments to be found in a Christian culture. While this use
of the term is still found, the renewed interest in the nature of
religious language both in philosophy and psychology has led
to the necessity to distinguish sign from symbol. This is now
being done with increasing unanimity.[1]

The origin of the word 'symbol' derives from the Greek, in
which it denoted such tallies as the two halves of a broken coin
which were exchanged by contracting parties, or any token
which established a person's identity such as a soldier's badge
or watchword. S. I. Hayakawa depends upon this etymology
when he defines symbol-making as 'the process by means of
which human beings can arbitrarily make certain things stand
for other things'.[2] This definition is, however, more appropriate
to the word sign, as we have described it. We shall see that a
symbol is not created arbitrarily in the way that a sign can be.
The symbol does, however, share with the sign the capacity to
stand for something other than itself, but in a way which opens

up possibilities which are closed to the sign. We have already noted that signs become really powerful, at least in a religious context, only when they are associated with a symbol. When the sign of the cross was associated with certain universal symbols, it became existentially powerful to such a degree that the designation of the cross as a symbol almost seemed appropriate. This is perhaps an added reason for the embracive use of the term symbol. It seems to be acceptable for things which apart from certain associations would clearly be regarded as signs. The symbol has a potential far above the capacity of the sign, and it is this that we must now explore.

THE INTRINSIC CHARACTER OF SYMBOLS

Symbols are not created, but born out of life. They do not come into being like signs as a result of the creative faculty of man's imagination. The symbols of darkness, light and water, for example, were given to man with his existence in the world. They were not even isolated by any arbitrary decision, for these elements in man's experience forced themselves upon him in a way he could not ignore. They were the powerful forces impinging on his being. In seeking to understand and come to terms with them, man attempted to reach through them to the reality which they mediated; he used them as symbols. Nor was their adoption in this way as key figures for man the result of a social convention, for the most powerful symbols have been universal. For example, the sun has been understood as a symbol of creative power in such scattered areas of the earth as Egypt, Greece and America.

Symbols therefore appear to be built into man's experience as such. This fact has been given considerable attention by the work of psychologists, particularly C. G. Jung, who noted the universality of symbolic motifs both in ancient and modern times. J. Daniélou argues from this fact that 'the only acceptable conclusion is that the existence of a common set of symbols in the various religions is due to the parallelism of mental processes', and goes further to arrive at the conclusion that 'this

hat the objective reality of the symbols themselves must
non ground as well.'[3] At all events, it is clear that the
universality of what we have called symbols indicates that they
derive from a common experience and a common manner of
responding to that experience.

THE VERSATILITY OF SYMBOLS

A most important feature of symbols lies in their richness of
expression. They have what Josiah Royce calls 'surplus
meaning', the ability to speak to man of many things. Whereas
a sign must refer specifically to one object, person or event, a
symbol is able to refer to a variety of things at different times
and places. Whereas the sign has a one-to-one relationship,
the symbol has a one-to-many relationship. In fact a true
symbol appears to be always capable of new applications and
evocative of new insights. Water confronts man in his existence
in many different ways. Sometimes water is cool and refreshing,
suggesting the beneficence of creation. In the midst of flood or
storms at sea, water assumes a malevolent aspect and symbolizes
the ultimate threat to man's existence. It is hardly surprising
that water should be a universal symbol and most ambivalent
in its meaning, at one time suggesting life and regeneration, at
another destruction and death. Even within the context of the
Christian faith, the richness of the symbol is apparent.
Daniélou draws our attention to this by pointing out that 'a
whole corpus of "death and resurrection" symbolism sur-
rounds the theme of water, from the Creation to the Last
Judgement, through the Flood, and the Atonement, and the
laver of regeneration'.[4] Thus we see, as E. Cassirer remarks,
that 'a genuine human symbol is characterised not by its
uniformity but by its versatility.'[5]

This ambivalence of symbols is partly due to differences in
geographical and cultural environments. The environment of
the Babylonians led them to stress the character of water as a
symbol of destruction, for they were constantly threatened by
the overthrow of their homes by flood. In Egypt and Palestine,

on the other hand, no such terror of water was normally experienced, and in these countries water usually symbolized the creativity of nature. This diversity of experience gave rise to what Erich Fromm calls symbolic dialects, a usage of symbols peculiar to a particular group of people or geographical environment.[6] In this context J. E. Smith stresses the organic relationship of symbols to historical situations, the variations in which give rise to different psychological needs.[7]

The significance of a symbol is not unlimited. It has both flexibility and constancy. The 'multiplicity of signification' is bounded by 'the natural qualities of the symbol'.[8] A symbol operates because it bears a relationship with that symbolized. This lays a limit upon its use. The symbol can only reveal what is present within it. The symbolism of fire possesses versatile content. It can represent reality in its devouring aspect. The Hebrews could speak of God as a consuming fire, even equating his name with fire.[9] Yet even this frightening aspect was seen as meaningful as a work of refinement or cleansing.[10] On the other hand, fire could represent God's energetic revelation of himself as in the story of the burning bush.[11] The early Christian fathers used it as an analogy in discussing the doctrine of the Trinity, drawing out the parallelism between the relationship of fire and flame and the relationship of God the Father and the Son. This versatility, however, was clearly restricted by the nature of fire itself, and its use is always related to the qualities inherent in fire as a physical phenomenon.

LANGUAGE FOR ULTIMATE REALITY

E. A. Nida remarks that 'language has been recognised as . . . in a sense a kind of model of the way in which people view their world'.[12] If this is true of language as a whole, it is certainly true in a most significant way of symbolic language. Even sign-language expresses man's understanding of the nature of things. Symbolic language, however, attempts far more than signs. It attempts to reach out to grasp that which is not immediately known. Symbols do not denote things which are already understood, but attempt to push forward the frontiers of knowledge and to grasp the reality of things, the real nature of life, the stuff of existence itself. They push beyond the frontiers of empirical objectivity and seek a subjective appropriation of the transcendent. They are not concerned like signs to deal with the observable and measurable aspects of human experience, but attempt to get beyond the empirical to meaning and value. Daniélou holds, for example, that 'the real significance of symbols' is 'to afford us access through the visible world into a higher transcendent plane of being'.[13]

Symbolic language operates for this task by taking images derived from the world of sense experience and using them to speak of that which transcends them. G. E. Wright expresses the point by saying that man 'does not encounter the world directly. He creates, or has created for him, a world of symbols through which he experiences, interprets, and perceives "truth" in the objects, processes, people, nations and cultural heritage in the midst of which he lives.'[14] The only tools at man's disposal are those which lie around in his experience. He is not content with the mere handling of these physical things, but is endowed with a passion for knowledge of the meaning which lies behind them and which he believes they can point to, of which they can be symbolic. This is a truth which has long been recognized in the history of philosophy. John Caird, for example, said: 'Faith speaks, and necessarily speaks, in the language of one world, the world of sense and sight, concerning the things of another world, the world unseen and eternal. It presents the spiritual to us through images borrowed from the sensible and external.'[15]

There can be little doubt that it is in the sphere of religion that this symbolic process is most obviously in evidence. It is the primary concern of religion to get beyond the appearances to the reality, but the language of religion has always found it necessary to make use of the language of appearances in order to speak of that reality. 'A religion', says Wright, 'is the structuring of a certain group of symbols which are understood to portray ultimate reality and the manner in which meaningful life is to be lived in relation to it.'[16] The Bible in particular is recognized as a 'vast structure of symbols and sign events which are expressive of the nature and purpose of God'.[17] We shall find that this symbolic language of the Bible constantly appropriates images derived from sense experience and uses them as windows on the transcendent reality which is its concern. The age of radical criticism in the later nineteenth century was characterized by the intent of many, both Christians and their opponents, to take all biblical statements as physical fact and argue their validity on that basis. Only with the recognition that these writings were often poetic and symbolic could the misguided arguments of that era be brought to an end. The use of apparently physical or sense statements as a means of expressing spiritual reality was largely responsible for this confusion in an age which tended to look back on the biblical era as peopled by men and women who lacked their own poetic and romantic sense. Progress in understanding scripture may in fact be said to be proportionate very largely to the extent to which its symbolic character is recognized.

In the age of rationalism in the eighteenth century and of materialism in the nineteenth century, it appeared to many that man had overcome the need for symbols and could know the world as it is. The success of science in its investigation of the nature of matter was so great that the intimate secrets of the universe seemed to be opening up. This attitude was often adopted not only in scientific but also in theological circles. John Caird, whom we have already quoted, goes on to say that 'it is only by rising above the symbolical or representative form that we can grasp the reality which they "half reveal and half conceal" '.[18] Many philosophers of Caird's day were impatient of the concealment of ultimate truth and believed that the symbolism of religious language could be swept away as the archaic survival of a less capable era. Others, however, had already recognized the permanence of the symbol and not merely in the religious but also in the scientific sphere. Thus Herbert Spencer remarked that: 'Ultimate religious ideas and ultimate scientific ideas alike, turn out to be merely symbols of the actual, not cognitions of it.'[19] In our own time this recognition of the symbol has increased, and many could agree with L. K. Frank when he says that science consists of turning the 'Secrets of Nature' into symbolic codes.[20] The importance of investigating the nature of the symbol is now recognized in many diverse fields of human exploration, in the social sciences, in psychology and in the history of religions. Symbols have constantly been the means whereby man has attempted to understand the universe and his place within it. For this reason the description of man and his history cannot be attempted without paying due regard to them. Efforts to approach the problems of reality without recourse to symbols have ended in failure. That branch of philosophy called metaphysics which is connected with the nature of ultimate reality is now in many quarters abandoned as impossible. Such a retreat into agnosticism, however, is unable to satisfy, for without a view of reality within which man can orientate his life, that life becomes meaningless. The necessity of metaphysics is derived from existence and cannot be abandoned. If however, there are no direct means of knowing or stating ultimate truth, man is forced to operate at the level of the symbolic. Symbols turn out to be the only way in which the nature of being may be explored and our relationship with it stated.[21]

In this endeavour man is confronted by a range of symbolic possibilities. The potential symbols in his experience determine the limits through which he can understand reality, and his receptiveness to these symbols determines his outlook. The history of man's use of symbols reflects his changing view of the universe and of his relationship to it. From this there emerges a most important characteristic of symbols, namely their power to direct our thinking and our orientation towards life. It is this characteristic which makes the development of symbol systems so interesting for understanding the development of man, and it will concern us a great deal later in our study. Thomas N. Munson points out that this is an important distinction between the sign and the symbol, for the sign merely points to something whereas 'the symbol directs our manner of thinking about an object'. He cites the well-known symbol of the shepherd which, when applied to the power ruling our lives, 'gears the mind to think of providence and divine care'.[22] The importance of this characteristic will emerge as we discover that the potentiality of certain symbols for laying bare the meaning of life varies considerably. Some symbols are potentially rich in discovery while others turn out to be restrictive.

THE EXISTENTIAL CHARACTER OF SYMBOLS

The existential character of symbols has already emerged quite clearly. They operate at the level of the subject and not that of objects. They are not part of our discursive discussions of that which lies outside the self, of our intellectual manipulation of reality as made up of series of objects. They are concerned with man's subjectivity and with the subjectivity of the cosmos itself. They work intuitively and directly out of man's experience of himself as self to grasp that subjectivity which lies in the whole realm of being. The symbol, says Munson, is born in and for an encounter, or, as Martin Buber would put it, for dialogue between the I and the Thou. The richness of the Bible in symbolism is very largely explained by the fact that it is a book which seldom indulges in intellectual debate about the nature of God but is constantly concerned to speak of man's relationship with God in person-to-person encounter. From this flow the multitude of personal-level symbols such as father, teacher, lover, nurse, guide. These are symbols which can only be constituted if man is seen as a partner in the relationship they indicate, even though the role may sometimes be a passive or a subordinate one.

The symbol of faith is the key, in fact, to the ability of man to participate in that experience which constitutes what we call faith. The dominance of particular symbols determines the level at which men enter into relationship with reality. When the dominant symbols are those of nature, such as light, darkness and fire, the level of personal relationship is inhibited.

B

When personal symbols such as father and lover are dominant, a truly human relationship with the order of being becomes possible. In either case the symbol provides the means of relating his subjectivity to reality, although the nature-symbols will not allow that subjectivity full play. The unsatisfactory character of nature-symbols for man is clear from the universal tendency to anthropomorphize them, to raise them to the level at which an I and Thou dialogue is possible. Fire, for example, was first venerated for itself, for its inherent power. For it to become a means of access to a truly human existence, fire had to become a god.

Because this relationship is only accessible through the symbols, the failure of the symbol for an individual results in his being barred from the attainment of a meaningful orientation towards reality. The importance of symbols in this context has been clearly recognized by many psychologists. Hans Schaer, for example, says that 'for many religious persons the symbol is *the* expression of faith and cannot be replaced by a better; and that only those who have found access of some kind to the symbol can have any idea of what religious experience means to such persons'.[23] Following the understanding of symbolism contained in the work of Jung, Daniélou points out that symbolism belongs to the structure of the self so that its use 'provokes an intuitive response in the soul'.[24]

The result of symbolic activity, therefore, is the attainment of emotionally experienced meaning. At the level of subjectivity, mere intellectual or logical construction, however impressive, is insufficient. That which may be known at the level of signs can leave the knower untouched in his being, whether it is algebra or ecclesiastical heraldry. Assent to a proposition is not an existential experience and correct theology is no criterion of a satisfactory faith-relationship. On the other hand, symbolic discourse is rooted in human experience as subject and results in deep psychological change. Symbols speak to the ontological anxiety of man, his concern to understand the roots of his own existence which he seems to hold under constant threat of non-being.[25]

The validation of symbols can only take place subjectively. From what has been said it is clear that one cannot create or destroy symbols by intellectual argument. Their persistence at times can even appear to be irrational. Symbols are adopted because they answer to the subjective needs of man and are validated in his experience. The appearance of irrationality is deceptive. Symbols must submit to existential criteria. Certain indications of the way in which symbols validate themselves can be discovered from the way in which they operate in human history.

The maintenance of a symbol over a long period of time is some indication of the satisfactory nature of the symbol. It clearly has the power to evoke a response in man. It continues to 'ring true' because it helps to make sense of human experience. Symbols have the power of gripping men, of laying hold upon them. We seem to have an example here of what Karl Barth would have seen as 'the analogy of grace', that operation whereby God confers on human language the capacity to speak meaningfully of himself to man.

From the history of symbolism we can have some fairly clear understanding of the results in the human soul which enable a symbol to prolong its life. First, those symbols which have been most evocative for man are invariably those through which he can encounter ultimate reality in a meaningful way. Almost every symbol of importance speaks of that which man ultimately comes up against in his experience. In religious language we would say that they speak of God in some way or of the powers which he opposes on behalf of man. Second, these symbols have the power to enhance the being of man, to create healthy existence, to open his being. Symbols are not retained which finally turn out to diminish man. Friedrich Nietzsche declared the death of God because the symbolic content of the concept had become for him and many of his generation a limiting and dehumanizing factor.

Life-giving symbols have the capacity to become demonic. When the symbol is taken literally, when the sense-object of the symbol is taken as the reality itself, then the symbol becomes a destructive force. This is that realm of Satan of which scripture so often speaks, the realm of idolatry. The worship of an idol is nothing other than the elevation of a thing to the level of God, of the symbol to identification with ultimate reality. The symbol of kingship has over a long period of time been capable of providing a satisfactory orientation of man towards reality, and yet it could become demonic.

When the symbol of kingship was used for God to the exclusion of counter balancing symbols, God was presented as a despot destructive of man's humanity. God became an idol to be smashed. A particular use of a symbol can therefore be declared invalid. Experience can show that it does not measure up to the facts. Two important criteria of falsity can be distinguished, corresponding to the factors which prolong the life of symbols. First, the partial may never be used for the whole; one symbol can never prove satisfactory when it excludes others. Second, a symbol has ceased to be valid when it results in the diminishment of man.

The ability of symbols to influence the life of men in such fundamental ways indicates the most important fact: that they involve commitment. Because they operate at the level of the subject, they demand response from men in their character as persons. When God is characterized as a father, the symbol calls upon men to play the part of sons. If the symbol of the husband is attributed to God, it implies the correlative that there is a wife, an image which Israel developed at some depth and which helped to shape the concept of religious chastity and loyalty. The shepherd symbol directed the Hebrew mind towards the need for a sense of trusting dependence on the part of man when confronted by God. The kingship symbol inculcated loyalty, respect and obedience. A symbol is never neutral, but always calls upon man to play his part in the dialogue between God and man which it opens up. In this lies the power of symbols to direct the life of men, to determine their moral behaviour and bring out their spiritual potentialities. Religion is specifically concerned with commitment. It requires the giving of himself by man to that which is revealed.

For this reason a religion marks men and women out according to their response or commitment. It is never content to assert its symbolism in a neutral way or require a merely intellectual assent. It insists that its symbolism must determine both the understanding and the way of life of its adherents.

NOTES

1 F. W. Dillistone has edited a collection of writings which attempt to clarify this distinction and other terms relevant here: *Myth and Symbol*, SPCK 1966; see also E. Bevan, *Symbolism and Belief*, Allen and Unwin 1938, republished by Fontana Books 1962; F. W. Dillistone, *Christianity and Symbolism*, Collins 1955.

2 S. I. Hayakawa, *Language in Thought and Action*, Harcourt, Brace 1949, Allen and Unwin 1952, p. 25.

3 J. Daniélou, *The Lord of History*, Longmans Green 1958, p. 133.

4 *Op. cit.*, p. 131. Compare the symbol of night instanced by Daniélou on p. 132.

5 E. Cassirer, *An Essay on Man*, Yale University Press 1964, p. 36.

6 Erich Fromm, *The Forgotten Language*, Holt, Rinehart and Winston 1951.

7 J. E. Smith, *Reason and God*, Yale University Press 1961, p. 229.

8 J. Daniélou, *op. cit.*, p. 132.

9 Deut. 4.24; Isa. 30.27.

10 Isa. 6; Mal. 3.2.

11 Gen. 15.17.

12 E. A. Nida, *Message and Mission*, Harper and Row 1960, p. xi.

13 J. Daniélou, *op. cit.*, p. 135.

14 G. E. Wright, 'History and Reality: The Importance of Israel's "Historical" Symbols for Christian Faith', in: B. W. Anderson (ed.), *The Old Testament and Christian Faith*, SCM Press 1964, p. 183.

15 John Caird, *The Fundamental Ideas of Christianity*, James Maclehose and Sons 1899, Vol. 1, p. 54.

16 G. E. Wright, *op. cit.*, p. 183.

17 J. E. Smith, *op. cit.*, p. 238.

18 John Caird, *op. cit.*, p. 54.

19 Quoted in the *Oxford English Dictionary*, s.v.

20 L. K. Frank, 'The World as a Communication Network', in: G. Kepes (ed.), *Sign, Image and Symbol*, Studio Vista 1966, p. 11.

21 See D. Emmet, *The Nature of Metaphysical Thinking*, Macmillan 1945.

22 T. N. Munson, *Reflective Theology*, Yale University Press 1968, p. 93.

23 Hans Schaer, *Religion and the Cure of Souls in Jung's Psychology*, Routledge and Kegan Paul 1951, p. 81.

24 J. Daniélou, *op. cit.*, p. 135.

25 See G. Zunini, *Man and his Religion*, Geoffrey Chapman 1969, which gives substantially the same view of symbol as that outlined in this chapter. Compare Paul Tillich's treatment of symbol in his *Systematic Theology* I–III, Nisbet 1953, 1957, 1964, and the discussion of it in W. L. Rowe, *Religious Symbols and God*, University of Chicago Press 1968.

3 Allegories and Parables

ALLEGORIES AND parables have often been confused because they are both narrative forms of symbolism. It is, however, important to maintain the distinction between them, for serious misunderstanding can result when a parable is taken as an allegory. In the history of biblical exegesis this became so common that the real meaning of Christ's teaching was obscured by the abundance of unintended correspondences which the church fathers were able to find. Only in comparatively recent times, through the work of C. H. Dodd and others, has the real nature of the biblical parable been recovered.[1]

The fundamental structure of allegories differs from that of parables. An allegory belongs to the category of the sign, the parable to that of the symbol. They represent the development of these two types of discourse in narrative form. If the criteria already established to determine the difference between signs and symbols are applied respectively to allegories and parables, the distinction between them emerges quite clearly.

ALLEGORIES

The most fundamental characteristic of an allegory, as I. T. Ramsey describes it, is that it 'tries to secure a one-to-one fit between two areas of discourse'.[2] A series of signs is set out against the reality of which they speak in an exact parallel relationship. Each element within the allegory is designed to denote a corresponding element in reality. The allegory given in Ezekiel 17.1–10 with its explanation in vv. 11–24 exemplifies this detailed correspondence, which is an essential element in

39

all allegorical discourse. The structure of the signs and their interpretation will be seen most easily in tabular form.

The Allegory (vv. 1–10)	The Interpretation (vv. 11–24)
A great eagle comes to Lebanon, takes the young twigs from the top of the cedar and carries them to the city of merchants, takes the seed of the land and plants it to become a low spreading vine.	The king of Babylon comes to Jerusalem, takes its king and princes and deports them to Babylon, takes a royal prince and makes a treaty with him allowing Israel the role of a subject kingdom.
The vine leans towards a second great eagle for sustenance, but will the vine flourish now it has been transplanted or will it be uprooted?	The prince rebels and asks help from Egypt, but can a treaty-breaker survive or shall not Babylon have its revenge?

A study of the passage will reveal not only the major correspondences given but also the subtlety of the wording of the allegory at each point. The reader would, for example, have little difficulty in translating the meaning of the first great eagle's 'great wings and long pinions, rich in the plumage of many colours', for the references to the long reach and power of Babylon's armies which had been successful in overcoming many nations needed no explanation from the prophet once the major clues had been given.

The allegory is also called a riddle in this passage, for the very good reason that until the major correspondences are given, the story is no more than an idle tale. To those who have not been initiated into the particular sign-language used, an allegory is no more than a puzzle. While the figures used in the allegory are appropriate representations, their inner meaning is an arbitrary one in the manner of signs.

When an allegory is provided with an explanation, as in Ezekiel 17, the matter of interpretation is done for us. In many cases however, allegory is not provided with a key or crib. This is the case, for example, with the Book of Revelation. This book has been a source of perplexity to exegetes throughout the centuries, for much of it is cast in allegorical form and many of the signs within it can no longer be deciphered with anything like certainty. We can presume that at the time of writing the narrative made good sense to most of the readers. Just as the original reader of Ezekiel 17 would understand the allegory more readily than ourselves because he was living in the conditions and situation portrayed by the allegory, so the reader of the Apocalypse would be able to relate the signs to the significant personages and events of the Roman Empire in the latter part of the first century. At this distance of time, many of the allusions which would have provided a basis of interpretation are lost, or have to be recovered by the slow process of archaeological and literary research.

The use of sign-language was in some cases probably demanded by the situation. The Book of Revelation and another largely allegorical work, the Book of Daniel, were written in the context of persecution and dealt with the political events of their day. By using the esoteric signs of allegory, the writers were able to speak freely about such matters without the content, which would have been regarded as seditious, being understood by the authorities. Only those with the same cultural background would be able easily to decipher the code-systems of these underground books. In this way the Jews of the Maccabean period and the Christians under hostile Roman emperors could encourage one another and speak of the slaying of the beast of oppression and the emergence of 'one like a son of man' who would set up the kingdom of God and his saints.[3] These books were intended for a restricted circulation among men and women who were initiated into the meaning of the signs.

It is clear, however, that the signs were normally chosen according to a certain logic. We have already noted the appropriateness of the description of Babylon as a great eagle and that the characterization of Israel in subjection as a 'low-spreading vine' is inherently suggestive of the real situation. In the same way the metals chosen as signs of the nations in the allegorical dream given in Daniel 2.31–35 are hardly fortuitous. The construction of this particular piece of allegory indicates more than a sequence of events; it suggests an evaluation of the nations to which it refers and a constant deterioration in the quality of the empires under whose sway the Israelites had been forced to live. The final characterization of the feet of the image as being made of iron and clay was undoubtedly intended to indicate the contempt which the Jews felt for their Syrian masters, whose desecration of the Holy City constituted such a final insult to the Almighty that the remnants of all the proud empires would become 'like the chaff of the summer threshing floors', to be blown away by the wind.[4]

It is typical of allegory that it should deal with the objective events of history, with political manoeuvres and economic disasters. The Pharaoh's dreams spoke of Egypt's economic difficulties, for which Joseph was able to plan because of his ability to read off the signs of the dreams. In such narratives we are not concerned with spiritual insight but with empirical fact and human ingenuity dealing with affairs. Allegories can light up the stark features of the situation, but they do not lead to the revelation of God. They speak of the known, and all that is required is a knowledge of the correct correspondences of which they speak.

PARABLES

The Hebrew word which is translated as parable derives from a root which denotes making some kind of likeness. A parable draws out a comparison between one thing and another. It can therefore be understood immediately and easily, because there is an obvious likeness between the parable and the real situation. In contrast to the allegory, no code is used and no key to its meaning is required. A parable can be used at any time by a speaker to any audience because it speaks in the language of universal experience.

Parables have this capacity to communicate meaning to all and sundry because they invoke the knowledge which all have of the situations of everyday life. They appeal to typical situations, to events which occur frequently in men's lives, to a fund of common knowledge. They can therefore characteristically begin with such expressions as 'Which one of you . . .?' When Jesus used his parables, he constantly relied upon his illustrations having a self-evident validity. He could say in effect that 'everyone knows this' or 'we are accustomed to doing this'. The images which he conjured up in the minds of his hearers were those which were familiar in the life of everyday. He reminded them of such common events as the loss of a sheep or coin, of the planting of seeds, the sowing of grain or the gathering of the harvest, of family quarrels, the division of legacies and the difficulties of hiring good workmen or servants. In this constant reference to common matters lay the appeal of the parable, which Jesus seems to have used as his principal mode of teaching in public.

The difficulty which we may sometimes have in seeing the point of a parable is likely to be the result of changing cultural circumstances rather than of any ambiguity in the parable itself. Because the parable draws on familiar situations, its reference to contemporary patterns of behaviour can make it archaic in time. Some of Jesus's parables depend upon a knowledge of contemporary customs. The parable of the wicked husbandmen relies to some extent on a common knowledge that landlords were often absent from their estates for most of the year, living in more comfortable climatic conditions in Italy. The story of the man who went in search of a kingdom, of deputations sent to prevent this, depended for its realism on a knowledge of local politics, of the location of ultimate sovereignty in Rome and of the way in which Jews of the time had to contend with puppet kings imposed upon them against their wishes. For this reason some of the parables only come alive when we gain by laborious historical research what was common knowledge to any Jew to whom Jesus might have spoken.

Such a knowledge of contemporary culture, however, is only required to understand the story as a whole. It is not required in order to set out the kind of detailed correspondence which is essential for the understanding of an allegory. A parable does not attempt to secure any exact parallelism or a one-to-one fit. When we are told a parable, we either *see the point* or fail to see it in a similar manner to the way in which we *see a joke* or fail to be amused. The story as a whole has a point or moral; the details are merely the clothing for it and have no independent value.

The point made by a parable, moreover, is not restricted to any one set of geographical or cultural circumstances. A knowledge of these (as we have seen) will help us to understand why the parable was put into its original form, but once the teaching of the parable is clear, it is one which conforms to the characteristic of symbol over against sign in that it can speak to many situations. It is for this reason that preachers have been able to make constant use of Jesus's parables throughout the ages and under vastly differing cultural situations. The lesson of each parable has been capable of being applied to life over and over again. This can happen because a parable states a universal truth, a truth which emerges out of the very nature of human life. In our day we no longer sleep on the floor of the living room in normal circumstances, but the midnight caller requesting help to deal with unexpected guests is still an inconvenient disturbance. It is of such typically human situations that parables are made, and they still highlight the existential character of life, the need for decision and compassion which can serve as an illustration pointing towards the character of God. In a parable we can see immediately a likeness in the characters to ourselves, see them having to make the kind of decisions forced upon us, and so we can still be illuminated by their message.

The parable authenticates itself in our experience. We do not accept its teaching because it satisfies the kind of criteria we apply to an argument. It appeals to our intuitive knowledge and to our imagination. It conjures up pictures in which we can see ourselves, and we know the truth of its teaching because we can look within ourselves and see its truth reflected there. As a symbol the parable moves on this intuitive, imaginative level of experience.

It is characteristic of a symbol that it should open up levels of experience otherwise locked away. The parable appeals to what is known and yet it opens up a new area of knowledge. On one level it lays bare our own true nature. As we see ourselves faithfully reflected in the story, we begin to see ourselves as we are. The parables of Jesus often caused men to turn angrily away from him. When he told the Pharisees the story of the wicked husbandmen, they recognized themselves in the story and became angry. He had told them nothing they did not already know in terms of history, but he portrayed it in such a way that it led his hearers to a new level of self-understanding. At another level the parable is used to open up a knowledge of that which lies beyond us. When Jesus used his parables to give his audience some idea of the nature of the kingdom of God he was attempting to do more than merely highlight their own existential experience. He was attempting to initiate them into the mysteries of the transcendent. For this purpose the analogical element within the parable came into play. Jesus compared a human reaction with a divine reaction, or rather he contrasted the volatile character of man with the eternally self-consistent character of the Creator. On this level also the parables opened up new levels of insight because as symbols they can point towards that in which they participate, with which they have an inherent relationship. The human is used to mirror, in however distorted a way, the divine.

Faced with a better knowledge of himself or of God, the hearer of a parable is forced into commitment or rejection. Symbolic language is never content with simply making a point in an argument. This is not the level on which it works. The parable is not content until a decision is made. An interesting example of this is found in II Sam. 12.1–10, which records a parable told by the prophet Nathan to king David. Nathan's parable leads the king to make a judgment on a certain type of behaviour. The story appeals to his inner moral sense and he sees the point of the parable very well. David is not, however, able to see himself in the parable. He is unable to realize that he has committed the very sin which he so loudly condemns in response to the parable. Nathan then has to say that the king himself is the man in the parable. The parable had been successful up to a point. It had not been successful in creating self-understanding. This has to be drawn out by the prophet, who cannot be content until David has committed himself to his own moral standards and judged his own behaviour in the light of them. This example gives us some understanding of the way in which the parables of Jesus functioned. The reactions to Jesus's teaching were varied. His stories were capable of being taken on different levels. Some thought he was always talking about other people, as David thought Nathan was speaking. Some realized only too well that they were a target for criticism embodied in the narrative but were not prepared to alter their way of life in response to the new insight they had achieved. Others again not only saw the point of the parable and applied it to themselves, but were prepared to act upon it. Of such people as these were his disciples made.

We can conclude our short study of the symbolic nature of parables with a brief examination of the story of Jonah. This has sometimes been taken for an allegory. While it is true that there are a number of correspondences between peoples and events in the narrative and the real situation in history, there is no detailed correspondence such as an allegory requires. The story is better taken as a parable. This particular example is of a satirical type which holds Jonah up to ridicule. The Jewish readers were invited to see themselves as being like the exclusive Jonah with his convenient theological equivocation in the face of the grace and mercy of God. The Jews of the day claimed that God was indeed the God of all men, and yet they remained inward-looking and, like Jonah, unable to face up to the fact that the divine favour was not a special preserve of the descendants of Abraham. The parable intends to open up a new understanding of the Jews themselves and of their God. In order to make its point, the story makes use of a good deal of humour. There was at one time much discussion about the whale which swallowed Jonah and vomited him up towards the direction in which he had been originally sent. The laboured researchers into the stomach capacity of sperm whales and the like failed to see the point or indeed the joke. Their inability to see the biting humour in the story was probably a simple reflection of an over-intense seriousness where matters of faith were concerned. The whale was a subordinate element in the story, but one which allowed the narrator to suggest in the most humorous terms that no man can escape the destiny which God has planned for him and that God will proclaim his judgment and mercy to Nineveh, Babylon (or Rome, Britain or America), in spite of any unwillingness among his chosen servants.

Parabolic teaching makes use of analogy for the purpose of illustration. Its method and function is aptly summed up by D. Emmet as being 'to bring out a relation by exhibiting it in a different context, which may be more familiar, or one in which the significance of the relation may be seen without prejudice'.[5] Parable is, however, only one example of the complex use of analogy; so to a consideration of the various forms and functions of analogical discourse we must now turn.

NOTES

1 C. H. Dodd, *The Parables of the Kingdom*, Nisbet 1935; J. Jeremias, *The Parables of Jesus*, SCM Press 1963; E. Linnemann, *Parables of Jesus*, SPCK 1966.
2 I. T. Ramsey, *Religious Language*, SCM Press 1957, p. 12.
3 Dan. 7.11 ff.; Rev. 19.20 f.
4 Dan. 2.35.
5 D. Emmet, *The Nature of Metaphysical Thinking*, p. 6.

4 Similes, Metaphors and Analogy

SYMBOLIC LANGUAGE depends on the presence of analogy within it in order to function. 'Where this analogical relation is ignored or exploded, symbolisation cannot be understood.'[1] If there were no correspondence between a symbol and the reality, its ability to speak of that reality would be gone. Symbols are able to participate in the reality because they share something with it, they are analogous to it.

The use of analogy has appeared constantly in human discourse. We often flatter ourselves into thinking that we speak of reality in a direct manner, but much, even of our ordinary conversation, is built up of words and phrases which on analysis turn out to be merely analogous. When we turn to the realms of science and theology it is virtually impossible to speak or write at all without recourse to this device. 'In the attempt to make the brute facts of experience intelligible,' says Milton K. Munitz, 'analogy plays a fundamental role.'[2] The attempt, for example, to speak of the phenomenon of light has led to the use of more than one analogy. One analogy was derived from the way in which particles of dust travel through the air. This gave rise to what was known as the corpuscular theory of light. Another analogy was derived from the way in which the sea forms waves on its surface. This led to the so-called undulatory theory of light. Both of these images were useful in that they accounted for some of the phenomena which had been observed. On the other hand, both failed to account for all the known facts. Light, as we now know, consists of neither particles nor waves, though these figures are still useful to describe certain aspects of the behaviour of light.

In the whole realm of discovery, analogy is a fundamental tool by which we can increase our understanding of the nature of things. As each new element in our environment is discovered, we are forced to rely very largely upon our ability to liken it to something already familiar. The function of analogy, for Munitz, is to make clear the unfamiliar and the unexplained by means of that which is already familiar and already explained.[3]

New discoveries can, of course, often be described in mathematical terms, that is, by reducing them to an already recognized sign system. Analogy, however, enables us to do more than speak in the language of signs. It makes it possible for us to picture or conceive, however inadequately, that of which we wish to speak. 'The scientist,' says Professor Toulmin, 'must be able . . . to look at the system of bodies he studies with a professional eye and "see" their behaviour in the way his theories require.'[4] The sign statement must be translated into an analogical statement in order to gain a perceptive 'view'. The use of analogy was particularly helpful to scientists like Sir James Jeans and Sir Arthur Eddington, who were most successful in communicating new scientific ideas to the general public. Toulmin points out the dangers inherent in this process.[5] When the layman is presented with these analogies, divorced from the mathematical formulation of the scientist, it is likely to cause some misunderstanding. The uninitiated may well fail to recognize the analogous character of popularizing statements and so confuse the analogy with the reality. Nor is this danger one to which the layman alone is subject. Scientists have themselves been misled. I. G. Barbour cites as an example of this the search for the 'ether', which was begotten by a literalistic understanding of the analogy of wave formations for the behaviour of light.[6]

The history of theology, like that of science, is largely made up of attempts to find satisfactory analogies. Like the scientist, the theologian has been forced to discard his images when they have led to a misleading line of thought. Just as there has been a tendency for a particularly useful analogy to dominate the scientific thinking of a certain era, so theological analogies have been made determinative at various times. In both cases, disastrous results have followed from the exclusive use of a particular analogy and the identification of the real state of affairs with it. The way in which analogies have developed in religion and theology will be the concern of later chapters in this book. Many religious controversies have been created by identification of a dominant analogy with reality. Despite the dangers, however, analogous language has proved indispensable as a means whereby the new and the unique may be mentally grasped in some measure by our minds and our perception sharpened. These dangers can only be overcome if the nature of analogical thinking is clearly understood and its limitations fully seen.

SIMILES

Analogy is self-evidently present in the use of similes. In a simile the analogy is declared. One thing is specifically said to be like another. Because the analogy is declared, there should be no misunderstanding of the analogical character of the statements, no danger of the simile being taken literally. If we are told that electrons behave within the atom like bees buzzing in a cathedral, we are immediately aware of the incongruity between the two. If we are told that the brain is like a telephone exchange, it is clear that the analogy would break down at many points. The similes are helpful in that they convey something of the nature of the reality to us by a striking comparison, yet the difference between the one and the other in each case is clear. We know that a simile cannot be used in an allegorical fashion. We cannot use each and every feature of the comparison, finding them in that which is being described. Rather, a simile functions much like a parable. It does not pose any detailed correspondence, but is intended simply as an illuminating picture which can highlight a basic feature.

D. M. Baillie uses a simile in his book *God was in Christ* to show the necessity of analogical language in speaking of religious experience. 'The attempt,' he writes, 'to put our experience of God into theological statements is something like the attempt to draw a map of the world on a flat surface, the page of an atlas.'[7] Cartography involves a transposition from one form which is three-dimensional to another form which is two-dimensional. In this way something of the nature of the reality is lost, but, on the other hand, a convenient method of description is attained. A similar process takes place when we are speaking of religious experience. Our language is largely derived from the things of sense, from the objective, empirical world in which we live as perceptive organisms. In spiritual or existential experience, however, we are in a non-sensuous realm, for the description of which our language derived from sense-experience can only function analogically.

It is hardly surprising, therefore, that the literature of religion abounds in the use of similes. The subject of religious experience is constantly saying 'it was like . . .'. Mystics have described themselves as being like burning logs in the fire, being united to God as a bride is joined to her husband, of passing through a dark night or of being transported as though they were in an alcoholic reverie. A psalmist uses a succession of similes to describe his experience in a prayer of supplication.[8] He speaks of his days passing like smoke or an evening shadow, of his bones burning as though they were in a furnace, of his heart smitten and withered like grass, as being like an owl of the waste places or a lonely bird on the house-top. Job described himself as having become 'like dust and ashes'.[9] Isaiah resorted to simile in order to describe the chastisement of Israel, speaking of his nation as being 'like a woman with child, who writhes and cries out in her pangs, when she is near her time'.[10] When men have wished to indicate the nature of their experience at depth, similes have proved a valuable tool. It is to be noted, however, that similes often turn into metaphors. The passage we have just quoted from Isaiah continues, 'So were we because of thee, O Lord; we were with child, we writhed, we have as it were brought forth wind.' The change from simile to metaphor is an easy transition, and it is noteworthy that metaphor plays an even larger part than simile in religious literature.

We must now consider the nature of metaphor and attempt to discover the reason why it is so often preferred in religious discourse.

METAPHORS

Metaphors have a direct quality absent from similes. They hide their analogical character. They are undeclared analogies. The metaphor appears to declare not merely a likeness but an identity, and in this lies both the strength and the weakness of metaphorical language. The weakness of the metaphor, or the danger that lurks within it, results from the hiddenness of the analogy and the possibility that the comparison will be taken literally. There is ample evidence that a large number of people have taken the metaphor in which God is said to dwell 'above the bright blue sky' quite literally. Even in the sphere of serious theology, the history of the doctrine of atonement bears witness to the danger that was present in the use of such metaphorical expressions as 'a ransom for many', a 'lamb without blemish' or 'our great high priest'. If a metaphor is sufficiently outrageous, it is not likely to be taken literally and used as a basis for theorizing and propositional thinking; but when metaphors are considered within a cultural situation to which they did not originally belong, misunderstanding is likely. The clear analogical character of the metaphor which was apparent to the original hearers may no longer be apparent in a later age. It is noteworthy that the metaphors used in atonement theology were undoubtedly outrageous when first used, and that the construction of theories out of them belongs to subsequent ages which became increasingly unaware of their outrageous character. In our common daily speech we use metaphorical expressions with such frequency that we fail to recognize them for what they are. We speak of a grain of truth, a cool reception, a biting wind or of being on fire with anger. The failure to recognize the metaphorical character of these phrases in our day-to-day speech involves little danger. When, however, our language is used to speak of less familiar and more problematic matters, the hiddenness of metaphors can cause difficulty. To speak of going *up* to town is not likely to cause confusion because the declaration that we are going to ascend spatially will not be taken literally. But when the word *up* appears in a religious context, misunderstanding does arise. The narrative of the ascension of Christ uses the spatial metaphor throughout, and Jesus is said to ascend to his Father. Religious people speak of their prayers ascending to God. If the metaphor is taken literally, as a propositional statement, then God is held to be located in space at a certain height. We are then faced with the situation which concerned Dr J. A. T. Robinson so much in his book, *Honest to God*, a situation in which the God of whom Christians speak is held to be 'up there'.[11]

The danger inherent in metaphors is the price which is paid for symbolic power. Metaphors are much stronger than similes, forcing perception upon us. The use of the word *like* cushions us against the impact in a simile, whereas the metaphor strikes home directly. It sharpens our perception in a vivid way and enables us to share in the vision of the user. Perhaps one of the strongest uses of metaphor appears in the narrative of the last supper. Christ's identification of his body with the bread and his blood with the wine was designed to create a revolution in the understanding of the disciples. Bread and wine were already familiar symbols to the Jews which were rich in connotation. The application of these symbols to Jesus was a startling innovation which opened up an entirely new range of meaning, sharpened the disciples' understanding of the events about to take place, and has been the means whereby countless Christians have been able to share in the bond of union thus made possible. On the other hand, the apparent identification of Jesus's body and blood with the bread and wine has led to a long history of metaphysical speculation and bitter argument at the propositional level. In this case the price paid for the use of metaphor has been very great indeed.

The function of the metaphor is not exhausted by its ability to bring about understanding. It shares with the parable the power to engage the audience in decision. When metaphors are used, for example, in St John's gospel, they are not merely illustrative, but imply acceptance or rejection. When Jesus claims to be the vine, he claims to be the true Israel, the vine of God. His identification of the disciples with the branches asserts that their life is one with his and nothing apart from him. The gospel presents these metaphors to the reader, who can only take them into his own usage when he is prepared to accept the claims they embody and commit himself to their truth. A simile may be used as a description which involves no more than some kind of evaluation. A metaphor, on the other hand, insists on being taken seriously at the deepest level, that of personal commitment. The way in which a simile appears to lessen the impact of an analogy in comparison with a metaphor may be illustrated by the way in which C. S. Lewis described his conversion experience. He says that God 'was the hunter (or so it seemed to me) and I was the deer. He stalked me like a redskin, took unerring aim, and fired.'[12] In this short passage we have the emergence of a metaphor whose potentiality for telling effect is mitigated by the employment of a bracketed qualification followed by a descent into a mere simile. For all the dangers which may be inherent in metaphorical language, the price must be paid if symbolic power is to be achieved. The prevalence of metaphor in the scriptures has undoubtedly been a major factor in giving them that quality of authority and response-evoking power which has maintained their position in the religious life of so many people.

ANALOGIES

In view of the prevalence of analogies in the symbolic language of religion, it is necessary to analyse the way in which they work in some detail. Only by being familiar with the precise nature of analogy can we avoid misuse and misunderstanding.

i *Strong and weak analogies*

We have already seen that an analogy is primarily constituted by the use of an image which corresponds in one or more respects with the reality of which it speaks. We can define this more closely if we observe that an analogy possesses both *positive and negative characteristics*. The positive content of an analogy consists of that which it has in common with that for which it stands. The negative content consists of those features which are not shared. In addition to similarity, there is dissimilarity. The extent to which there is a correspondence determines the strength and usefulness of an analogy.

An analogy which has few positive characteristics is weak to the point of being fanciful. If the structure built by Noah were compared to a fish, the analogy would fail to convey any understanding to the reader. It would have the capacity along with fish to survive in a time of flood, but apart from this there would be little positive content in the analogy.

If Noah's ark were compared to an Old English broad-beamed ship of unwieldy proportions, we should almost have a straightforward description of the structure. Such a statement is informative but is a *weak* analogy. The ark was intended to be some sort of floating vessel, and the only negative characteristics in the analogy derive from the fact that the ark, according to the information given, would have been most unlikely to have been given a certificate of seaworthiness.

A *strong* analogy for Noah's ark is provided by describing it as being a floating house. It had features in common with a house as we know it, and yet it was intended to survive in time of flood. The analogy conveys something of the size and shape which the ark would have had, and suggests its lack of propriety as a sea-going vessel. On the other hand, the ark was not constructed out of the materials normally used for house-building in ancient or modern times. The analogy is strong and illuminative because it possesses both positive and negative characteristics.

ii. *Types of analogy*

There are two major types of analogy which differ according to the kind of content which constitutes their positive characteristics. These two types were distinguished by St Thomas Aquinas in the thirteenth century, and have been generally recognized since that time. St Thomas named them the analogy of proportion and the analogy of proportionality. Later theologians have preferred to call them respectively the analogy of attribution and the analogy of proportion.

Whatever name is given to it, the first of these types consists of those analogies in which a predicate which properly belongs to a subject is used as a predicate of another subject in an analogical fashion. When the word 'wave' is attributed to the subject 'light', it has been transferred from its proper subject, 'the sea'. In technical language we say that the predicate'wave' has been transferred from its prime analogate 'the sea' to a secondary analogate 'light' and has become an analogue because it is being used in a related though not identical manner. This is possible because the analogue has a positive content: light shares with the sea certain characteristics in movement which can be described as wave formations. But there is also a negative content in the analogue. The word 'wave' is not being used in an identical sense, for light does not possess waves in the same manner as the sea. The waves of the sea are created by vertical movement only, while the 'wave' of light is conceived as travelling through space.

This type of analogy is the kind we were considering when describing Noah's ark. In each case we took a secondary analogate, fish, an Old English ship and a floating house, and compared them with the ark. Each of these comparisons made use of certain features only. Attributes of size, shape and function were predicated of the ark. Each analogy was able to contribute some of these attributes. Our most satisfactory analogy for the ark, a floating house, was a construct of our imagination made up of attributes properly associated with a raft or ship combined with others derived from a house. The first gave us the characteristic of floating and the other the implied size and shape.

The second type of analogy is made when the relationship between two pairs is seen as similar. We speak of vision being to the eye what intellectual understanding is to the mind. In this case we have used the word 'see' analogically. We have derived it from the sense experience of seeing with the eye and applied it to the mind. We have transferred the word 'see' from its prime analogate, 'eye', to a secondary analogate, 'mind'. This analogical usage is so common that it appears frequently in ordinary conversation. We speak of seeing the other person's point of view, of seeing the point, of seeing the joke. Sometimes the analogy is spelled out for us as in I Peter 2.5, where we are exhorted to allow ourselves to be like stones built into a house. At other times the analogy is hidden. The psalmist for example, speaks of his life being 'on the verge of death', which hides the analogy of relationship which we can set out in full as:

> As a man may be on the verge of a precipice,
> So my life is on the verge of death.

The word 'verge' is used of a secondary analogate 'death' in order to bring out the quality of the psalmist's situation.[13]

An extension of this type of analogy is found in what is known as the analogy *duorum ad tertium*. In this form of analogy two analogates are given a common analogue because they both have the same relation to a third analogate to which the analogue properly belongs. Thus we may speak of being on the verge of an important decision, on the verge of marriage as well as being on the verge of death. The phrase 'on the verge' is properly used, however, only of a precipice or a spatial edge of some kind. All other uses are analogical.[14]

iii. *The uses of analogy in religious discourse*

Both types of analogy have been used for two quite different

purposes. One of these has formed the basis for the construction
of a natural theology; this is the argument from analogy. This
method of building up a knowledge of God proceeds by the
examination of nature and argues to certain propositions about
the creator on the presumption that both types of analogy can
validly be used. The analogy of attribution is used as the basis
for inferring certain facts about the attributes of God. It is
thought that the creation must reflect something of the character of its creator and that therefore there must be an analogical
relationship between the attributes of the creature and God. In
this way it has been held that faculties of man, such as love,
purpose, etc., are also found in God, at least in a related sense.
The analogy of proportionality has similarly been used to
argue that relationships which exist within the created order
provide an analogy for the relationship between God and the
creation. The most famous example of this is probably W.
Paley's use of the watch, which suggested that God was
related to the universe as a watchmaker to a watch.

The use of analogy as a means of argument to establish the
nature of 'reality' or God has been subjected to a great deal of
criticism in recent decades. John Hospers roundly declares that
the argument from analogy is always false.[15] Dorothy Emmet
takes a more judicious view and claims that an analogy may
constitute a valid argument when 'the relation illustrated is
sufficiently alike in both cases for it to be possible to draw
conclusions from the one case to the other'.[16] But she goes on to
recognize that this cannot be the case with metaphysical
statements, because we are not then dealing with 'parallel
cases of a homogeneous type'. That this prevents the attainment of a knowledge of God by any argument from parallel
cases has long been recognized. In recent years the point has
been made most forcibly by some theologians, notably Karl
Barth, who, having contended that God is 'totally other',
refused to indulge in any form of natural theology. They have
argued rather that knowledge of God can only come by
revelation and that no propositional arguments of any kind can
ever arrive at the God of religious faith, but only at a mental

construction. John Baillie opposed the total denial of natural theology as presented by Barth, but nevertheless rejected the argument to God from analogy in his Hibbert Lectures.[17] He held that we do not gain our conception of perfection from this world because we do not experience it in this world. We could not even have arranged our human approximations in an ascending order and then lengthened the line to obtain an idea of the perfect, because without the idea of perfection already being present to us we would be unable to construct such a line. For Professor Baillie, therefore, our knowledge of God's perfection was the result of revelation. This, he held, was given 'in, with and under' the knowledge which we have of the finite. The two kinds of knowledge come to us together as one experience. Therefore, he argued, when we use such terms of God as wise, good, person, etc., this is proper language only when used of God and improper when used of men. These words would not then be attributed to God by analogy, but God would be their prime analogate. In this he followed the champion of the *analogia fidei* over the *analogia entis* or the argument from analogy, Karl Barth, who held, for example, that God is the 'incomparable prototype of all human creaturely fatherhood'. This approach to the problem of our knowledge of God turns the argument from analogy on its head and it is asserted that we are using analogical language when speaking of the creature, not when speaking of God.

The second purpose for which the way of analogy is used, according to Van A. Harvey, is to answer the question, 'How can one make significant statements about the infinite in concepts that are derived from the finite?'[18] This second usage of analogy appears within the total structure of symbolic language so that man may speak meaningfully about God and his acts. This language (as we shall see) emerges out of religious experience in which disclosures of the nature and acts of God take place. Because these disclosures are of that which transcends the sensual and objective plane of our existence, they cannot be spoken of in the language derived from that plane except in an analogical way. They have, however, the quality of giveness on which Karl Barth and John Baillie insisted. This second usage implies, like the first, that there is an analogical relationship between the nature of God and that which appears within the created realms, but it does not proceed by logical argument. Symbolic language emerges out of convictions already attained, out of experiences already grasped. It does not attempt to arrive at convictions by any kind of propositional logic. The prophets of Israel were propelled into their work by experiences which we normally term their 'call'. In this initial experience they were confronted by God, they encountered the divine. We gain a sense of the overwhelming nature of these experiences even from the brief descriptions which scripture affords. They are at first like Peter's at the transfiguration of Christ, who did not know what to say. When writers do find words in which to describe their experience, they resort to the language of symbol. Isaiah spoke as though all the familiar sights of the temple came alive. The seraphim embroidered on the temple veil took to their wings, formed a choir of praise and touched the prophet's lips with a live coal from the altar of sacrifice. The description of God himself is couched in the symbolism of royal majesty and extended to convey the sense of his pervasive presence. Out of the experience Isaiah came to a new understanding of the holiness of transcendent being and of its demands upon his own life.[19] The experience gave rise to the symbols. In no way can we imagine Isaiah deducing his new conception of God from that which had been familiar for most of his life. Rather, it was the experience which provided the understanding and the symbols in which it could be communicated.

The difference between the two uses of analogy now becomes apparent. The first usage relies exclusively upon the cold power of reason. It attempts to handle the transcendent within the categories of objective and abstract thinking. The second usage, on the other hand, is embedded in symbol and subordinate to the symbol. The symbol appeals to the imagination, not to the reason. It points man towards the transcendent and essays to lift him beyond the realm of objective thinking. Nor can the analogy within the symbol be isolated from it and handled as though it were part of a propositional argument. Symbolic language severely limits the analogical element, qualifying it and shaping it in order that it should not be used discursively. The symbolic use of analogy is akin to Anselm's faith seeking understanding rather than to understanding seeking faith.

The symbolic use of analogy has been employed most frequently in discussing the nature of certain events and in speaking of the nature of God.

The Hebraic-Christian tradition is centred upon specific events in the history of men. Symbolic language makes use of analogy in speaking of all these events. The way in which it operates, however, is clear from a consideration of its use in connection with that event which created the Christian faith, the resurrection of Christ. The modern reader owes a debt of gratitude to Professor Wolfhart Pannenberg for the way in which he has replaced this affirmation at the centre of the Christian faith once more.[20] We owe him a particular debt for the way in which he makes clear the function of symbolic language in the description of this event. Pannenberg insists that the resurrection of Christ was an event in ordinary history. That event was, however, to date a unique event and as such it could only be spoken about and have meaning if certain elements were present in the understanding of it. One of these elements he cites as an adequate metaphorical expression. Because it was a unique event, it could not be classed with other events of the same kind. It could only be compared to events of a similar kind. It could only be spoken of analogically. He points out that an adequate metaphorical expression lay near to hand. Isaiah 26.19 had already spoken of the dead living again in terms of an awakening from sleep. When the experience of the disciples validated the belief in resurrection which was already a tradition in the thought of many Jews of their time, they naturally turned to this expression as a means of explicating the nature of that event to themselves and conveying it to others.

This analogy, however, is not presented as a logical construct but as a metaphor. We have already seen that a metaphor has a range of power which transcends that of formal logic. The daily experience of rising out of sleep was capable of being a powerful image when used as a metaphor. It was an evocative image associated with feelings of new opportunities and the constant revival of human powers. To examine the biological factors in the process of awakening from sleep would be totally misguided in attempting to attain the meaning which they were trying to convey. Such a line of thought could only lead to some idea of resuscitation whereby a corpse was revivified and continued to live the same kind of life as before. This is certainly not what they meant. They wished to convey the message that Christ had conquered death as the night is conquered by the new day. In order to make this clear they found it necessary to qualify their use of the analogy of awakening from sleep.

The gospel narratives of the resurrection make strange reading when understood at the objective, spatial or biological level. We read of a body passing through closed doors, of appearing and disappearing in a moment, of a body which can be touched, of a body that must not be touched, of a man who eats fish and walks upon water. Many misguided writers have attempted to reconcile these various features as though they were data for the construction of a biological hypothesis. While such an event must have had a content which may at some time be expressed in biological terms, it is fairly clear that this is not the kind of information which the evangelists are trying to provide. They make it quite clear that the event is not to be regarded as an example of a common biological event. On the contrary, they are asserting its oddness. They are employing one of the most frequently used methods of qualifying their analogy, that of contradictory images. No one of these images is to be taken without the others, and none of them are to be taken as scientific data. If a biological description were successfully attained, it would not serve the purpose of an evangelist. The evangelists wish to convey something more than this, something which a scientific or objective description would not touch. The stories operate at the level of the subject. They speak of personal confrontation, of the perception of meaning and of the obliteration of the fear of death. They describe an experience in which men come to know that death is overcome and transcended by Christ. Of this they can only speak in a confusion of symbolic terms which may reach out and grasp the reader so that he can share their insight.

Although the Bible is almost totally concerned to speak about the acts of God rather than of his nature, in doing this it inevitably employs images which suggest the nature of God symbolically. In both cases words have to be used in a new kind of way. When considering the resurrection we discovered that the word 'awaken' was used in a way different from its normal usage. It was applied to another kind of event and hence became an analogue. Similarly, in speaking of God himself, words have to be used in an analogical fashion. What clearly cannot be done is to speak of God univocally, in words used in an identical way. Our language is derived from our sense-experience of objects within the universe and is therefore inapplicable in its ordinary sense to that which cannot be identified with any object. If words were used of God univocally, we should be indulging in a form of idolatry, making something within the universe into God. If God is other than an object within the universe, and all the great religions have been agreed upon this, then no word derived from such objects can be used of God in an identical sense.

The Bible is constantly aware of man's inability to speak of God univocally. God is asserted not to be an object of sight – no man has or can see God. God in his reality is hidden from man and the Hebrews went to great lengths to symbolize this truth verbally and dramatically. Their laws forbade the representation of God in any form. No attempt was ever made to describe God in propositional, discursive terms. There was a clear recognition that the being of God could not be laid bare. Rather they spoke of God as hidden by a cloud which man could not penetrate, and symbolized this by erecting a great veil between the people and the Holy of Holies.[21]

The realization that God is not an object within the world nor any kind of being alongside other beings in the totality of existence has led theologians to use the analogy of proportionality in ways which would make this clear. Dean Inge spoke of God as the canvas on which the picture of history is painted. In this way it conveys the idea that God is not one object within the picture, but rather what Paul Tillich tried to convey by saying that God was the Ground of Being. Similar uses of this kind of analogy are those in which God is spoken of as having a relationship to the universe similar to that of space-time, as the metre is related to a poem or a key to the music in which it is played. Dietrich Bonhoeffer made use of this analogy to illustrate the closely related theme of the relationship between the love of God and earthly love. The passage from his letter is worth quoting at some length as an example of this use of analogy:

> There is always the danger that intense love may cause one to lose what I might call the polyphony of life. What I mean is that God wants us to love him eternally with our whole hearts – not in such a way as to injure or weaken our earthly love, but to provide a kind of *cantus firmus* to which the other melodies of life provide the counterpoint. One of these contrapuntal themes (which have their own complete independence but yet are related to the *cantus firmus*) is earthly affection. . . . Where the *cantus firmus* is firm and clear, the counterpoint can be developed to its limits. The two are 'undivided and yet distinct', in the words of the Chalcedonian Definition, like Christ in his divine and human natures. May not the attraction and importance of polyphony in music consist in its being a musical reflection of this Christological fact and therefore of our *vita Christiana*?[22]

Another common example of this type of analogy is that in which God is compared to the author of a play. Thus C. S. Lewis wrote that God 'is related to the universe more as an author is related to a play than as one object in the universe is related to another'.[23]

Quick took the analogy further and compared Shakespeare with more modern dramatists to make the point that whereas Shakespeare's own personality was not allowed to intrude so that the characters could be themselves, in modern drama the tendency was for the dramatist to be constantly speaking through the characters. He then uses Shakespeare's art as an analogy for God and the universe saying that 'perhaps such an illustration may help us a little way towards understanding how it is that a world which we affirm to be in all its points an expression of the divine mind should nevertheless often seem to a superficial view entirely to conceal it'.[24] Quick here hints tentatively at the idea of God we find in Paul Tillich and John Macquarrie of the God who *lets be*.

Any analogy must, of course, break down, however well conceived. Analogies must be qualified in all sorts of ways. Thus Lewis modifies his analogy in order to take account of the incarnation. For this purpose he makes specific use of the way in which Dante not only wrote the *Divine Comedy* but also made himself one of the characters in the drama. Even so, he has to note that the analogy is imperfect, for the characters in Dante's work are not, like men, free to act as they will.

Even in the use of the same basic analogy there are differences in its employment by the two writers. Quick attempted to find an example of a feature in Shakespeare, the freedom of the characters to be themselves, which Lewis failed to find in his analogy taken from Dante. Lewis was led to use Dante as his example because he wished to portray a feature, that of the incarnation, for which Quick was not attempting to provide. Each form of the analogy has its merits, and yet neither is entirely satisfactory. One analogy contradicts and yet complements the other. No situation within the universe is likely to serve as an exact replica of the situation in which God is related to the universe. On the other hand, the situations adduced are not being used when applied to God in an equivocal fashion, being made to mean something entirely different. Rather, it is asserted that some elements within the analogue are also attributable to the relationship of God to the universe.

The necessity to make use of various analogies causes the element of paradox to appear in religious discourse. One image is always contradicted by another because no image is adequate in itself. Even such a dominant analogy as that of love in Christianity has to be balanced by the complementary analogy of justice. In this way any theological statement is qualified by the presence of paradox. This element of paradox is not to be understood as logical contradiction to be removed by the elimination of one of the terms within the paradox. For certain types of philosophy, this way of thinking has led in the discussion of determinism and free will to one school of thought attaining logical consistency by denying free will and to another achieving it by denying determinism or providence. The paradoxical language of religion recognizes that this procedure moves away from the truth and seeks rather to embrace all the facts of experience in the recognition that slavery to the will of God is perfect freedom. Such a transcendence of the problem is not achieved by logic but arises out of the source of all symbolic language, the experience of God by man in the depths of his being.

Theological statements are further qualified by the addition of such words as eternal, infinite, everlasting. These adjectival qualifications are used to indicate that any analogous language for God must be purged of negative characteristics before it is applicable to God. We have already seen that analogical language is held to be valid for talk about God because it is believed that finite beings reflect the character of God in varying degrees. Theologians have therefore used what is known as the way of eminence; they have arrived at statements about God by raising statements about man to a pre-eminent level. This does not mean that finite attributes are merely enlarged so that God is spoken of as a kind of superman, but proceeds by the removal of limitations. The qualifiers are present to indicate the lack of limitation in God, especially the lack of imperfection. The ability of the theologian to do this, as John Baillie pointed out, is not the result of logical argument but is possible because the vision of perfection is vouchsafed to man as a revelation from God. Jesus could rely upon his hearers being aware both of their own imperfection and of the perfection of God. In consequence he could contrast the perfection of God's love with the limited compassion exercised by the average Jew. His teaching did not consist of logical argument but of an appeal to what was known in the depths of the human soul. Our awareness of our own imperfection embodies our knowledge of perfection and asserts the necessity of the addition of limitation-removing qualifiers to our analogies when attributed to God.

Analogy proves itself to be an inevitable and God-given tool in religious discourse. To be effective at the level of faith, however, it must be raised above purely rational speculation to the level of the symbolic. For analogy to speak not merely to the mind of man but also to his heart, it must be subordinated within symbolic models which have for him the quality of revelation.

NOTES

1 A. M. Farrer, *Finite and Infinite*, Dacre Press 1943, p. 94.

2 Milton K. Munitz, *Theories of the Universe*, Free Press of Glencoe 1965, p. 5.

3 Munitz, *op. cit.*, p. 5; compare I. G. Barbour, *Issues in Science and Religion*, SCM Press 1966, p. 167, and D. Emmet, *op. cit.*, p. 3.

4 S. Toulmin, *The Philosophy of Science*, Hutchinson 1953, p. 165.

5 Toulmin, *op. cit.*, p. 11.

6 I. G. Barbour, *op. cit.*, p. 159.

7 D. M. Baillie, *God was in Christ*, Faber 1948, p. 109.

8 Ps. 102.3–11.

9 Job 30.19.

10 Isa. 26.17 f.

11 J. A. T. Robinson, *Honest to God*, SCM Press 1963, chs. 1–3.

12 C. S. Lewis, 'The Seeing Eye', *Christian Reflections*, Geoffrey Bles 1967, p. 169.

13 Ps. 88.3 (Revised version).

14 Cf. the article on analogy in Van A. Harvey, *A Handbook of Theological Terms*, Allen and Unwin 1966; A. M. Farrer, *op. cit.*, pp. 88 f.; E. L. Mascall, *Existence and Analogy*, Longmans Green 1949, pp. 92–121.

15 J. Hospers, *An Introduction to Philosophical Analysis*, Routledge and Kegan Paul, 1956.

16 D. Emmet, *op. cit.*, p. 7.

17 John Baillie, *The Sense of the Presence of God*, Oxford University Press 1962, p. 116.

18 Van A. Harvey, *op. cit.*, p. 16.

19 Isa. 6.

20 See W. Pannenberg, *Jesus – God and Man*, SCM Press 1968, pp. 74–88.

21 Ex. 8.10; 9.14; 33.20; Deut. 33.26; II Sam. 7.22; I Chron. 17.20; Ps. 86.8; Isa. 40.18; 46.9.

22 D. Bonhoeffer, *Letters and Papers from Prison*, revised ed. SCM Press 1967, p. 162.

23 C. S. Lewis, *op. cit.*, p. 168.

24 O. C. Quick, *Doctrines of the Creed*, Nisbet 1938, p. 45.

5   *Models*

MODEL IS a much-used word at the present time. It was
used first in studies of scientific language and imported into
theology by I. T. Ramsey, where it has proved of great value.[1]
The brevity of the word probably accounts for some of its
popularity, making it possible to avoid cumbersome phrases
such as patterns of intelligibility, principles of interpretation
and categories of understanding. However, the apparent
simplicity of the word must not blind us to the fact that it is
capable of a variety of meanings. Initially the most important
distinction which must be drawn is between descriptive and
analogical models.

DESCRIPTIVE AND ANALOGICAL MODELS

Descriptive models are used when we have or think we have
an exact knowledge of the real thing. They are used to depict
things which already exist. A railway enthusiast, for example,
may attempt to construct a replica of a particular section of
line on a small scale and go to great lengths to reproduce
what he has observed. They may, on the other hand, depict
something which is not yet an observable fact. An architect
often has such a model constructed in order to show a client
the kind of building it is proposed to erect. In this case the
subject of the model is not yet a fact but a picture in the mind
of the architect. Yet again, we may have a picturing model
in our minds when we imagine what something is like which
we can never observe. We have, for example, a mental picture
of the solar system although we cannot see it as we picture it

in our minds. What all these have in common is that they rest on the assumption that we can describe something which either is or could be an observable fact at some future date or from a particular vantage point. They are believed to represent exact knowledge of something.

Analogical models are used when we do not possess a clear picture in our minds of how something would look if we could observe it, or when we wish to speak of something which could not be observed at all. An analogical model, therefore, makes no attempt to provide a direct and undistorted picture of the real thing. It indicates certain characteristics in a graphic manner, but is not expected to provide a description of each and every feature of the original. It is called a model and not simply an analogy because this indicates that the analogy is being used to suggest a correspondence not merely between one particular thing and another but between one set of circumstances and another. The analogy is extended to cover a wider field.

Sometimes the analogical character of a model is made explicit. It is not claimed that the model gives more than a partial insight, or assumed that it tells the whole story. In consequence, the use of one model does not preclude the use of others to illuminate the subject from a different point of view. In this case the analogical character of the model is fully recognized. On the other hand, the analogical character of a model may not be acknowledged. It then becomes a pseudo-descriptive model and its use creates the illusion that an exact and complete understanding has been attained when in fact this is not true. Moreover, such a usage creates considerable difficulty because no other analogical model is accepted as valid or necessary. The user believes that his model excludes the need for complementary concepts.

LIMITED-RELEVANCE AND CONTROL MODELS

Models are not only distinguishable on the basis of their claim to be descriptive or analogical. Both of these types of models are divided according to the extent of the task they are considered capable of performing.

A model may be seen to have only a *limited relevance*. It is not taken as offering an explanation beyond a defined and restricted field. The phenomenon of radiation, for example, is a complex one, but some idea of its nature can be given by the use of a model in which it is compared with ballistics. Albert Einstein attempted to depict the nature of radiation by comparing it with the flight of arrows. Max Planck compared high frequency radiation with the firing of massive bullets and low frequency radiation with the firing of small shot.[2] In these expressions we note that one basic comparison underlies a number of particular analogies. We can therefore speak of a model being in use. It is, however, a model whose relevance is seen to be restricted to the problem of defining the nature of radiation. The users of the model do not imply that it would necessarily be of use in a different context.

Another example from a specifically religious body of language is provided by the Old Testament. Here we frequently come across phrases which are linked together by a common idea which constitutes the model being employed. Yahweh is referred to as a lover in search of his bride and as a husband caring for his wife. Israel is described as the beloved bride of Yahweh who becomes an adulterous wife.[3] The model provides a pattern of language which enables the prophets of Israel to characterize certain aspects in the relationship between Israel and her God. No claim is made that the model is exhaustive; on the contrary, it is complemented by a number of imageries which point out other aspects in the relationship.

On the other hand, a model may be used as a basic interpretative idea. In this case little limitation is placed upon the relevance of the analogy being used and it is allowed to exert a dominating role and become a *control model*. The German philosopher Friedrich Hegel provides us with an example. In the nineteenth century Hegel used a model derived from the mechanics of learned debate. He saw the course of history as being like a constant argument in which each creative moment represented the statement of a proposition and each revolutionary event a counter-argument. The conflict between opposing sides usually resulted in a compromise or synthesis of their views, but this merely prepared the way for the next stage in which the compromise became the proposition to be challenged. History was thus seen by Hegel as informed by a dialectical movement. Although he intended in his own mind merely to describe the facts, he did in fact impose upon given data a model or interpretative idea in order to make sense of the confusing mass of historical facts. The model proved its possibilities in that Hegel was followed by men who found it fruitful in a number of different contexts. Hegelian theologians followed his lead in using the model as a way of stating certain Christian doctrines such as the Trinity, the Incarnation and the Ascension and used it in the interpretation of New Testament history. Others took Hegel's model along quite different lines and developed a materialistic dialectic of history which provided a starting-point for programmes of economic and political revolution.

These two uses of models are not, of course, unrelated. Whenever a limited-relevance model is employed it is likely that there is an underlying control model embodied in the very methodology which has led to its construction. How we understand the particular is largely determined by the way in which we think of the universal. The control model may not be acknowledged. Because it forms a presupposition to a pattern of thought we can be unaware of its presence precisely because it is pervasive. Hidden though it often is, however, the control model is the key to the language system being employed. It determines the kind of limited-relevance model which is used and thus controls all our attempts to capture the truth.

The division, for example, between a scientific and a religious approach is traceable to the employment of distinctive control models. They lead to quite different questions being asked and to quite different kinds of answers being accepted. The difference in the character of the limited-relevance models already given as examples is apparent. The scientist is likely to use models derived from such things as radiation, whereas religious literature makes plentiful use of analogies drawn from the field of human relationships. This indicates that each is dominated by a control model very different from that used by the other. But the controversy which has frequently raged between science and religion has not simply been due to the existence of dissimilar control models. Argument has only developed when one side or the other has claimed that its model is exclusively relevant, or when the analogical character of the model has not been avowed. Even a control model is subject to limitation in that it only looks at the whole of things from one perspective and its fundamental analogy has to be supplemented by models constructed from another perspective.

SYMBOLIC MODELS

All the types of models which we have so far considered may come to have symbolic value. Just as anything may become a symbol because it has the power to evoke a personal response in a man, so a model may become a powerful symbolic pattern of thought. The way in which descriptive models come to have symbolic significance can be illustrated by the impact which changing ideas of the solar system have had. In the ancient world the sun was normally thought of as being small in comparison to the earth and the earth itself was regarded as being in the centre of the system with the sun circling round it. The Copernican revolution in astronomy placed the sun at the centre and the earth was then understood to be quite small in comparison to the sun and to revolve round it along with a number of other planets. Later the enormous size of the cosmos was increasingly realized, and the solar system in which the earth is placed was then seen to be but one of a large number of such systems. From a purely scientific point of view these changes in our knowledge of the universe were clearly a steady progression towards a deeper realiza-

c*

tion of the truth. On the other hand, we note that each change has been greeted with a great deal of emotional language. The assertions of astronomers have apparently had an evocative quality, for their propositions have been contested or enthusiastically taken up with an intensity which betrays personal motivation. Human beings appear to have felt very much involved at the personal level with astronomical discovery. In other words, the descriptive models of astronomy have been symbolically powerful.

The reason for this is not difficult to discern. Even a casual study of iconography shows us that there have long been two ways in which it is possible to suggest the importance and value of something. One is to place it at the centre of the picture, especially in such a way that a number of lines converge upon it. The second is to depict the central object as being much larger in size than everything else in the picture. Ptolemaic astronomy had given man a picture of the world which corresponded perfectly with these traditional iconographic ideas. The earth was at the centre of creation and it was the largest sphere in the system. There was a perfect correspondence between man's sense of his own importance, value and responsibility in the universe and the current world view. When the Copernican revolution placed the sun in the centre and made it the larger object, this seemed to imply a radical reassessment of man. At this point the symbolic significance of the earlier world-view becomes apparent. Post-Copernican man has felt that he cannot really be of any ultimate value simply because he is relatively diminutive in an infinitely large universe and an inhabitant of a minor planet which is merely one among countless others. He has continued to assert his own value and responsibility, but has been forced as it were to do so in defiance of the model which he himself has constructed out of his observations. The model was not created for symbolic purposes but was the picturing model demanded by the evidence. It was not intended to say anything about such subjective matters as man's search for the meaning of the universe or of his own role within it but, as a fundamental tool of human thought, the helio-centric model had, inevitably, powerful symbolic value.

Man has a twofold relationship with the world. On the one hand he is a physical entity and must live in a world of objects. On the other he is a spiritual being who must establish personal relationships. These two aspects of man's being confront the world in quite different ways. Any effort which man makes to understand the world as an It is accompanied by the fact that man himself is not only an It but also a Thou. Any world-view which he constructs, therefore, has importance at the subjective level. He has to live in the world as a person and so the descriptive and analogical models which he constructs usually have symbolic significance. He may attempt to conceive the world in purely objective terms, but he cannot escape his own subjectivity. This approach to the world, however, is a comparatively recent one.

Before the rise of a scientific attitude some two thousand five hundred years ago, man appears to have had a different order of priorities. Today we construct our theories first and afterwards discover what effect they are having on our souls. In ancient times, on the other hand, there was little desire to know about things in and by themselves. Man was determined by his own subjectivity. He had not yet learnt to think about the universe without concern for his own place within it or even to hold such concern in abeyance until he had com-pleted his investigations. Consequently we find that the models which he created were not intended to be taken as descriptive; indeed, their paradoxical nature makes this impossible. They were symbolic models attempting to portray reality as he experienced it as a subject.

At this point one simple illustration of a model created solely for symbolic purposes must suffice. In the mythology of the ancient world we frequently hear of land, air and sea routes which traverse the whole of creation. One cannot read very far through one of its stories without hearing of the sun riding his chariot through the sky or his ship of the night along the dark river beneath the earth, of gods descending to earth on a rainbow or of men taking the road which leads through a cave in the mountains down into the darkness of the netherworld. It would seem that the universe possessed a whole network of routes so that one could travel to any part of it with more ease than is today advertised by our travel brochures. Yet it is clear that the roads are not such as could be surfaced with tarmacadam and the subterranean passageways are not imaginary equivalents to underground railways. Because they constitute a symbolic model it is impossible to set out simply the ideas and emotions which these routes through the cosmos conjure up. One suggests the meeting of the sacred and the mundane, another speaks of the meaning of death, while yet another tells of the pride in which a man would elevate himself above his kind and be a god. They speak of many things, but together form a model which, though it has nothing to do with the shape, size or weight of the universe, nevertheless depicts aspects of the world as it offers itself to man's consciousness. In it he may find a god as well as a demon, a heaven as well as a hell. It is a world in which above all man is never alone, because there are roads along which he may travel to meet the meaning which is seeking him out.

THE USE OF MODELS IN SCIENCE AND RELIGION

The peculiar character of religious language can be further clarified by a consideration of the different sources from which models may be derived. Any model may attain symbolic significance if it evokes a response at the personal level of human experience. Because they are derived from a variety of sources, however, the character of their symbolic message and their potentiality as the medium of religious insight is also variable. Although it is an arbitrary classification, the common division of data into physical, biological and personal will be a convenient way of handling the issues which are raised. In each case we shall note how a particular type of data was used in the creation of symbolic language in the ancient world, then how the same kind of data is handled by the scientific method, and finally how attempts to use the language of science in religion can only be done by a return to the distinctively religious use of personal being as a control model.

The physical world has always been a fruitful source of symbol. We need only think of the prominent part played in religious language by images drawn from light and darkness, height and depth, sea and river, sunshine and storm. Pre-scientific man perceived these things directly as impinging upon his life and as such they had great symbolic power. He did not consider them apart from himself. Their communicative power lay precisely in the fact that they were seen as part of his world, communicating with him the meaning of life. In the mythology of the ancient world the objects which we now think of as exclusively physical were endowed with personal significance. They were subsumed under a personal model which enabled them to be in the same world as experiencing man. Physical phenomena were regarded as manifestations of personal activity and responded to in a personal way. The image of man's subjectivity, therefore, constituted the control model in the use of the physical in ancient religion.

With the advent of physical science the world was viewed in a different way. The personal model was gradually excluded. Nature was observed apart from its existential significance for man. The scientist was looking for a way of describing the world accurately as it exists apart from man's involvement with it. For this purpose it was necessary to look for a model which was derived from the world and not from man. The ancient Greek philosophers attempted to see everything as a variation of one kind of physical being. One thought all things to be a form of air, another that they were constituted of fire and another that they were all ultimately reducible to water. They looked for their clue to the nature of reality among the elements of nature. This was the beginning of that process in which everything is seen as being fundamentally physical. Today the physicist speaks of everything as reducible to a form of mass or energy. As the physical came to dominate men's minds and provide the control model for understanding, it became increasingly difficult to find a place for man as a subjective being because the way in which science had chosen to view the world excluded as its primary principle any kind of subjectivity. The energy model of the physicist appears at first to bear some relationship to the power model of religious thinking. It is only possible, however, to speak of God in terms of the energy immanent in the universe if it is endowed with personality characteristics. If God is merely equated with the energy of the physicist, indispensable elements in the religious idea have to be abandoned. The term God becomes super-fluous because it makes no additional statement. Energy can only be used as a symbolic model for religious purposes when it is seen as the action of personal being. In consequence the apologetic use of the physicist's model has credited universal energy with such personal characteristics as freedom and purpose. To be of use in religious language, cosmic energy must be seen as a force creating and preserving value. Once this is done, however, the model ceases to serve an apologetic purpose, for it involves the addition of categories of thought which have been rejected in order to produce the methodology of science.

The phenomenon of life played a much greater role than the physical in the development of religious symbolism. For primitive man everything in the universe was 'alive'. Even those things which seem to us to be merely dead matter were conceived as having in them the flux of universal life. The experience of the phenomenon of life in himself and in animals created for him a model which controlled his perception of the inorganic. Rocks and rivers were living things. His mytho-logy has life for its constant theme, speaking of its origin, its passing and its existential significance. Life seemed to primitive man, as it still does to us, a mysterious thing. In it he could perceive the activity of the sacred in the world. God had breathed his own life into the world so that what had been dead came to pulsate with the very life of deity. The whole world was not merely alive, however, but also personal. The multitude of deities in mythology testifies to the necessity in primitive religion to subsume all under the personal control model. Only when the universe was conceived in this way could it achieve existential significance for man. As personal the universe could be encountered as a Thou. Only then could his thinking be religious.

In the scientific treatment of life the procedure reverses the relationship between life and the physical. Not only is the personal model excluded, but the tendency has been to treat the phenomenon of life under categories of thought derived from the physical. The relative success of physics and chemistry has tended to raise them into a position of dominance over the biological sciences. Life, therefore, has come to be described in physical or chemical terms. In his *Introduction to Philosophical Analysis*,[4] John Hospers sets out the differences between the organic and the inorganic realms in a manner which is not untypical. Although his aim is clearly to show the differences between living and non-living, he nevertheless describes the differentiating characteristics of living things in terms derived from the inorganic. Life is subsumed under the physical model and the understanding of it dominated by its terms. Such an approach, of course, cannot even have a distant relationship with life as man experiences it existentially or as religion expresses it symbolically.

When biological science, however, is not demoted to be a mere department of chemistry or physics, it does seem to offer itself for symbolic purposes. Many Christians saw the theory of evolution in particular as offering real enlightenment. A religious naturalism based upon evolution envisaged God as the restless phenomenon of life ever recreating itself and seeking new forms. Here again science provided theology with a conceptualization of the immanent activity of God. Once more man could think of the universe as primarily a living thing. Men could recapture that sense of the universe as on fire with life and pregnant with the new that was still to come.[5] But once again we find that a model drawn from anything other than the personal level was insufficient. Henri Bergson became a noted exponent of a religious philosophy based upon the idea of evolution, but he was ultimately forced to supplement a purely biological outlook by adding concepts derived from the personal. In *The Two Sources of Morality and Religion*[6] we find him speaking of God as not merely a life-force but also as Love. Bergson and others discovered what had been known to the religious consciousness of ancient India and embodied in the symbol of Shiva as *Nataraja*, the Lord of the Dance. The play of life only has religious significance when it is seen as the expression of personal activity.

At each point we have been led to see that for religion the only adequate kind of language is that which derives from the personal. It is therefore *the phenomenon of man* which has always provided the control model for religious language. One of the most obviously recurring features of primitive religion in particular is that it speaks of virtually everything in human terms. Everything is not merely alive but also personal. The wind blows, the seas rage and the crops grow at the behest of a personal will conceived on the analogy of man's experience of himself. The human model has so grasped the religious imagination that God has often been given human form so that the wind is the breath of his mouth, human events are brought about by his hand and human souls are drawn at death into his bosom. These anthropomorphic expressions gave substance and warmth to the personal model. As theology became sophisticated it was embarrassed by such phraseology, but provided we remain aware of its symbolic character, no other language seems capable of conveying so well the way in which God reaches out to man.

When man is submitted to the control model of scientific investigation, the very characteristics which made it possible to create significant anthropomorphisms in religious language tend to disappear. Man himself can only be the source for religious model-making as one who experiences himself and not as an object observed from the outside. Scientific procedure, by contrast, views man as an object and inevitably excludes even here the use of the personal model. It rejects in consequence the most appropriate tool for the understanding of man in the interests of a consistent methodology. Its models are derived from the non-human, with the result that man is dehumanized. He is described in the terms of physics and chemistry. His subjectivity is either reduced to a physical category or dismissed as unreal.

The scientific study of man, therefore, has not contributed the basis for any kind of theological apologetic, because it eliminates that with which religion is concerned. In fact religion constantly protests at the reduction of man to physical or animal terms. One suspects that much of the uproar which greeted the work of Charles Darwin in the nineteenth century was much more a protest against the reduction of man by the elimination of his distinctive subjectivity than a protest against Darwin's theory of his origins. The theory of evolution seemed to argue that as man was descended from ape-like ancestors, he was therefore no more than an animal. This was of course an example of 'the fallacy of primitivism' to which E. S. Brightman referred,[7] but it was a conclusion generally drawn.

Analogies may, then, be drawn from any level of which man has experience. John Macquarrie is really too cautious when he says that 'the symbols that are drawn from the level of personal being have the highest adequacy' for religious purposes.[8] Symbols drawn from elsewhere are only of use in religious discourse when they are given a personal dimension. A scientific methodology inevitably eliminates this dimension and its language can never be used in religion without first being baptized by personality. Because the object of the scientist's study is the same world in which man has to live out his life, the scientist will always have something to say to existential man, but in appropriating it religion must invest it with characteristics which science has taken great pains to eliminate. The universe has to come alive and encounter man in his existence, otherwise it is to him merely dumb.

The importance of the different control models used respectively by science and religion can further be seen in the way in which the former places man outside the universe while the latter seeks to provide for a total participation in it.

The models of science are *observer models*. Professor Toulmin, speaking of the use of models in science, says that 'the acceptance of the model is justified in the first place by the way in which it helps us to explain, represent and predict phenomena under observation'.[9] This description is clearly of an observer model, one which is constructed about things which are the objects of our observation and thought. Everything is therefore viewed as an object, even man himself. This being the case, those elements which are part of man's subjective experience, freedom, decision, responsibility and the like, can have no place. Instead, everything is brought within the orbit of an objective model, placed within a causal system which rules out freedom by predictability.

The models of religion, on the other hand, have to be *participator models*. They are models which enable us to think of the cosmos in such a way that man as personal being is able to see himself as a fitting part of the whole. They make room for man as a subject of his own inner being and as one who is only completed by entering into relationships with all that is exterior to himself. The personal model controls all the lesser models of religion precisely so that man is not thought of as being an alien in the world. It ensures that the cosmos is perceived as personal and therefore as that with which man can have the relationship on which he depends. In the object world constructed by scientific theory there is no place for man as he knows himself. In the subject world of religion man is able to see himself as participating in a world of personal relationships. To this end, every analogy used in religious discourse must find its place ultimately within the personal control model.

THE MODEL OF THE SPIRIT

The argument just developed is exemplified by the use

religion makes of the word spirit and its equivalents. In the Hebrew language, for example, the word we translate as spirit is *ruach;* it possesses an ambiguity which is essential for its religious function. Its use enabled the Hebrew to span the areas we have designated as physical, biological and personal, seeing all as the expression of a living and personal God from whom both nature and man are derived.

Ruach was the creative energy which had moved over the waters of the primeval ocean and brought all things into being. It was the power which pulsated through the universe and held it in being. But *ruach* was not left as an abstract concept. The wind which blew now softly and now violently seemed to the Hebrews to represent so exactly what they understood the power of God to be like that the wind, too, was called *ruach*.

When a Hebrew died he was spoken of as having 'given up his *ruach*'. The word also denoted the principle of life which came from and returned to God. This, too, had its symbolic expression. God had breathed into Adam to make him a living soul. As the wind symbolized the activating energy of deity throughout the universe, so breath represented the portion of God's life which he lent to man and took back to himself at a man's death.

Finally, *ruach* was also used to designate that peculiar subjectivity of man whereby he was constituted a self, a subject of experience, a mind and a seat of emotion. For the Hebrew, therefore, a description of a man's *ruach* was also a description of his mental outlook and his disposition. This, too, had come from God, who was thus the source of man's wisdom and intelligence, his skills and craftsmanship, his conscience and sense of value and even of his ability to experience the awe and wonder which pointed him towards the source of all being.

The possession of such a key word with multivalent symbolic power was not, of course, the prerogative of the Hebrews. In ancient Egypt the god Amon was spoken of as acting in just these ways, and Evans-Pritchard describes how the Nuer use the word *kwoth* in a very similar manner.[10] A constant feature of mythological expression seems to be that it should include some means of stating that the world is the work of one Spirit and that man in particular possesses a special likeness to the source of all being because he participates most fully in it. The Ashanti of West Africa express the idea picturesquely when they tell of how the creator Odumakuma poured juice into the eyes of animals and men to give them life and how he breathed his spirit only into the faces of men. In such a story there is an eloquent recognition of the distinctiveness which man possesses and his peculiar likeness to the creative principle. Conversely, the story recognizes that only in those characteristics peculiar to human subjectivity do we find the clues to the construction of a model capable of revealing the real nature of the world in which we live. The cosmos is not reduced to physical terms nor is man reduced to the level of the merely animal. On the contrary, the personal character of man is understood to be inexplicable unless it is seen as having its source in the very nature of being itself and as therefore providing an essential characteristic of any control model through which being is to be understood.

THE FUNCTIONAL VALUE OF MODELS

Although the use of models in science and religion differs in significant ways, it is possible to see both uses as primarily functional. They are created so that men can act in a certain manner.

In science, the function of a model is not merely to provide understanding but also to enable the scientist to exploit the knowledge which he thus gains. The planetary theory of the atom was not constructed for the pleasure of having a mind's eye view of the atom, but so that practical use could be made of this knowledge. This theory, which thought of the atom as being like the heliocentric solar system with the electrons revolving about the nucleus like the planets round the sun, was created to explain certain observations and to enable further experiments to be carried out which would be of technological value.

For such a model to function adequately it is not necessary that it should contain more than analogical truth. Atomic research does not depend upon the planetary model being descriptively accurate. In fact the possibility of creating descriptive models has been largely abandoned in modern science. The models which were once created in the belief that they were descriptive have given place to models which are recognized to be merely functional. The physicist is indeed happiest when he is allowed to express his findings simply in terms of mathematics, the purpose of which is clearly to create working formulas rather than to describe how things really are. Underlying this preference of the modern physicist is the idea 'that the fundamental processes of nature cannot be depicted as happenings in space and time'.[11] This fact is not always apparent to the layman because, as Toulmin remarks, scientists often leave out the words 'as it were' and this leads to misunderstanding.[12] Gas, for example, is described as a collection of minute particles moving with high velocity in all directions. This description does not, however, provide a picture of gas, but only an analogical model which serves a useful function in scientific experiment.

A model may function quite satisfactorily in one context while being quite useless in another. When we plan a journey by car, we assume for the purposes of the operation that the earth is flat. In this context our other picture of the earth as a sphere is irrelevant. If we were planning a journey into outer space, however, the spherical model would be both appropriate and necessary.

In religion we find a comparable state of affairs, although different objects are in view. The scientist requires models which will ultimately prove of technological value. Our car driver or space-man requires models for operations in space and time. The theologian, however, requires models which are primarily valuable for their existential content. Religious models exist to give a symbolic picture of reality of such a kind as to provide man with a way of orientating his life in the world. The control model of religion (as we have seen) exists precisely for this purpose. It furnishes men with such a way of looking at the universe that they can relate themselves to it meaningfully.

Religious symbols do not exist simply for the enlightenment of the soul. The prophet presumes that any insight into the nature of God carries with it implications for human life. Each vision of God entails an attitude toward life and implies the necessity for a secular implementation. The lover model not only gave the Israelites a way of seeing their history as meaningful but also suggested certain lines of action. A response to the model entailed the application of certain concepts embodied in it to their political and social life. It established in both spheres the idea of covenant loyalty. On the political front this was held to mean that international bargains once made should not be broken. More directly, we can also see that the development of a monogamous concept of marriage in Israel was bound up with the imagery which the prophets had declared. The symbolic model thus provides a framework from within which certain obligations and commitments arise.

Theology recognized many hundreds of years ago that it could not provide descriptive models, but that all its talk was at best analogical. This was, of course, more obvious in dealing with the intangible world of the spirit. Just as the subjectivity of man does not lend itself to picturability, so the theologian knew that he could not describe that subjectivity of the universe which he called God. What he could do, however, was to furnish a number of complementary images for the spiritual life of man, each having value in so far as it was capable of serving the development of man's potentiality for spiritual life.

Each symbolic expression in religion has enclosed within it an aspect of man's experience of the personal dimension. The shepherd imagery expressed that sense of dependence which man inevitably feels in the face of the givenness of life. As a model it enabled him to accept a dependent role because it set his life within a personal relationship. That on which he was dependent was declared to be not a blind, impersonal force but caring personality. The shepherd model, however, only reflected one element within human experience and by itself would have encouraged a self-destructive passivity. It was therefore complemented by other models in which quite different aspects of human experience could be given due weight. One of these was the vineyard model which appears frequently in the Old Testament. This suggests that man is also under obligation in his life. It is an image which stresses man's sense of responsibility. As a model it implies that man is not only a child of God but also a partner with him in the ongoing process of the universe.

The power potentiality of a symbol depends upon the extent to which it corresponds to man's experience. That experience, however, constantly changes. The models which serve best in youth fall into the background in later life. The imagery which served ancient man so well may no longer speak to men in the twentieth century. The amazing variety of symbolic forms corresponds to the richness of human experience of the personal. A model, therefore, which is appropriate in one context is useless in another. The symbols of religion cannot be expected to speak to each man at every moment of his life. He is not continuously in a state of rebellion and the imagery of God as judge is not therefore always immediately meaningful. Nor is he continuously gripped by guilt and in need of the symbols of forgiveness. There is in religion as in all life a season for everything, and great harm has been done to men, as Dietrich Bonhoeffer stated so well, by the imposition of ultimate categories upon men engaged in the penultimate.[13]

THE COGNITIVE VALUE OF MODELS

The functional and existential value of models is readily seen. We must now consider the relationship between the symbolic models of religion and factual reality. The cognitive status of scientific and religious statements has been debated at great length and has resulted in considerable difference of opinion.

Many hold that the validity of a model is exhausted by its relative functional ability. On this view science presents us simply with ways in which we may make use of the world without making statements about the way it is in reality. Similarly, some theologians under the influence of either existentialist or analytical philosophy have held that we must be content to regard religious language as making statements solely about the inner life of man. Religious language is then seen as merely descriptive of the subjective reactions of man to his environment. Thus to speak of God as shepherd would indicate that the speaker felt a sense of dependence, but would not imply that there was anything exterior to man on which he was dependent. It is granted further that religious statements may express an intention to act in a certain way. To say that God is love, for example, would indicate an intention to live a loving life. To characterize God as judge would be a way of declaring a concern for justice in the world. On this view it is held that religious statements do not say anything about reality but merely embody the personal preferences of individuals.[14]

If positions such as these are maintained, however, we would have to say that religious language is not what it has purported to be. There can be no doubt that the scriptures of world religion have all intended to make assertions about the nature of reality. If religious statements were reduced to descriptions of inner feelings or statements of human intent, the bulk of that writing which makes up sacred scripture would have to be abandoned as perverse. While much attention is devoted to the human appropriation or reception of the divine, the assumption is always that there is a reality which is being appropriated and a Thou who is being confronted. Religious experiences declare themselves to be perceptions of reality as personal. Standing before the altar in the temple at Jerusalem, Isaiah believed that he was in the actual presence of God.[15] It was to him a moment in which a reality was disclosed. If that reality is denied, then he did not experience anything but the projections of his own subjectivity. Yet his message is included in scripture in the belief that the words, 'Thus saith the Lord', were not a fabrication of a deluded mind but resulted from an encounter with ultimate reality.

Religion stands or falls by the answer to the question concerning the cognitive value of religious language. Religion has always been a structure in which man has embodied his perception of the world as meaningful to himself. In it he has recorded his awareness of being confronted by that which stands over against him as personal being. In consequence the current breakdown of confidence in man's ability to speak of anything beyond the observable and the functional has inevitably meant the loss of both religion and personal significance for many people. If religion cannot be accepted as speaking meaningfully of that which is real, it no longer retains any function. It is clearly impossible to speak of a relationship with the world as a mediation of personal being if we may not speak about that with which the relationship is to be formed.

With the loss of religion which asserted a reality beyond man of such a character that man could enter into relationship with it, modern man has been forced to attempt the construction o meaning out of himself. He has been left to find an equivalent for deity within himself. As a result he has attempted to produce an understanding of himself as at once the one who needs and the one who provides for the need. Within his own subjectivity he must perforce be that other to himself and teach that he must be true to himself, respond to himself and be responsible to himself but without any reason for being true, for making a response or for responsibility. Man is thus locked in the prison of his own subjectivity.

It would appear, however, that the cause of such a retreat into human self-sufficiency is often found in a wrong understanding of the nature of the reality asserted by religious language. Religious symbols do not assert a reality other than that which is also assumed by scientific man. What they do assert is that the one reality has a dimension which is not exhaustively described in the objectifying language of science. It asserts that in addition to being apprehended as an It the world may also be apprehended as a Thou. The cognitive assertion of religious symbol therefore is that what the scientist describes in quantitative terms must also be reckoned with in qualitative terms.

Religion is often judged as though it were in competition with science and spoke of another reality, of another world. But the God of whom religion speaks is not a being or an object. Religious statements may not be analysed as though they were scientific. Such a process eliminates the distinctive character of religious language and brings it into an alien framework where it is absurd and superfluous. Religion speaks of the same reality, of the same world, as that investigated by science, but in such a way that its subjective and personal dimension is made clear. The true centre of the argument between religion and non-religion is not to be found where discussion rages as to the existence of a person or thing, but where man decides whether the world which confronts him is mere object to his subjectivity or whether it possesses a subjectivity answering to his own. His decision at this point is not merely about what he himself will be, but about whether there is that which lays upon him the burden of personal response because it is personal being.[16]

VALIDATION AND RESPONSE

The truth or untruth of a model as a correspondence with reality can only be known by its ability to function. The technologist uses the models of science on the assumption that they make genuine statements about the nature of things and is satisfied with those models when they produce the kind of results which they led him to anticipate. Similarly, in religion a man can only assume the validity of its characteristic model if in use it opens up that personal dimension of experience which it led him to expect.[17]

There is, however, a fundamental difference in the way that

models are validated in religion as against science. This derives from the fact that the control model of science is one which sees the world as object while the control model of religion sees it as subject. The validation of the first consists in its ability to manipulate objects within the world. The validation of the second cannot proceed in this way, for when a subject is manipulated it has become an object. Religious statements cannot, therefore, be submitted to the kind of verification procedure which a scientist may apply to a hypothesis. Both the hypothesis and the religious statement may be born of an intuitive and perceptive moment, but they differ radically in that the scientific hypothesis discerns a relationship between objects while religious disclosure opens up a confrontation between subjects. The verification of religious statements must therefore be undertaken in ways which are quite distinctive.

First, we have to note that if the control model of religion has any validity it would be impossible for it to have that kind of consistency which is demanded of a scientific model. If reality is perceived correctly as possessing subjectivity, its description must allow for that essential ambivalence which characterizes free selfhood and which can only be stated in symbolic terms. The first hopeful sign to the religious consciousness is that it is impossible to submit all areas of human experience to objective consistency.

Second, the character of the religious model determines the kind of verification procedure which can be applied to it. As the religious model provides for participation by men the model can only be validated by participation. It cannot be subjected to criteria from outside itself, for this would be to submit it to another kind of model. In order to enter into a relationship with the world as the personal model sees it, a man must shed those objective categories in which he has attempted to see and control the world as an It. In the language of religion itself, he must climb the ladder into the cloud of unknowing in order to discover that dimension of cosmic reality which he calls God. The personal relationship which religion speaks of can only be known by participation in it. Talk about God has to be replaced by encounter with God. Just as the personality of other human beings can only become real to us when we commit ourselves to a relationship with them, so the selfhood of deity can only be perceived when we allow ourselves to be taken up into communion with God.

Third, we must locate the point in such a procedure at which the element of faith enters in. The mere response to the world as personal does not constitute in religion that which men call faith. It is possible to see the cosmos in the light of the personal model of religion without attaining religious faith. When the disasters of human life call forth a response of hate, when God is vilified out of the depths of human misery, the world is being perceived in a personal way but such a response does not embody that trust which is faith. Faith has never been satisfied with a mere cognition of cosmic selfhood.

Personal relationship between human beings is experienced as something in which the self is fulfilled. Indeed a man's capacity for selfhood is only known in encounter with another self. The need for self-discovery appears to be built into the very nature of subjective freedom, and is only possible in a relationship with that which is other. In isolation selfhood dies, because it cannot feed on communion. A true, personal relationship, therefore, is said to exist when the potentiality for personhood is being actualized in it. This perhaps gives us a clue as to the way in which the religious model appropriated in faith can be submitted to a verification procedure appropriate to its nature. If the apprehension of the cosmos as truly personal is valid, it must inevitably manifest itself by the promotion of personality in man. That potentiality for being a person which man discovers to be within himself will be nurtured by his confrontation with the universe as personal.

Participation in dialogue with the universal Thou is always an ongoing process. Religion always recognizes that man lives between the times and before the end. In that present where man is always located, the fulfilment for which he looks has never arrived except in part. Moreover, he has experiences which appear to point away from fulfilment towards destruction. In this situation it can only be a matter of faith that the experience of opposing negation is playing an ultimately creative role by eliminating that self-destructive element in man's subjectivity which asserts itself at the expense of object-ifying all that is not-self. Faith alone can trust that man's fulfilment as a person is being created by the experience of the shadow-side of deity and that the *no* which God says to man will in the end turn into a triumphant *yes*. The descrip-tion of such faith, therefore, is necessarily couched in the language of eschatology. It asserts that the destructive exists only in order to be creative. The present is seen as a participa-tion in a battle which is finally won by creative power.

Thus, in the final analysis, the religious model as it is accepted in faith can only be validated eschatologically. Men may attain a degree of certainty by what religion sees as a foretaste of the end-event. There may be the comfort of a partial triumph in the blossoming of real selfhood, a moment of authentic existence or beatific vision, but man cannot know until he has finally allowed himself to be known.

NOTES

1 I. T. Ramsey, *Religious Language*, SCM Press 1957; *Models and Mystery*, Oxford University Press 1964; *Christian Discourse*, Oxford University Press 1965.

2 Sir James Jeans, *The Growth of Physical Science*, Cambridge University Press, rev. ed. 1950, p. 329.

3 Notably in the book of Hosea.

4 J. Hospers, *Introduction to Philosophical Analysis*, p. 282.

5 Rom. 8.22.

6 Henri Bergson, *The Two Sources of Morality and Religion*, Macmillan 1935.

7 E. S. Brightman, *A Philosophy of Religion*, Skeffington 1947, p. 29.

8 J. Macquarrie, *Principles of Christian Theology*, SCM Press 1966, p. 132.

9 S. Toulmin, *The Philosophy of Science*, p. 37.

10 E. E. Evans-Pritchard, *Nuer Religion*, Clarendon Press 1956, pp. 1 ff.

11 Jeans, *op. cit.*, p. 336.

12 Toulmin, *op. cit.*, p. 169.

13 *Letters and Papers from Prison*, pp. 177 ff., 190 ff.

14 See Paul van Buren, *The Secular Meaning of the Gospel*, SCM Press 1963; R. B. Braithwaite, *An Empiricist's View of the Nature of Religious Belief*, Eddington Memorial Lecture, Cambridge University Press 1955.

15 Isa. 6.

16 See J. A. Martin, *The New Dialogue between Philosophy and Theology*, A. and C. Black 1966, for a review of positions recently developed on the cognitive value of religious statements.

17 See P. L. Berger, *The Social Reality of Religion*, Faber 1969, pp. 180 ff.

6   Myths

THE MISUNDERSTANDING OF MYTH

IN COMMON language, to say something is mythical is to declare simply that it is untrue. This usage is a legacy from a long period in which the nature of the myth was not understood. Because the meaning hidden within the myths was undecipherable, they were dismissed as unworthy of further consideration. There appear to have been a number of reasons for this of which it is possible to isolate at least four.

(i) At one time our knowledge of the myths was totally derived from a study of ancient literature. In particular, the literature of the Greeks and Romans was well known in a period which was dominated by the idea of a classical education. Mythology came to be regarded by many as virtually synonymous with this literature. This, however, was most misleading because the literature had come into being when the Greek and Roman age of myth was already in decline. The myths had already become the basis for great fiction. Their influence on the thought-forms, ritual and social structures of the people was merely a legacy of the past, and much of this was not understood in the classical period of Greece and Rome. We were more aware of the difficulties which the classical world had in believing in the gods of the myths than of any living faith which these myths might once have enshrined. The result was that scholars came to the conclusion that myth was no more than imaginative fiction. It was noted that there were many similarities between the myths in Hesiod and Homer and the stories of dragons, beanstalks and the like which were told to children. It seemed possible, therefore, to treat the myths as though they were of no more consequence than the horror entertainment provided by the films of Dracula and Frankenstein which made use of some of the traditional motifs.

(ii) Allied to the relegation of myth to the realm of the fairy-story, was the operation of a control model which had come into use in the modern period of history. The western world came to think of itself as the result of an evolutionary process in which the crudities of the past had been largely eliminated. It had adopted the idea of progress as its control model. This became so generally accepted that it was possible to refer to the ancient world as the childhood of the human race. The makers of myth, therefore, were judged by reference to the standard of the west's comparative excellence. Consequently, much of the early work in the field of mythology was rendered suspect because it seemed to assume that what was ancient was necessarily naïve, simple and childish. There can be little doubt that this has often caused writers to postulate the existence of absurd ideas among primitive men because they were expecting to find them. This is particularly evident in some of the descriptions of savage religion given by missionaries of the nineteenth century.

The use of the model of progress led in particular to the formulation of a theory of religious development which ignored the multivalence of mythology. This can perhaps be best illustrated by seeing how two lines of progress were held to have taken place with the one influencing the other. Man's social structures seemed to have developed towards an ever-increasing degree of centralization from loose family structures through clans, tribes, nations to empires. Alongside this picture was placed another. Religion was seen as having passed through a similar process of centralization starting from a vague animism through spiritism, polytheism, monolatry to monotheism. The parallelism between the two developments thus stated appeared further to suggest that man's social development had created his religious ideas. Logically, therefore, the great religions of the world today are monotheistic because man is politically unified. Put in this way the thesis already appears to be doubtful. While we may not dismiss the idea that there has been a development in both social structure and in religion with the one influencing the other, it would seem necessary to balance a recognition of this fact with another. A number of apparently contradictory features can exist together.

(iii) The understanding of myth has also been seriously hindered by an attempt to relate it to scientific ideas. When this has happened, the conclusion has invariably been that good myth was poor science. Myth has been seen as representing a pre-scientific way of thinking. Primitive man has been thought, on the one hand, to have failed to make use of a valid methodology while, on the other hand, he has been expected to have been concerned with that kind of understanding of the world which we expect science to provide. Myths have, therefore, been classified according to the scientific questions they were held to be attempting to answer. Some were called aetiological myths because they asked the question of origins. Others were called cosmological myths because it was assumed that they were primarily trying to describe the physical universe. In particular, it was argued that the myth-maker created gods to whom he could attribute those occurrences in nature which were inexplicable to him. Thus this approach did not recognize in myth a different way of thinking from that of science, although historians had gone to great lengths to show that scientific thinking was a phenomenon of the modern world, dependent on the emergence of an empirical method, on making accurate observations and of logical deductions. But the use of an empirical method would not have answered the questions raised by the makers of myth. It is not even clear that we should think of myths as being answers to questions at all. Rather, they appear to have been statements of immediate apprehension. At all events, it has become clear that myth and science work in two quite different areas of human concern and that a comparison between the two is misleading rather than enlightening.

(iv) Finally, it is important to recognize that one of the

D

greatest barriers to an understanding of myth is the fact that we may no longer share the kind of faith which gave rise to it. The myths embody a religious outlook on the world. If this is not shared by one who seeks to interpret the myths, there is at least a strong possibility of misunderstanding. In many works on primitive religion, in fact, we can often detect a polemical attack upon religion as such. Thus often the attribution of naïvety to mythological man is the means used by a propaganda aimed at notions which an author wishes to discredit, and he oftens believes his purpose accomplished merely by showing ideas to be extremely ancient.

RENEWED UNDERSTANDING OF MYTH

In the last few decades, various studies have entirely altered the situation and given us some real insights into the nature of myth.

A large number of scholars have investigated the thought and life of societies in which myth appears to be alive. This has resulted in an entirely new appraisal of mythological culture. When myths are seen in their effect upon a people's way of life, we gain some insight into the purpose of these stories. Moreover, when we have gained knowledge of certain basic ways in which myth operates we find that the familiar ancient texts begin to speak in quite a new way. Meanings which we might never have guessed become plain. Perhaps the most important discovery which has resulted from this is that we are no longer able to assume that a people must be either monotheistic, polytheistic or animistic; they may be all of these at once.

Archaeology has also made a significant contribution. It has given us much more precise information about the ancient cultures in which myth was a dominating element. In particular, it has illuminated the role of myth in primitive man's understanding of death by its uncovering of ancient burial rites and funerary architecture. From this evidence we gain the clearest understanding of the way in which mythological man was totally involved in his world of myths.

Much important knowledge about myth has been gained by psychological research, particularly by the work of C. G. Jung and his school. This has shown that mythological ideas are rooted in the depths of the human mind and have been the means whereby universal man has expressed his most fundamental ideas, hopes and fears. It has reinforced the view that an understanding of myth can only take place when it is seen as an instrument of subjective rather than objectifying man. Perhaps more than any other study, psychology has shown that mythology embodies a distinctive kind of language which we must meet on its own ground.

A most important result of the recognition that mythological thinking is distinctive has been the growth of respect for pre-scientific modes of thought. We are now beginning to understand that the pre-scientific mind was not necessarily savage, barbarous or backward, but capable of real insights into the nature of what it means to be alive. While myth was judged exclusively in relation to scientific accuracy, an appreciation of mythological insight was precluded. When intelligence is exclusively equated with the use of modern scientific techniques there naturally results such a denigration of ancient man that it is impossible to take seriously anything which he produced. A sympathetic understanding, on the other hand, reveals that while much may have been gained by the advent of science, much has also been lost. The study of mythology can therefore be an enlightening experience, if our false sense of superiority can be abandoned and we accept that the language of myth is not now our language, but one the discovery of which can be a relevatory experience. In order to accomplish this, however, we need to discover the nature of this distinctive form of communication.

MYTH AS SYMBOLIC

Perhaps we can come to a better understanding of myth by recognizing it as belonging to that kind of language which we have called symbolic. There may be some primary basis for this in the fact that it has provided the substance of drama in both the ancient world and the modern. In the theatre which was born out of the rituals in which the myths were enacted, that which is done cannot merely be dismissed as fiction. It grapples with the real at the level of personal apprehension. Drama opens up the subjective dimension of the objective. That which takes place in a confined space speaks of that which occurs in the great space of mankind. In the objects which serve as stage setting and furniture, a few act out a confrontation which the many live out with the It of the world and strive for personal meaning. In some measure even a demythologized drama retains a symbolic character, a capacity to speak of something beyond itself.

If we compare mythological language with the forms of symbolism we have already discussed, it will be apparent that here we have a language complex which gathers within itself all the features of symbolic discourse.

First, the myths give ample evidence of their belonging to the category of symbol rather than of sign. They are rich in meaning, capable of constant reapplication and reach out in all directions. They possess that characteristic multivalence of symbol which makes it possible for them to speak of many things at once. Osiris, for example, was to the people of Egypt a vegetation God, the fertilizing waters of the Nile, the judge and protector of the dead, the principle of eternal life and a symbol of loving concern. The goddess Nut, while less rich in potentiality, nevertheless manifests the same symbolic characteristic. She supports the vault of the heavens with her body and yet at the same time she is herself the very firmament. By a typical anthropomorphism she also becomes the mother of the sun to whom she gives birth each morning. The gods of a myth may be many things at once. Their story may tell of how things began and at the same time show how things always are. They may portray the constant battle of human life on the political and the psychic level. They speak of things which evoke awe, wonder, terror and beatitude. They deal with the emergence of life, the meaning of sex and the passage through death.

The myths are never trivial because they are concerned with the meaning of human existence at the deepest possible level. They speak of man's confrontation with the elements of nature, his struggle for survival and the most intimate events which take place within the human soul. With one voice the myths declare that the meaning of the superb joy and the disastrous despair which man can experience is not to be found in a simple empirical observation. They are suffused with emotion because they arise out of the depths of human experience where the barriers of objectivity are removed.

We are never given the author of a myth. Like the icons of Byzantine Christianity, myths are unsigned, because they are the medium of revelation rather than of man's self-expression. They are born out of the common life of man, out of his confrontation with the world which speaks to him in the symbols it creates. In this lies the explanation for the fact that the themes of the myths are both timeless and universal. They have local form and colour provided by the imagery appropriate to a particular time and place, but they emerge from the universal rather than the individual consciousness. For such stories there can really be no human author. They are accepted by those who use them not as the creation of men but as handed down from the gods themselves.

Second, myths are akin to parables in that they operate symbols in narrative form. Unlike the parable, however, the myth is not simple but complex. Whereas the parable attempts to achieve one moment of enlightenment, the myth acts as a constant source of revelation at every point in life. The myths are closely related to those crucial moments in human life which are dealt with in archaic societies by rites of passage. The insight embodied in the myth is applied at each point, to birth, to the second birth which is initiation into adulthood, to marriage and to death. The myth in fact provides a framework within which the whole of life can be understood.

The likeness of myth to parable necessarily means that we should not treat myths as though they were allegories. The myths are not understood by the discovery of any code. The difficulties which we may have in interpreting them are not due to the lack of an esoteric key. Invariably they arise because we are unaware of the original meaning of the words used, of the associations which certain elements had in the minds of those who created the myths, and even because some geographic or botanical fact is unknown to us. Granted the intimate acquaintance with the local scene which the myths assumed, the only hindrance to their understanding lay within a man himself. The one necessity was spiritual perceptivity.

The third symbolic feature of mythology of which note must be taken has probably given rise to more misunderstanding than any other. The myths operate analogically at the level of metaphor and not of simile. This metaphorical structure is consistently maintained, and so the analogical character is never apparent. They never speak in simile of one thing being like another, but as though they gave a direct description of the world and a transcript of ancient history. It is hardly surprising, therefore, that many should have fallen into the trap of thinking that the myth-makers were attempting to write science or history. This would have been avoided, perhaps, if the significance of the humour born of ambivalence had been appreciated.

A recurring feature of mythological narrative is a play upon words. In Egyptian mythology, for example, we are told that men were born from the tears shed by the sun-god Ra. When this story was told, the Egyptian recognized the play upon words because the word for man sounded like that for tears. In the Hebrew Genesis we are told that 'the Lord God formed man of dust from the ground'.[1] The use of tears and of dust in such contexts was clearly intended to be evocative and to suggest a certain insight into the character of man. Similarly, the Hebrew story of the creation of Eve out of one of Adam's ribs implied a concept of womanhood. T. Boman points out that for the Arab 'rib' means 'bosom companion', and so this may have been a play upon the ambivalence of the term.[2] Certainly the writer was not making a literal statement, for nowhere is it suggested that man lacks one of his ribs. The device is simply one of evocative metaphor.

A consistent metaphorical structure was not, however, merely a convenient technique on the part of the story-teller. It was essential. Mythological thinking does not perceive the universe indirectly, but directly and as one. It makes no distinction between the symbol and that which is symbolized, because the meaning is given in the symbol. The sky can be spoken of as though it were identical with the numinous transcendence of the High God, because the immensity of the sky itself mediated a sense of transcendence. The existential meaning of the myth was not clothed in the symbol, but perceived through it. The thing or the event and the meaning which the myth sought to lay bare were therefore one in mythological thought, and this was best expressed in the medium of metaphor.

Lastly, we must note that myths work within a framework of symbolic models. These models provide the space in which the drama of the myth can be acted out. Taken as descriptive models the mythological cosmographies merely appear absurd. The mythological use of models can only be understood when it is accepted that they are being used symbolically. The mountains, oceans and rivers of the myth do not belong to geographical science. While the way in which they are conceived is influenced by experience of a local terrain, they are handled as images of cosmic and not local structure. As symbol the part may stand for the whole, so that tiny areas in which a ritual is acted out can represent the cosmic magnitude. Moreover, the myths never speak of the world in which their action takes place as though it were simply neutral. The very stage of the drama is made part of the drama itself. The models used by myth portray the cosmos from a human, personal perspective and as that which can and does respond to man. The various parts of the universe, therefore, are actors in the drama and are never allowed to become mere stage scenery in which men lose themselves in a world neither beneficent nor hostile. The symbolic model thus forms an essential unity with the mythological narrative because it is part of it.

SYMBOLIC FEATURES PECULIAR TO MYTH

Myth incorporates not only such symbolic forms as we have already noted, but also some which are peculiar to itself.

The stories are always ones in which some, at least, of the actors are gods. It is this feature which makes myth so distinctive when compared with other forms of literature. If we are to achieve any real understanding of myth, therefore, we must discover what precisely the myth-maker intended when he referred to the gods and what role he assigned to them. Because we live in a world which we normally use in an objective way, it is difficult for us to appreciate a language which is consistently subjective even when speaking of things which we think of as inanimate. Numerous writers on mythology have assumed that primitive man made the same kind of distinctions as are now made between animate and inanimate matter. In consequence they have presupposed that the gods of myth were thought of as beings in space and time in addition to those which we normally encounter in the world. The gods of mythology, however, were invariably the result of an animistic attitude which saw everything in the world as imbued with personal life. Some of the mythological gods were really living stage properties, trees, rivers, mountains and oceans. Others were the elemental forces of nature such as storms, thunder, sunshine and rain. Yet others were expressions of the various manifestations of creativity. Because these things are not now normally understood in a personal way, their identity with the gods of myth has not always been appreciated. Instead, writers have spoken of the god of the tree as though it were believed that a deity paid occasional visits to the tree when he thought fit or was brought there by some ritual magic. This led to the further misunderstanding that these disembodied gods must have been credited with other bodies in which they inhabited another world. By this time, all contact with mythological understanding had been lost.

The cause of much of this misunderstanding is to be found in the fact that studies of mythology have often been based on literature which was created when myth was no longer alive. Many quite ancient texts reveal themselves already to have lost the animistic insights of myth and to have been produced by a degenerated form of mythological thinking which is best described as magical.

If we hold on to the fact that myth operated within a symbolic model which perceived the cosmos as personal, we can arrive at an understanding of myth which does more justice to the evidence. We can then understand that the gods of mythology do not belong to another world but confront man in his world, and that the universal Thou is potentially present in everything. Seen in this way, the apparent journeyings of gods to and from their natural habitat begin to fall into place. When the Israelites spoke of God departing from Israel or drawing near to them, it is really inconceivable that they were describing the journeys of deity in space. We note that the nearness or absence of Yahweh to the Israelite depended upon himself. The location of Yahweh was an existential fact. God drew near to the receptive Israelite but departed from the man who had enclosed himself in his own self-sufficiency. Similarly, in the myths we may discern that the presence of deity in a tree or river did not denote that the god had arrived but that man had perceived divinity there. When the place no longer mediated the personal Thou of the cosmos, the god had gone away.

If we follow this through we can also see that the talk of many gods is a description of man's perceptiveness rather than of reality. It has been increasingly realized that underlying the apparent polytheism of mythology there is usually evident a sense of the unity of things. The myths form a symbolic complex which sets forth the diversity in which the one discloses himself. This can be illustrated by the mythology of the Ngadju Dayak of Borneo. Here we have a story which speaks of cosmic mountains, of the first humans, Mahatala and his wife Putir, and of two hornbills which are connected with the tree of life out of which men first came. These are the 'actors' of the story, but it emerges that they are all one, symbolic expressions of the one

D*

Spirit under various aspects. The mountains are both the loca-
tions of the gods and themselves the gods. Mahatala and his
wife Putir represent the male and female principles of the same
deity in an anthropomorphic form, while the two hornbills set
forth the divine principle theriomorphically.[3] The apparent
polytheism of the myth is created by the variety in which man
experiences the divine which he nevertheless recognizes ultimately as one.

The attempt to create out of mythology a pantheon of
beings is doomed to failure by the way in which the gods are
constantly confused one with another. There can, strictly
speaking, be no pantheon of gods because each one is merely a
symbol standing for one aspect of the one deity. At Heliopolis
in Egypt, Ra was also Atum, while his wife Rat was merely the
feminine aspect of himself as the name clearly indicates. The
same principle operative in the cosmos may be called by many
names, but its essential unity is also seen.

The name by which the one divine principle is designated has
an existential significance. In the Rig Veda the Creator is
called Indra, in the Brahmanas he is named Prajapati, while
later still he is Vishvaharman. Now it is undoubtedly true that
such changes of name probably reflect the way in which one
culture overcame and dominated another. We must not,
however, suppose that the people were asked to change their
gods. In the nature of things this is impossible, for a god has no
reality for a man apart from an existential appropriation.
What was being changed was the symbol. The new name could
only achieve dominance when it came to possess that evocative
nature which a symbol must have to be operative.

A further clue to the way in which myth conceives of the
gods may be provided by the way in which they speak of battles
between the gods. Some of these stories, of course, merely
reflect the struggle of cosmic forces with one another. One
particular form of mythological contest may, however, represent something quite different. In many of the myths one
of the lesser gods attempts to usurp the throne and become
lord of all the gods. It is possible that this in particular repre-

sents an existential truth. The High God who occupies the throne is generally recognized to be the symbol of that unity which we now see is assumed to exist behind the variety of divine manifestations. The lesser gods, on the other hand, represent those partial disclosures of the sacred. A revolt on the part of one of the lesser gods, therefore, would constitute an attempt to see the whole in the partial, the fullness of deity in some particular. In the terms of religion itself this would be the essence of idolatry, because it raises up that which is a created medium of divine disclosure to the rank of deity itself. In the condemnation of the usurper the myth declares that every god must keep his place; a thing, however evocative, can never be allowed to take the place of the infinite.

These observations suggest that space in the myths is not a measurable but a symbolic space. Distance is equivalent to existential separation, failure to perceive the immanent presence of deity. The existential separation between God and man may be portrayed in terms of two different kinds of space. The division between man and his maker may be stated in horizontal terms. In Genesis it is represented by Adam and Eve being cast out of the garden of Eden. They are sent away to another land, one in which they will not meet God walking in the cool of the evening. The same symbolic use of space is made in Chinese mythology when the heavenly realm is said to be in the isles of the west across the sea. The symbolic distance may also be represented as vertical. Deity is 'located' at a great height. The mythology of certain African communities makes it clear that vertical separation is the result of man's action or sin. Parrinder cites several examples which stress the idea of overfamiliarity with deity as the cause for its having removed itself away from close contact with the world of men.[4] We may perhaps discern in this feature a recognition of that oft repeated lesson which men must learn, that neither the subjectivity of another human being nor of God can be domesticated to our use. A genuine personal encounter and relationship is only possible when the integrity of the other's transcendence is maintained. Whatever we may make of the reasons given in the myths for the separation they speak of, it is at least clear that the distance involved is symbolic of existential experience.

The myths also use a symbolic time. It is one of their characteristics that they relate events which are said to have taken place in primordial time, in the time of the beginnings. The myths are invariably connected with creation. Mircea Eliade goes so far as to say that myth is always an account of creation or cosmogonic.[5] Yet this interest in origins is not scientific. The myths do not provide alternative solutions to the various theories proposed to account for the way in which the universe or the world came into existence. They do not look back beyond a particular point in time and ask what happened in the historical time before that point. Rather, they are placed as events before time began. In this way they can be understood as archetypal events, as events which can be interpretative for all the happenings which take place in man's time. The time of the gods, like their space, is symbolic, although it serves a different purpose. It is a way of stating that everything which happens in historical time is to be understood as a recurrence of the cosmic pattern revealed in the myth. The man who possessed a living myth, therefore, was not bewildered by the apparent contingency of events. Everything was explicable and meaningful in the context of the myth.

This is most obvious when we find myths operating as paradigmatic models. The story tells how things were done in the beginning and it is understood that this shows how things are always to be done. The gods teach men how to be born, how to sow, to marry and to die.[6] The insights embodied in the myth are especially concerned with those moments in human existence in which man asks anew the meaning of his life. Each of these moments has to be seen in the light of the genesis of all moments. The myth, therefore, attempts to portray the essence of existence and in so doing to display a pattern of behaviour which can be constantly rediscovered. Thus the creation story is told again and again to become the basis for the 'rites of passage'. In this way it is understood that life is not to be lived fortuitously but in a way decreed by the gods and exemplified by the ancestors of the human race in primordial time.

In particular, the myths represent their own function in their constant description of a man's search for immortality, for the nectar of the gods. The story sets forth man's awareness of his own finitude and his need for infinity. It portrays the search as one in which man is constantly foiled in this life, as though the gods were jealous of their possession. The climax of the myth, however, assures him that he may ride in the barque of Osiris in an eternity which completes his end and gives meaning to his present.

We can now see how religious language is built up from isolated symbols which find their place in patterns of various kinds. The myth represents the most complex form of these symbolic patterns. In it we find emblems, symbols, parables, metaphors and symbolic models. We may say that just as the model gathers within itself the various static elements of symbolism, so the myth gathers together the dramatic elements and portrays them within the framework of a symbolic cosmic model. The advantage which this gives the myth over other forms of symbol lies in the fact that this enables it to be cosmic in every respect. As Munson puts it, myth 'enables man to grasp his situation in its totality'.[7]

The portrayal of the cosmos, however, is not undertaken impartially or with the observer's eye, but with passion and with the participant's eye. The object of the whole exercise is to conceive of the way in which man as subject fits into the whole of things. For man to fit in he has to find the sense of things; hence the fulfilment of myth is in the disclosure of a cosmic meaning within which each individual can find his own. Man is seen as playing a part in a cosmic drama to which his role is essential. The myth overcomes the finitude of man by setting him in an eternal framework. The finitude of the present is taken up into the infinity of the eternal. The myths speak to birth and death, to man's existential anxiety, and attempt to lay bare the meaning of existence.

THE GREAT COSMIC MYTH

The mythologies of the world have provided almost endless tales of creation. When they are examined, however, certain features seem to recur frequently to produce a story which can claim to be virtually universal. This story we can call the great cosmic myth and use it to exemplify the fundamental character of mythological language.

The story usually begins with a picture of a great ocean existing in primordial time. It stretches as far as the eye can see and reaches down into infinite depths. Man's varied experience of water gave the symbol that ambivalence which made it possible for the primordial ocean to represent two quite different things at the same time. On the one hand, the ocean suggested chaos and destruction as man had experienced it flooding his home and sweeping all life away in its terrifying strength. On the other hand, water was also experienced as the source of life for himself, his cattle and his crops. Consequently the primeval waters always seem to have a dual nature. Although a symbol of primordial chaos, the vast, bottomless ocean which was always a threat to man also had within itself the capacity to nourish life. Floating on the waters of the primeval ocean, therefore, we find the seminal egg from which the whole of creation would spring, as in Greek mythology. Alternatively, the waters in their dual aspect are enclosed within a shell as in the Rig Veda, which tells of how Tvastr breaks open the shell releasing both the forces of destruction and the creative principle, the god Indra, contained within it. The duality of the waters is also portrayed in Hindu mythology by drawing a picture of it as a snake, Shesha, in whose coils the creative and preservative principle, Vishnu, lies resting. The snake or serpent as a symbol of both death and immortality is a common representation of the primeval waters precisely because it served to portray their dual nature.

As the creative principle present within the waters was activated, the earth emerges out of the ocean, for primitive man saw the existence of dry land as the first requisite for life to come into being as he knew it. In Egypt the idea of the primeval hillock or mound was probably suggested by the way in which land appeared in the middle of the Nile as the waters receded. At Hermopolis this primordial event was represented in the sacred enclosure by a lake to symbolize Nun, the primeval water, in the midst of which was a miniature island with a hill in the centre called the 'Island of Flames'.[8] The idea was not confined to Egypt or dependent on the phenomenon of the receding Nile waters. It appears also in Sumeria, Japan, Borneo and elsewhere. In many of these traditions we have the same basic idea which is expressed in North European mythology by describing the earth as a mountain, called Midgard in this instance, surrounded by the deep sea into which the world serpent has been flung where it circles the world, biting its own tail. The serpent and the ocean are, of course, one and the same.

The next point in the story usually concerns the birth of the gods. Sometimes they emerge out of the primeval ocean as in Homer or are born of the earth as Enlil was in Sumerian mythology. The appearance of the gods in myth indicates the arrival of distinctive elements within the creation. In these stories there is a consistent recognition of an underlying unity out of which all things emerged. It was a unity, however, which had within itself the potentiality for that differentiation which constitutes the world as man experiences it. The original unity is usually represented as sexless being or as bi-sexual. When the gods appear, the division of the primordial unity has begun, and this is represented by showing the gods as either male or female. In China this process was described in a manner typical of mythology. The original chaos, it was said, was enclosed within the egg of a hen. When the egg hatched there emerged the primordial deity, P'an Ku, who was also the primal man and coiled-up time, because in fact he was everything which was to be. With the release of P'an Ku and the beginning of man's time, the unity is broken. P'an Ku is said to have divided the earth from the heaven. He himself ceases to exist but from his body come the various parts of creation, earth, sky, gods and men.

Once the separation has taken place there invariably follows a battle which represents the interplay of cosmic forces and the existential struggle of man with his ontological anxiety. In the separated state, the deep waters are now simply the principle of destruction, for the principle of creativity and life has departed. For life to continue, the deep must be kept within bounds, and so Oceanus in Homer is kept at bay lest it bring the creation to nought. The deep retains its dreadful power and the great serpent Apep who lives in the depths of the mythical Nile is capable of swallowing the ship of Ra, causing the dreaded eclipse of the sun, the source of life. In order to overcome the monster of the waters the myths provide a number of dragon-slayers. In Phoenician mythology Baal overcomes Yam when he attempts to attain a total destructive power. In North European mythology the serpent-dragon, Tafnir, is slain by Sigurd the Volsung. In Babylon it was Marduk who overcome the great sea-monster, Tiamat, when it threatened to obliterate mankind in its flood. In Aztec mythology the snake is devoured by the creator, Huitzilopochtli, in the form of an eagle. In the Vedas the serpent-dragon coiled round the cosmic mountain is destroyed by the creator, Indra.

This primeval battle sets forth the struggle in which man is constantly involved. The primeval waters are only held in check, not eliminated. They remain a constant threat to man's existence. Thus when the North American Indians speak of Nanbozho, Manabush or Wisaka as having overcome the powers of the waters, they see this as merely the initiation of the cosmic drama.[9] The struggle would be repeated indefinitely, and its story was to evolve into numerous forms in the derivative folk-lore of the world. Many a Saint George would be knighted for having saved mankind from the threat of the fire-breathing dragon.

The myth was told as a story of the beginnings, of creation, but it represented what was to be eternally true both in the physical and the spiritual realm. Man would have to struggle with flood and tempest, heat and drought in order to maintain physical life. Equally he would have to join battle with his own fears, especially with the threat of ultimate destruction symbolized by the man-eating serpent or hippopotamus. Sometimes this existential significance is made clear for us. When the Phoenician dragon, Tannin, the commander of snakes, is also said to be Mot or death, we can see clearly that the cosmological narrative has its importance in myth largely because it represents man's struggle with the ontological anxiety which threatens to destroy his soul. The actors or gods in the story of the myth are the features of world scenery, the ocean, the mountain, the sky and the earth. They are also the elemental forces in nature, the wind, the earthquake and the volcano. They were only these things, however, as they presented themselves to the consciousness of man. To that consciousness the world could appear both beneficent and destructive, kind and also cruel. Hence the gods of the myths either have a dual character like the ocean which gave them birth, or exist in pairs of opposites. Yet the myth generally asserted an elementary faith. Against the threats to his existence the maker of myths set forth a belief that the principle of creativity would hold the monster at bay that man might live on the earth, and even in death return not to a mere void but to a primeval ocean which was also the source of life.

NOTES

1 Gen. 2.7.
2 T. Boman, *Hebrew Thought compared with Greek*, SCM Press 1960, p. 95.
3 See M. Eliade, *The Quest*, University of Chicago Press 1969, pp. 77 f.
4 E. G. Parrinder, *Religion in Africa*, Penguin Books 1969, pp. 31 ff.
5 Mircea Eliade, *Myth and Reality*, Harper and Row 1963, pp. 5 f.; *Patterns of Comparative Religion*, Sheed and Ward 1958, p. 416.
6 *Patterns of Comparative Religion*, pp. 410 ff.
7 T. N. Munson, *Reflective Theology*, p. 98.
8 J. Černý, *Ancient Egyptian Religion*, Hutchinson 1952, p. 44.
9 *The Quest*, pp. 141 f.

PART TWO

Mythological Models and the Sacral Society

7 Cosmological symbolism
in the myths

THE EARLIEST form of religious language appears to have been that of myth. It is necessary, therefore, to begin our study of the way in which religious language has developed by paying particular attention to mythological culture. In our subsequent studies it will then be possible to see how mythological ideas continue to recur and to influence later developments. On the other hand, we shall be able to note the way in which important changes took place in the development of religious language as the symbolism of the myths was put to new uses.

We also need to examine the way in which the various types of symbolic expression were able to complement one another and to form in this way a total language for religious expression. Mythological culture provides us with our first example of the way in which the vocabulary of symbols was put together as it were into grammatical form. Any one symbol taken in isolation would be misleading. In order to appreciate the true nature of symbolic discourse we must see how each symbol fits into the whole and how various forms of expression can come together into a structure which obeys a logic peculiar to itself. For this purpose, therefore, we shall note how fundamental mythological ideas were put together into a complex of ideas which could be expressed in religious architecture and social structure.

The fundamental ideas of mythology were concerned with the nature of the cosmos. The world was a place in which men and women had to live and so it was from the beginning most important to formulate some ideas about it. This was not done as we might do it today. Mythology does not attempt an observer's description of the universe, and therefore no attempt is made to be consistent in the manner of a hypothesis reconciling various observed facts. Our study of symbolism has already shown us that we cannot expect to find a simple unity of expression, but a complex of complementary ideas. Religion appears to express itself in a variety of symbolic formulations which are not antagonistic to each other, but stand in mutual support. The concept of a supreme deity, for example, does not exclude the idea of a number of lesser deities or angels. Both the idea of unity and of multiplicity may find a place together. As R. E. Clements points out, a god might be thought of both as lord of a particular place while at the same time being worshipped as the creator of all things.[1] In the same way the cosmological symbolism of mythology does not form a tidy unity, but is made up of a number of limited insights which are held simultaneously. The reason for this, of course, is that these symbolic descriptions were understood to be analogical and hence only a partial statement of the truth. Symbols were placed alongside one another so that the defects in each would be made good by others. The cosmological symbolism of mythology, therefore, consists of a number of paradoxical but related images which reflect the multi-dimensional character of religious experience.

Yet despite the variety and multiplicity of mythology, we can reasonably expect to discover some controlling ideas. It has often been assumed that each people created a distinctive language of their own and that any similarities had to be accounted for by assuming that there had been some cultural influence of one upon the other. Ethnological explanations, however, are not always necessary and sometimes most unlikely. It seems much simpler to suppose that we find the same basic ideas recurring in different cultures because they are derived from the common experience of mankind. Symbols are made out of the obvious, and while the nomenclature may vary considerably, the symbolic content is often the same. Consequently we find light, darkness, water, earth, mountain, man, woman, navel, womb, bird, tree, cow, serpent and other such fundamental notions wherever we turn.

It even seems possible to go further than this and to attempt the discovery of mythological control models. We have already noted that all religious language prefers the use of subjective and personality terminology, and so we can expect to find the analogy of man as one of the controlling ideas. At this point our task will be to see how this model was applied to cosmological understanding. It was, however, clearly supplemented by others which served an integrating function by gathering to and round themselves an assortment of universal symbols.

THE ARCHITECTURAL MODEL AND THE COSMIC MOUNTAIN

The first of these other models came into being when it appeared useful to think of the universe as though it were a huge building. The analogy was a natural one, for the majority of architectural structures were designed as dwelling places, while obviously the universe was also a structure in which man had to live. The houses of men, of course, varied a good deal throughout the world depending on the nature of the terrain on which they were built. In the architectural model, therefore, we find features which are drawn from a diversity of sources. The various elements did not have to create the kind of model which could have been turned into an actual house because its purpose was symbolic. A number of contradictory features could be included because they were able to highlight different aspects of the way in which man saw himself enclosed within the cosmic building.

The idea of the universe envisaged in the myths has often been described as being that of a three-storeyed building. It as been held that primitive man thought of there b eing a heaven above the earth as a kind of upper storey and of a place below the earth constituting a kind of basement. Yet while there is an element of truth in this description, it is nevertheless somewhat misleading when applied to the earlier stages of mythological thought. The idea of a three-storeyed building is not likely to have arisen until civilization was somewhat advanced. What we find in many strands of mythological material is an idea which appears rather to suggest the construction of a tent.

The form of tent which seems to have been used as an analogy for the universe was one which consisted of a canopy supported by a pole at each corner and by a larger pole in the centre. The canopy was used to represent the sky, and the poles stood for the mountains which reached up to the sky and could be thought of as holding it aloft. When seen in this way a number of otherwise puzzling features of mythological language become clear. It explains why we regularly find five mountains mentioned, and why there is continual reference to the four corners of the earth. It also explains why poles or pillars could represent the mountains. Most important of all, the analogy of the tent gives us the reason why the sky is always seen as pressing down upon the mountains and hovering precariously over the earth.

The tent image does not really allow for three storeys in the universe. At first heaven is merely the sky in this symbolism and the hell of later days is only the ground beneath the tent into which the poles are driven.

The cosmic tent, however, was not placed in the kind of situation which we would expect. It is not located in a deserted space but is set in the midst of an ocean. It will be remembered that in the cosmogonic myths the earth was said to have risen out of the great sea. Another basic idea was, therefore, added to that of the tent. The earth consisted of land which rose like a mountain out of the sea to a high point in the centre and having lesser mountains round the base like a wall to keep out the watery floods. The joining of the two imageries meant that the tentage making up the walls of the earth were regarded as mountains as well as the posts at the four corners.

In view of this it is also misleading to speak of myth as having been based upon a notion of a flat earth. The question as to whether the earth was like a plate or a sphere was apparently irrelevant, because it did not have any existential or symbolic significance at this time. In so far as the shape of the earth was considered, it appears to have been thought of as an octohedron. A four-sided pyramid with a square base rose up out of the waters, while hidden from sight was another such pyramid reaching down into the depths of the ocean.

Even when mythological thought did not attain such precision as this, there was always the idea that there was a high point, the summit of the central mountain and therefore the centre of the universe. This centre was not, of course, primarily a cosmological centre but a symbolic one. When this is not seen, the cosmography of myth becomes absurd. Herodotus, for example, scorned the maps drawn up in earlier days because he took mythological symbolism for cartography.[2] The centre may well be considered the most important symbol contained in mythological cosmology. The world was understood as a place into which the sacred constantly poured itself, which it created so that there might be life and that there might be man who could commune with the divine. As the summit of the central mountain was the point at which the earth met the sky, it was naturally considered to be the location at which the sacred manifested itself, for the sky is regularly synonymous with the father deity. The centre was, therefore, always the place of theophany.

The symbolic nature of the mountain becomes clear when we see that it was considered irrelevant to locate the actual centre of the universe. Wherever men lived there was also a centre, a place of meeting between the divine and the human. Any local hill or mountain could serve to represent the cosmic mountain, and in consequence we find that there were innumerable centres of the universe. Any mountain could be the home of the gods, and if this mountain was called Olympus there would be many mountains of this name, as in fact there were in ancient Greece. If a natural mountain was not available to serve symbolically as the focal point of human life and the place at which a man could commune with the gods, he built an artificial replica for himself. Thus the men of the plains in ancient Mesopotamia built their cosmic mountains which we call ziggurats.

As the mountain represented symbolically the point at which the divine and the human met together, it was natural to speak of the top of the mountain as the dwelling place of the gods. In the mythology of Northern Europe, for example, the gods were said to live in Asgard surrounded by a protecting wall guarded by Heindall, who lived near the rainbow bridge by which the heaven of the gods was reached.[3] In man's symbolic replicas of the cosmic mountain this was represented by the building of a shrine on the summit of a ziggurat.

There was a natural link between this concept and the idea that man was in a sense cut off from the divine, in that he did not live constantly at the top of the mountain in communion with the gods. Man was aware of being denied something for which he craved and this suggested that he had lost something which had once been possessed. This was symbolized by the myth of expulsion out of the paradisal life lived by the gods on the central summit. The gods lived in the garden of Eden while man was excluded from it. Ezekiel 28 sets out this imagery very clearly. The prophet tells the King of Tyre that he had been 'in Eden, the garden of God' where he had also been 'on the holy mountain of God, in the midst of the stones of fire', but as a result of his iniquity God had cast him out 'as a profane thing from the mountain of God', and driven him away by 'the guardian cherub'.[4]

Around the idea of the cosmic centre there arose a number of different symbols. One which relates to the architectural model is that of the hearth fire which was located in the centre of the type of mud-hut once used which had a hole in the top of the cone-like roof through which the smoke could escape. The centre, therefore, could be symbolized by fire. This imagery had the advantage of suggesting how at this point the worship of man rose up through the sky and into the realm of the gods. Thus in the Rig Veda and elsewhere we find that the god of fire is said to be at the centre of the earth.

The centre also possessed a well or lake from which rivers flowed down into the world of men. The Navajo Indians of North America, for example, show a lake in the centre of the world out of which grow the precious stalks of maize, the symbols of life and fertility. Other symbols are also found which we must consider in another context.

The existential significance of this symbolism is not difficult to discern. We naturally feel that if we could reach that point from which we could survey the whole of cosmic life, then we would understand. This, however, is denied us, and thus mythological man believed that there was a knowledge which was confined to the gods, a sacred knowledge which was denied to him. The over-towering peaks of the mountains inspired him with awe and so were fitting representations of his sense of the exaltation and otherness of the divine over against himself. Yet the centre also meant that there was a point of contact, and this reflected his sense that divine knowledge was occasionally granted to him. He could only periodically ascend into the mountain of the Lord and meet his God. He was also aware of the way in which he was dependent upon the stream of life which flowed from a beyond into himself, and this was well symbolized in the cosmic rivers which came down from the cosmic mountain.

There was, however, another aspect of man's life for which symbolic provision had to be made. He was also one whose life and meaning were constantly threatened, and this, too, was embodied in the architectural model.

The mythological portrayal of the emergence of the earth as a victory over the sea-dragon found its corresponding expression in the model. Frequent allusions are made to the pillars on which the earth rests as though it were like a house built upon stilts in the midst of the marshes or a river. These pillars are described as the foundations of the earth which are firmly placed in Tehom or the Great Deep. When the Psalmist says of the earth that God 'has founded it upon the

seas and established it upon the rivers',[5] he is both reiterating
the cosmic myth in which the cosmic forces of destruction
had been overcome and reflecting the way in which the model
embodies the result of the victory. The existence of the earth
above the great waters is a lasting testimony to the defeat of
the primeval dragon.

Similarly, the perimeter of the cosmic mountain locates
another point at which the elemental forces of destruction
were overcome. On the shores of the universal earth are the
symbolic walls or lesser mountains which keep the sea at bay.
They act like the walls of a prison for the monster of the deep,
so that he will not wreak destruction over man in his flood.
God had 'assigned to the sea its limit, so that the waters
might not transgress his command' and 'marked out the
foundations of the earth'.[6] For the author of Proverbs, the
pillars standing in the deep and the walls limiting the preserve
of the sea were clearly complementary symbols of the same
idea. God had made a place where life might flourish.

The idea of a space won by God from the forces of destruction
is also fundamental to our appreciating the way in which the
myth speaks of pillars and mountains supporting the sky. In
order to perceive the symbolic significance of this we must
remember that the great waters were not only thought of as
being beneath and around the earth but also above the skies.
The picture of pillars and mountains supporting the heavens
was therefore another way in which the victory over the great
monster was portrayed. The myth speaks of this coming
about because the dragon-slayer not only killed the sea
monster but also sliced its body into two parts. One formed the
underground waters of the model, while the other part constituted the threatening storm waters which poured down upon
the earth. By keeping these two parts of the dragon apart,
man was able to have a space in which to live. The role of the
divine in this operation could be given theriomorphically, as
in Egypt, where the goddess Nut was said to support Ra the
sun-god in the heavens in her form as a cosmic cow whose
four legs held aloft the firmament which was her body. The

idea attains an architectural form when the sky is spoken of as a kind of ceiling or tent canopy stretched over the earth which has windows through which the sweet waters of the rain could pass.[7] In Psalm 104 the imagery referring to the heavens is fittingly combined with that of the foundations of the earth. God has 'stretched out the heavens like a tent' and 'laid the beams' of his 'chambers on the waters'.[8]

So we have an idea of the earth as a vast building whose interior constitutes a place of safety free from the terror of Leviathan. The symbolism of light and darkness was introduced to heighten the contrast between the abode of men and the fearsome waters. The earth is lit by the sun and the stars which Yahweh has placed in the sky, while in Egyptian myth the sun-barque is a vessel of light which sails safely through the terrors of the dark sea which threatens to engulf it. In the symbolism of the cosmic mountain the dangerous terrain inhabited by wild beasts outside the cities of men and far from the 'centre' became a kind of no-man's-land, a place situated between the habitable earth and the cosmic moat, in which man was spiritually close to the realm of evil and in danger from the demonic powers.

The borderlands of evil, however, were not merely thought of as lying in those areas close to the cosmic moat, but also as being even closer to man in the depth beneath his feet. This was the abode of the dead, of those who had been gripped by the power of non-being. Their habitation was a place of darkness in which men were mere shadows of their former selves. It was spoken of as a vault beneath the earth, called by the Greeks Tartarus and by the Hebrews Sheol. The way in which the underground came to symbolize the place of the dead needs little imagination. The custom of burying the dead beneath the ground led to a natural association between the threat of non-being and the depths of the earth. The Hebrews therefore likened their Sheol to a pit dug in the ground[9] or to a water-hole,[10] and just as it was often customary to imprison men in such pits, the dead are spoken of as being prisoners[11] on whom the iron gates of Sheol had been closed.[12] To be buried and to descend into Sheol were identical statements, except that the latter interpreted the meaning of the former. As the source of life Yahweh was he who could shatter 'the doors of bronze' and split 'the bars of iron'.[13] A passage in the book of Jonah illustrates very fully how such symbolism was employed. Jonah cries to Yahweh from 'the belly of the fish' which represents 'the belly of Sheol' and 'the heart of the seas'. Here he is cast out from the presence of God and unable to even look upon the temple of God, for the deep has overwhelmed him 'at the roots of the mountains', and he is down in a land and a pit where the bars seem to close over him for ever.[14]

The symbolic complement to the Sheol of death was the heaven of God. Heaven, the sky and God were virtually understood as synonyms. Even in the New Testament the kingdom of heaven is interchangeable with the kingdom of God. The supreme deity in mythological thought is regularly associated with the sky and sometimes merely called the sky, as for example in Africa. In the Old Testament the sky imagery persists and Yahweh is constantly associated with symbols derived from the sky. The clouds are his chariot in which he rides 'on the wings of the wind'.[15] Similar usages are found universally.

The terminology of mythological thought, however, usually leaves us in no doubt that it is strictly improper to speak of God as located in any particular place. Evans-Pritchard remarks, for example, that the Nuer raise their hands to the sky, but they do not think of themselves as speaking to the sky but to what it represents in their imagination.[16] God, moreover, is usually held to be temporally transcendent to the heaven in which he is said to dwell. Either the whole architectural structure is said to have been his work or he is said to have given birth to it out of himself. He is therefore the Beginner and Unending, as the Akongo of Africa express it.[17] When Isa. 51.6 says that Yahweh is one who remains when both heaven and earth pass away, a thought is expressed which seems to be implicit in most mythology.[18] God is also held to be transcendent to heaven in a spatial symbolism which negates space. While he may be said to dwell in the heavens, he is also declared to be beyond the heavens, for, as Solomon declared, heaven could not contain God.[19] He is not only far away but beyond all distance. On the other hand he is in all things and in all places. The multivalence of mythological symbolism serves to express the idea of God's omnipresence which achieves classic expression in Psalm 139, and a humorous exposition in the Book of Jonah where the prophet is made to look ridiculous because he thinks that he can 'flee from the presence of the Lord'.[20]

The complex simplicity of early thought eventually gave way to a concept of a more ordered structure. The Jews, for example, developed the idea of dividing the heavens into three, the heavens of God, the stars and the meteors. Later Judaic literature became even more extravagant and, possibly under the influence of astrological ideas, divided the heavens into seven. The gnostics even went so far as to speak of there being as many heavens as days in the year. Later uses of the model, however, tend to betray an attitude which accorded ill with the original intentions of myth. They lean towards an objective analysis even when faced with the complexity of existential experience. The architectural model discernible in the mythological writings is not analytical, never objective but frequently subtle. This enabled it to say things in many ways and so to allow for the variety inherent in man's confrontation of the universe. In the myth a man could ascend the cosmic mountain or climb the heavenly ladder of the rainbow to meet his God. That same journey could also be across the great river, for it passed through the waters of the cosmic Jordan. The model thus provided symbolism for that immediate apprehension of the sacred in the midst of life and for the final appropriation of man by God which is accomplished through descent into the jaws of the death dragon. The use of paradoxical and complementary images was, moreover, one of the ways in which the mythological model qualified its statements and avoided the misunderstanding of literalism.

THE LIVING WORLD

The architectural model failed badly in one respect: it suggested that the universe was dead. The myths were primarily concerned with how life came into being, and so other models were used to show that the world brought into being by the cosmogonic act was alive. Models derived from the realm of the inanimate were supplemented by others which were capable of showing that the universe pulsated with the breath of God. For convenience, typical models can be set out in an ascending order of ability to convey this quality.

On the same level as the architectural model we can note another which we find in Chinese mythology. The earth was conceived as the body-work of a chariot. This was square in shape and so did not conflict with tent imagery. Rising up out of the middle of the chariot was a pole at the top of which was the umbrella representing the sky. In this model the phenomenon of life was entirely absent.

Another model which could be used in a way which accorded very well with the architectural model was that of the primordial egg. The egg suggested something which had within itself the capacity to give forth life, and it therefore provided an obvious analogy to the cosmogonic situation. At first we have nothing but an apparently dead object, but when it breaks up there appears something which is alive. In addition, an egg possessed a most useful feature which enabled it to complement the idea of the primeval waters. Inside an egg was water out of which the living thing appeared. In consequence we find in a number of mythologies the concept of a primal egg which is split into two parts like the cosmogonic monster to form the two parts of creation. The top half of the egg is used to represent the sky covering the earth above, while the bottom half of the egg retains the waters of birth on which the earth floats.

The idea of the universe as a tree takes the process a stage further, and constitutes one of the most frequently recurring images. Although the tree is often said to be in the garden of

God or Eden, this is another cosmic symbol and is co-terminous with the whole of creation. This is clear in the mythologies of South Borneo and of the Toba-Bataks of Sumatra. One of the best known examples of this usage, however, is found in North European mythology. The tree, Yggdrasill, represents the cosmos as a whole while also functioning in the manner of a symbol in many other ways. It is the source of life and immortality, a shelter from ontological evil and has the power of healing. As a cosmic symbol, its roots reach down into the earth, the realm of the dead, but from the roots also comes a spring from which life is nourished. Mimer's well was located at the roots of the tree, and in Ireland the Boyne and Shannon were said to flow from it. Its trunk reaches up from the centre of the earth to spread its branches in the heavens. The tree could be represented simply by a post with steps cut into it, or by a ladder. Once again we have an imagery which provides a connecting pathway through the cosmos. We also find a now familiar symbol in the serpent who attacks the roots of the tree and a new symbol, that of the eagle, who lives in the branches, in which souls are born, and opposes the destructive work of the serpent.[21]

Although a tree conveyed the idea of a living universe, it is obvious that myth-makers usually found it a deficient symbol. The plant or tree is therefore further supplemented by the model of animal life. In the Upanishads the universe comes into being when the primordial horse is sacrificed. The animal model was used to bring certain features of the architectural model to life. In Egypt, the sky and the pillars supporting it were likened to the body and legs of the cow Hathor, while in India the supports for the sky were said to have been elephants.

The myths made use of animal forms in all sorts of ways, and very few generalizations can be made. It is often said that the animal kingdom was not differentiated from the human, but although human characteristics are often attributed to animals, there would appear to be significant reasons why a god was thought in one context to be an animal and in

E

another to be human. The characteristics of certain animals seem to have appeared appropriate to designate certain aspects of the cosmos. The use of elephants as heavenly supports in India, for example, was clearly a representation of brute strength. The ability of birds to escape the spatial limitations of man naturally suggested an analogy of divine transcendence. The symbolic use of animals therefore, would seem to have been determined by specific requirements.

In order to show the character of certain cosmic elements, however, it was often necessary to resort to the creation of monsters. These extraordinary beings were made to combine a number of features in a way which was never actually found in creation. This seems to have been a way of suggesting that the cosmic power they had in mind could not be adequately represented by anything which really existed. Some animals were natural images of destructive force or tremendous power, but if it was desired to characterize a primordial energy, the myths frequently resorted to talk of fabulous animals.

Symbolic figures drawn from inanimate objects and from plant or animal life appear throughout the world's mythology. The human form however constituted the control model.

THE ANTHROPOMORPHIC MODEL

Although we find a bewildering variety of symbolic formulations which range through the threefold classification of inanimate, organic and human, all mythological imageries seem to be ultimately subordinate to anthropomorphism. The natural elements were not worshipped as mere forces or energies, but were regularly endowed with the peculiar characteristics of man. In this way the sun, the moon, stars, wind and river were turned into gods. This tendency achieved its most overt expression in cosmic anthropomorphism. The whole of creation was thought of as a giant human being. It was usual to speak of the primal being as male and so we have the symbol of the primal man. The idea appears in one of its simplest forms among the Godon of Mali and the Upper

Volta. They speak of a shapeless mass of clay being thrown into primordial space where it took the form of a body lying on its back.[22] This constituted the earth on which man lives and out of which he has come.

The various parts of creation were made out of different parts of the primordial anthropos. In China we find a number of different explanations of P'an-ku, but from these it seems worth noting some particularly significant ones. The four 'corner' mountains are derived from his head, arms and feet, while the 'central' mountain is his belly. The sun and the moon are his eyes, his breath the wind, and his voice the thunder. One story attributes the changes in the weather to his varying moods. In Northern European mythology the primal man is named Ymir, and here again the earth or Midgard is formed from his body, his flesh becoming the land, his blood the sea, his bones the mountains, his hair the trees and his skull the vault of the heavens. In the Rig Veda he is named Purusha, and not only do all the parts of creation come from his body, but also the various castes which had developed in Hindu society.

These descriptions clearly implied that creation came into being by the death of the primal man, and so we find that cosmogony constitutes a self-sacrifice on the part of the primordial being. He has to suffer himself to be dismembered in order that creation may come into being. The idea of the originating sacrifice could take many forms. Another is perhaps represented in the picture of Odin who is hung on the cosmic tree, an idea which a Christian Europe was to find most significant.[23]

The primal man becomes many things besides the cosmic structure itself. He is also the first man who is moulded out of his flesh, the earth, and made alive by himself. He is set to tend the garden of God situated on the top of the cosmic mountain as in Phoenician and Hebrew myth. In his appearance on the earth of his body, he becomes not merely one but two, the first man and woman, whose derivation from a properly androgynous being is indicated by speaking of them as 'one flesh' or brother and sister as in the Indian myth of Yama and Yima.

The basic idea behind all this imagery is of course, that man is held to be a microcosm of the universe or the best analogy by which to understand the whole. Thus in Zoroastrian literature the body of man is said to be the measure of the world. Consequently it can use man as a symbol of the creative principle Ohrmazd, from whose body the world comes as Gayomart. From it derives that fundamental anthropomorphism which has characterized religion throughout its history and proved a valuable analogical tool until its symbolism ceased to be appreciated and became an embarrassment.

The idea of the primal being as the source of life naturally suggested in particular the female analogy. The male role in the creation of life did find an important place as lingam pillars, representing Shiva in India and Fál in Ireland, for example, but the female imagery not unnaturally tended to predominate. Consequently the primal being is often described as a woman in this context. The Jains spoke of the world as a woman with her arms raised. In Greece Gaea was the gigantic and deep-breasted earth-mother who gave birth to gods and men. In Irish mythology a woman named Banba settled in the land before the great flood and survived the deluge on the island mountain which was, of course, herself.[24]

The female analogy made it possible to speak of man's relationship to cosmic being in ways not provided by the male form. In particular it suggested a way of symbolizing the emergence of man out of the primal being as a birth process and of his death as a return to the womb of birth.

The first of these usages is well illustrated by the mythology of the Pueblo Indians.[25] The originating deity is named Awonawilona and the process of creation is begun when he impregnates the sea. As a result green scum forms on its surface which eventually becomes the solid earth. In anthropomorphic form the deity thus becomes the sky father and the earth mother. The appearance of man in creation is then described as a birth out of the fourfold womb of the earth.

It is pictured as an ascent from the place of generation in the depths of the earth, up through the place beneath the navel, the vagina of earth and the womb of birth, to the surface of the world. In the world man is then nourished by the milk from the breasts of the divine mother-earth, and the breath of the sky brings fertilizing rain.

At death, mythology usually speaks of the soul returning to the womb of origin. Eliade points out that the Kogi of Sierra Nevada hold that the tomb is the access point to the cosmic mother and the funerary ritual makes it clear that death is a process in which the gestation of birth is reversed.[26] The Aramaic language may preserve this idea by using the word tomb as a euphemism for the uterus in which the embryo lies.[27] In ancient Egypt the souls of the dead were received by Hathor, the heavenly cow, in her mountains at the source of the Nile.[28] In this way the Egyptians indicated that the reception of the dead took place at the same point symbolically from which everything derived, from the top of the cosmic mountain and from the tree of life. Moreover, in presenting death in this way there was the idea that it was a process in which a man or a woman became one with the divine again. Thus the dead Egyptian was shown by various visual symbols portrayed in the tomb to have become Osiris if a man and Hathor if a woman.[29] The sarcophagus chamber in Egypt could be identified with the womb of Nut in her form as the cosmic cow, for the name means 'House of Horus' and indicated that the tomb was in fact a 'bethel' or place of God's presence. Death was a rebirth, usually spoken of as taking place in the lower world, as among the Hopi.[30] On the one hand the place of the dead was like Irkalla in Babylonia, a 'house of dust and darkness',[31] but it was also the cosmic mountain in the depths of whose hollows ran the watery deep of Apsu, which was the source of primordial life. When this imagery was used, the dead were identified with the serpent dragon and this was indicated by painting or carving the monster on the coffin or the tree which held the corpse, as at the Alamannic cemetery of Oberflacht.[32] The significance of this symbolism in which the dragon receives the dead into the grave mound which it guards is most fully brought out, however, in the womb imagery provided by the anthropomorphic model.

Finally, the differences between the male and the female forms of the model were ignored in the symbolization of the centre of the world as the navel of the anthropos. The idea would naturally occur to one who was thinking of the earth as a body lying face upwards. The navel was common to the male and female forms and, moreover, was an appropriate representation of the place of origin. The idea found wide expression. We have already seen how the Pueblo Indians connected the womb concept with the navel. Irish mythology regarded Uisnech as the navel of the earth. In ancient Greece we find it in a map drawn by Anaximander which shows the oracle of Delphi as the centre of the earth which is, of course, surrounded by the River Oceanus. The central point is indicated by marking it with the omphalos stone or navel symbol.[33] The same idea appears in Ireland, Greece, Indonesia and Peru. In Hebrew scripture the word navel appears twice as a symbol of the centre. Ezekiel 38.12 uses it to express the centrality of Zion: Childs remarks on this passage that the writer intends the reader to perceive an apt comparison between the umbilical cord as that through which the life flows into the foetus and the centre of the world, Zion, at which the divine creative and sustaining power enters the earth.[34] In Judges 9.36 f. we have the second passage which shows how the navel concept was naturally associated with other symbols of the centre in the Hebrew mind. Abimelek and his men suddenly appear out of ambush to attack the city of Shechem. When Gaal, Abimelek's enemy, sees the attackers appear, he tells the ruler of Shechem that men are coming down from the tops of the mountains and from the navel of the land. He also remarks that one company is coming from 'the direction of the Diviners' Oak'.[35] Not only has the mountain summit been naturally associated with the world's navel, but it is also closely linked with an oracular tree. The navel of the earth was not only the place which symbolized the passage of divine life into the world, but also as the centre it was the place at which knowledge of the sacred was revealed.[36]

The various models of the myths supplement one another and in this way correct distortions liable to arise when one model is used to the exclusion of others. In particular, it was necessary to inject life into the world of the architectural model by the use of analogies drawn from living things. If the architectural model had been used by itself it would have led men to think of the world as a dead, insensitive thing in which life and personality were alien intruders. The organic model brought the world to life and the anthropomorphic model imposed on it a character, a personal dimension which enabled men to confront the cosmos as subjective and responsive being. All mythological models were constructed out of man's search for a meaningful relationship between himself and the cosmos. The architectural model provided the idea of a space created by God in which he could live and confront the sacred while the anthropomorphic model provided for such an intimate relationship with the whole that man could expect to find the divine in the depths of his own being.[37]

NOTES

1 R. E. Clements, *God and Temple*, Basil Blackwell 1965, pp. 2 f.

2 See R. S. Brumbaugh, *The Philosophers of Greece*, Allen and Unwin 1966, p. 22.

3 H. R. Ellis Davidson, *Gods and Myths of Northern Europe*, Penguin Books 1964, p. 29.

4 Ezek. 28.13, 14, 16; see A. G. May, 'The King in the Garden of Eden', in: B. W. Anderson and W. Harrelson (eds.), *Israel's Prophetic Heritage*, SCM Press 1962.

5 Ps. 24.2.

6 Prov. 8.29.

7 Gen. 7.11; 8.2; Mal. 3.10.

8 Ps. 104.2, 3.

9 Job 33.18, 22; Ps. 30.9; Ezek. 32.25.

10 Ps. 40.2.

11 Isa. 24.22.

12 Job 17.16.

13 Ps. 107.16.

14 Jonah 2.1–6.

15 Ps. 104.3.

16 Evans-Pritchard, *Nuer Religion*, p. 321.

17 E. G. Parrinder, *African Traditional Religion*, SPCK 1968, p. 34; see further E. W. Smith (ed.), *African Ideas of God*, Edinburgh House Press 1950.

18 Compare Ps. 102.25–27.

19 I Kings 8.27.

20 Jonah 1.3.

21 See Ellis Davidson, *op. cit.*, pp. 190 ff. and A. and B. Rees, *Celtic Heritage*, Thames and Hudson 1961.

22 Parrinder, *Religion in Africa*, p. 29.

23 See Ellis Davidson, *op. cit.*, p. 220, and E. O. G. Turville-Petre, *Myth and Religion of the North*, Weidenfeld and Nicolson 1964, pp. 42 ff.

24 Rees, *op. cit.*, p. 115.

25 See C. Burland, *North American Indian Mythology*, Paul Hamlyn 1965.

26 M. Eliade, *The Quest*, pp. 138–41.

27 See E. S. Drower, *Water into Wine*, John Murray 1956, p. 71.

28 See Parrinder, *Religion in Africa*, pp. 78–87.

29 H. Frankfort, *Kingship and the Gods*, University of Chicago Press 1948, pp. 175 f.

30 E. A. Nida, *Customs, Culture and Christianity*, Tyndale Press 1963, pp. 164–68.

31 E. O. James, *The Ancient Gods*, Weidenfeld and Nicolson 1960, p. 179.

32 Ellis Davidson, *op. cit.*, p. 161.

33 R. S. Brumbaugh, *op. cit.*, p. 22.

34 B. S. Childs, *Myth and Reality in the Old Testament*, SCM Press 1960, pp. 86 f.

35 Judg. 9.37.

36 See M. Eliade, *Patterns of Comparative Religion*, pp. 374 ff.; *The Myth of the Eternal Return*, Routledge and Kegan Paul 1955, pp. 12 f.

37 Valuable information and interpretation of matters relating to this chapter will also be found in S. G. F. Brandon, *Man and his Destiny in the Great Religions*, Manchester University Press 1962; J. Duchesne-Guillemin, 'Some Aspects of Anthropomorphism', in: S. G. F. Brandon (ed.), *The Saviour God*, Manchester University Press 1963, pp. 83–96; E. G. Parrinder, *West African Religion*, Epworth Press, rev. ed. 1961.

8 Symbolic Architecture

THE RELIGIOUS value of the models used in the age of myth
is evidenced by the way in which they played an essential
role in the various aspects of human life. They not only gave
man a view of the universe but determined his mode of response
to it and provided the basic ideas for the construction of sacred
places in which that response could be given symbolic form.

Cultic ritual embodied the myth in the life of the people.
This has become increasingly clear with the study of peoples
for whom myth is still alive. The creation myth in particular
played an important part, for it contained the essence of man's
understanding of things. The re-enactment of this was fundamental. The events of the cosmic creation were acted out at
the New Year festival in which the world was made anew
after the death of the old cosmos or the return to the primeval
totality. In Mesopotamia, which seems to have been the
original home for numerous derivative celebrations, the
Enuma elish narrative of the creation myth formed the basis
of the celebrations in which the people entered into a renewed
world-order.

Rituals of creation, however, required an appropriate
scenery in which to take place. The stage-setting had to imitate
the symbolic models in which the myth itself was framed. As
a result we find that the setting for cultural activity is a symbolic
translation of the model into physical terms. As the myth was
a formulation which enabled a cultic ritual to give meaning
to the life it accompanied, so the provision of a symbolic
setting laid out in accordance with the model reinforced and

E*   137

controlled the ritual drama. Ritual could best bring men into line with the real order of things if it was enacted in a structure which set forth the nature of that reality. Hence the symbolic model created a symbolic architecture in which the cultus could be performed. Temple and ritual together were then able to proclaim both the cosmic structure and the creative activity informing all things. All that was done on the eternal scale and on a cosmic dimension was then seen microcosmically in sacramental activity which drew all men within itself and mediated to them its life and meaning.

The architectural setting of a people's worship is therefore likely to tell us something of their world-view if we are able to read its symbolism.[1] This, however, has often been found difficult to do because the nature of symbolism was not understood. In order to appreciate the symbolic significance of temple architecture we must approach it with an understanding of the way in which symbolic communication functions. We must not expect to find in a temple a scale model. There can be no translation of cosmic understanding into exact physical terms. The architect of a symbolic building was required only to point towards or hint at the cosmic structure. Moreover, a temple was not necessarily a copy of only one model but could embody a number of features derived from several models. These supplemented one another, and so the architectural forms sometimes contain what appear to be conflicting motifs. The temple may be at the same time a mountain, a palace, a tomb and a living organism. Again, the symbolic features are likely to have more than one meaning. As symbols they can point in many directions. We do not therefore find a tidy example of one particular model, but a confusing richness of expression, although one model may dominate the rest.

THE GATE OF HEAVEN

The site of a temple was not chosen by men but designated by a theophany of some kind. Although the sacred might manifest

itself in every place, the spot which was to be a people's perm-
anent means of contact with the divine had to be revealed.
Zion was the place in which Yahweh chose his Name to dwell.[2]
We find the most characteristic form of such a choice in the
story of Jacob.[3] In the course of a journey to Haran, Jacob
spends the night at a place called Luz where he has a dream in
which its character as a meeting place between heaven and
earth is made known to him. This is symbolized in the dream
by a ladder which connects earth with heaven and forms a
passageway for the ascent and descent of the angels of God.
When Jacob awakes, he knows that Yahweh is in that place,
and declares that 'This is none other than the house of God, and
this is the gate of heaven'.[4] He sets up a pillar which he anoints,
and renames the place *Beth-el*, the house of God. Here we have
the basic features of a theophany for the choosing of a temple
site; features which occur frequently in various religious
traditions.

The imagery of a ladder or stairway often appears, for it is
an obvious way of suggesting a means of connection between
the worlds of gods and men when they are being conceived
under the architectural model. Stairways form an integral
part of early temple structures. The idea of a connection
between two spheres is also given under the image of a bridge.
The essential idea in both these forms is simply a connection
between the sacred and man. They indicate that in these
places men may meet their God. Man-made ladders, stairways
and bridges were, however, merely copies of a symbolic idea
and there was a natural phenomenon which seemed to
represent it far more adequately. This was the rainbow.

In the Hebrew tradition the rainbow was the sign of a
covenant or relationship established between Yahweh and
man with the promise that the destructive waters of Leviathan
would never again threaten the total destruction of the earth.[5]
In the Hindu myth the rainbow is specifically characterized
as a bridge between men and the gods, and in the symbolic
architecture derived from Hindu mythology, bridges were
built as the means of access to some temples in a way which

suggested this. These bridges were built with balustrades in the form of cobras with multiple heads called *nagas*. Paul Mus pointed out that these were intended to recall the comparison made in India and East Africa of the rainbow with a multi-coloured serpent with its head reaching up to heaven or conversely dipping downwards to drink water from the sea.[6] The two ideas could be combined, and the descent of the Buddha from the thirty-third heaven to preach to his mother could be represented by a rainbow stairway whose sides were formed with *nagas*.

The designation of a temple as a gate of heaven is also very common. This was a very simple way of suggesting that it was the means of entering into the presence of God. Where-ever men have built temples, they have constructed a gate of God and this has even provided the designation for the city it served. Babylon, for example, was Assyrian for 'gate of God'. which was translated as *Bab-el* in Hebrew. The theophanous character of such a place was not only indicated by its name. Quite often a gate was built, the symbolic purpose of which was obvious by the fact that it served little useful purpose, although constructed to enormous proportions, as in a number of Persian mosques. More frequently we have doorways which proclaim their significance simply by leading into an inner shrine housing the image of the god. It was not always con-sidered necessary to carry out the symbolism in a detailed way. The rainbow stair could be indicated simply by a picture drawn of it on the lintels of a sanctuary doorway or by a figure of Indra whose bow was the rainbow. Whatever device was used, the message remained the same as that given at the consecration of a Christian church to the present day when it is declared in the words of Jacob that 'this is the gate of heaven'.

Sometimes the location of the doorway was determined by the position of the temple in relation to the rising sun. The sun has played an important symbolic role in religion over a very long period. It symbolized all that was good and beneficial to man; it was both actually and symbolically a source of life.

If the temple was constructed in such a way that the first rays of the rising sun struck through it into the shrine lighting up the image within, this could symbolize the coming of God to his temple. This device highlights a very important feature of the symbolic architecture of temples. God is thought of both as dwelling in the temple and also as coming to manifest himself there.[7] God is always present with man in the midst of his life and community, but there is not a continuous sense of his presence. The nearness of God is only experienced on particular occasions. The symbolism of the architecture attempted to convey this understanding of the divine as being a presence, an absence and a coming derived from the existential experience of man.

The theophany or man's experience of God in a moment of his life thus determined the kind of structure which he built for the purposes of worship. It was necessary to emphasize, however, that what he was doing did not derive from himself but had the quality of being given, that it was a revelation. Just as the siting of a temple was revealed, so also was its structure. If the temple was to be a symbolic copy of the total reality this was essential. Cosmic truth was inaccessible to man and known only to God whose 'house' the totality was. The plans for a temple building are therefore vouchsafed in a dream or in the sacred scriptures, given by God.[8] Only then could the temple be a valid representation which would enable men to meet their God. The temple had to be a setting forth of the cosmic whole or, in symbolic terms, it had to be at the centre.[9]

THE MOUNTAIN TEMPLE

The microcosmic symbolism of mythology accounts for the way in which innumerable places are dwellings of the gods. The centre of the earth can be virtually anywhere, providing some kind of theophany has taken place. Such a divine dwelling place is not exclusive except in the cause of nationalism, but permits the reality of other centres. There is nothing odd, therefore, in the fact that we find the gods located in different places even among one people. The commonest form of location is the mountain, a natural feature which recurs on a world-wide scale.

We have already seen that a cosmic mountain was considered a form of the universe. On the principle, therefore, that the macrocosm was shown forth in numerous microcosms, we have the idea that any mountain could represent the cosmic reality. There was no need, in fact, to build anything at all, because any high place could be a place of worship. The prevalence of 'high places' in Canaanite religion is well known to readers of the Hebrew prophets. As Clements remarks, any local mountain could serve as the symbol of the cosmos.[10] On the other hand, particularly striking heights were naturally favoured in that they appeared to capture the nature of reality in the fullest way. The mountains whose tips seemed to disappear into a beyond possessed that sense of mystery, a penetration into infinity, which inspired man's awe and wonder. The great mountains like the Himalayas, Mount Etna or Mount Fuji were therefore particularly communicative to man of cosmic reality. In this connection it is interesting to note the embarrassment of the Hebrews when speaking of Zion, the height of which could hardly compare even with the Alps, and the need to speak of it as being destined to become the high cosmic peak eschatologically. Zion served the Hebrews, however, as Zaphon served the Phoenicians. The Greeks also lacked one outstanding mountain for their purpose; hence every mountain was the home of their gods. They were all 'Olympus', a pre-Greek word for a mountain.

A natural mountain, then, was a normal place for the location of the gate of heaven. But its symbolic message needed to be made plain, and so we find that mountains were often submitted to a vast amount of labour to make them speak more eloquently. Mountains could be excavated as at Ellora and at Mamallapuram in India, to become plainly temples of Shiva.

As men settled in plains and built their cities near to adequate water supplies, the use of natural mountains became more difficult. It was important for a human community to be at the centre of the earth and to have its 'gate of heaven', and so artificial mountains were built and the city laid out around it. The intention to create a mountain was evident from the care men took to plant trees upon it, sometimes even ensuring that these were the same as grew upon the mountain serving as their model. Some of the earliest of such artificial mountains were built in Mesopotamia and called ziggurats. The name tells us that they were intended as 'hills of heaven' or 'mountains of God'. At Nippur, the ziggurat of Enlil was called 'house of the Mountain, Mountain of the Storm, Bond between Earth and Heaven'.[11] Here we see in the names given to it how the ziggurat was the focus for a number of ideas concerning a place of theophany.

When the form was totally under human control, symbolic elaboration was able to proceed easily and incorporate various motifs. One of the commonest of these was to create a number of stages or terraces in the ziggurat. The clue to the meaning of this is found in the fact that sometimes each stage was a repetition of the whole and even included the doorways as for example at Phnom Bakheng. This conveyed the idea of a series of worlds lying within or on top of each other and stretching upwards and inwards into the infinite. Such a concept was naturally favoured by the fundamental religious ideas emanating from India.

Mesopotamia may have been the original home of much of this type of architecture which is found developed in India and south-east Asia. The basic idea of the mountain temple, however, is probably not restricted to those cultures dependent on Mesopotamia. At all events the imagery does appear in widely separated areas. The Dinka tribes of the Southern Sudan believe that the building of a mound can be a means of creating a meeting between the divine *nhialic* and the human,[12] and the architectural pattern based on the mythical model appears both at Angkor Wat and among the Dayaks of Borneo. Staged towers and pyramids are found all over the world, in

India, China, Egypt, Mexico and Peru. The mountain-temple constantly appears as a fundamental architectural form.

At Angkor Wat, the temple-mountain of the Khmer civilization was an elaborate replica of mythical cosmology with individualizing features derived from the natural structure of Mount Meru which was their control model. The central temple was intended to represent Mount Meru itself and five towers imitated its five peaks. The mountain is symbolically the whole world, and so Angkor has an enclosing wall which is intended to represent the mountains at the edge of the world. Surrounding the wall is a moat to symbolize the ocean beyond. The sea motif appears frequently and its importance is obvious from the inscription describing the temple of Mebon Oriental which reads; 'In the middle of this sea, which is the sacred pool of Yasodhara, he erected a mountain, with a summit like that of Meru, covered with temples and sanctuaries plastered in stucco.'[13] Sometimes the creative, purifying and destructive water is merely indicated by placing a jug of water at the entrance.

Amongst the Dayaks of Borneo we find the same ideas, but in a less elaborate form, and associated with the ordinary dwelling houses. Here the village and the house are thought of as replicas of the universe, located at the centre. A steep roof suggests the primeval mountain and the house is erected on the back of the watersnake which symbolizes original creativity. The house is topped by a symbolic umbrella signifying the the mythical tree of life.

The portrayal of the cosmos is not complete without some indication of the underworld. The soaring mass of stone must be complemented by at least a suggestion of the foundations of the earth laid in the deep waters. In Indian cosmology, Mount Meru was held to extend under the earth and under the sea and this had to find a means of expression. The base or lowest terrace of temple buildings was covered with bas-reliefs which suggested the ocean or the demonic, and then covered over with a second layer of decorated stone. In this way the hidden underworld was incorporated into the cosmic

replica.[15] Herodotus was therefore speaking the symbolic truth
when he asserted that the tower of Babel had a subterranean
part which extended into the earth as much as the visible
tower rose toward the heavens. Again an inscription makes
the symbolic message clear. At Angkor, Jayavarnman VII, who
restored the structure, declared: 'The first pierced the brilliant
sky with its pinnacle, the other reached down to the unplumbed
depths of the world of serpents. This mountain of victory and
this ocean of victory built by the king, simulated the arc of
his glory.'[16]

THE COSMIC ORGANISM

The organic model of the universe also made a contribution
to temple architecture. When the dominant idea is of the
universe as a huge body it produces a characteristic temple
architecture. In certain Indian temples the structure is created
in such a way as to suggest various parts of the body. The roof
is curved to represent the trunk of the body, while the summit
is said to symbolize the throat and skull. Sometimes faces
were carved in the summit to make this clear.[17] In these
Indian temples there was often a 'womb-house', a 'germ-cell'
or an 'embryo of the world'. This was a small sanctuary in
which was kept the sacred image buried deep within the
masonry.[18]

The imagery being employed centres on creativity as expressed in the birth process. Because the source of cosmic being was
a unified totality, it was necessary in the myth to think of the
primordial originator as androgynous. Corresponding with
this, the one image can perform the function of being the
ultimate source of all things. As we move outwards in many
temple structures, especially in those characteristic of the
Indian medieval period, we find the godhead is divided into
male and female. Now the cosmic creativity is seen as the
result of an embrace between the male and female principles
which emanate from the one originating deity in the myth.
This is portrayed sometimes with gross sensuality in the

sculptured reliefs decorating the temple walls. To portray this, temples are even built in pairs and joined together in a masonic representation of the marriage knot tied in the clothes of a bride and groom.[19]

The life and ritual of man was understood to imitate the cosmic process seen in this way. In sexual activity man might participate in the divine creative activity and attain that kind of union which seemed to be the prerogative of the divine. Hence many ancient rituals incorporated symbolic acts of a sexual nature. Of far more importance, however, was the fact that the natural course of human life could be understood in terms of the myth. Dayak custom brings several features together for this purpose, uniting the symbolism of buildings with both the myth of the primeval waters and the imagery of cosmic creativity. When a young girl is initiated into womanhood, she enters an initiation room which is understood to be in the primeval waters into which she descends to become the primordial watersnake. When she later gives birth to a child she again enters a room which is symbolically located in the primeval waters, and in this way the act of birth is shown as a participation of mankind in the cosmic creativity. At death the Dayak is placed in a coffin which is made in the shape of a boat, and painted on its sides we find again a water-snake, the primordial tree and the cosmic mountain to indicate the return to the divine totality from which man was born.[20]

Another way of indicating the significance of death is found in the use of the stupa. This was fundamentally a burial mound built in stone and topped by the symbolic umbrella. It was thought of as a kind of architectural body built to replace the mortal flesh of the deceased. It was a tomb, but one which was thought of as housing life rather than death. There was often a ceremony of 'making alive' carried out at burial. In Cambodia, images of the dead were made and 'animated' by ritual acts before being placed in the funerary temple. In Egypt, the embalmed corpse was submitted to the ceremony of the *opening of the mouth* before being placed in its 'eternal house'.[21]   In the third century BC Shi Huang-ti

built a funeral temple for himself which makes its character
as a representation of the cosmic body quite clear. It was
built at the foot of Li-shan mountain, of which it was a symbolic
replica, as the mountain itself was a symbolic image of the
cosmos. The sarcophagus had a base which represented the
natural features of the earth, while the ceiling represented the
heavens. A mechanism was even installed to produce miniature
oceans. [22] Jeanette Mirsky cites the great stupa of Sanchi as an
example of one in which the mound is thought of as encasing a
pillar or lingam of Shiva symbolizing divine creativity. [23]
This imaginary pillar was envisaged as rising from the ground,
passing through the image in the 'embryo' sanctuary, up
through the solid tower to emerge through the ring-stone as a
pedestal for the symbolic umbrella. [24] In this we have an
example of the capacity of symbolic language to convey its
message by indirect methods and to combine a number of
evocative motifs.

The way in which a variety of symbolic motifs may be
incorporated into the cosmological architecture of a culture is
exemplified by the description given by Eliade of the Kogi of
Sierra Nevada. [25] The world is conceived here also as a pyramid-
like hill which can be embodied in miniature in the similar
shaped hills of Sierra Nevada and by the building of their
cultic houses which are located at the centre and able to
function as places of theophany. The world is also conceived
both as an egg created by the universal mother and as her
uterus. Consequently Sierra Nevada and each cultic house
and dwelling place is a replica of this. The tomb is also the
access point to the cosmic mother, and the funerary ritual
makes it clear that death is a process in which the gestation of
birth is reversed so that the dead return to the cosmic mother.

COSMIC ARCHITECTURE AND THE
HEBRAIC-CHRISTIAN TRADITION

Examples of the kind of symbolic architecture we have
discussed are drawn most readily from the fertile crescent

during the ancient period and from Indian-dominated cultures in the far east. We do, however, find examples in other cultures, although they are often subordinated to new motifs.

There is cause for thinking that the temple of Solomon possessed a cosmic significance, although there is much dispute about particular features. The bronze sea can hardly have fulfilled anything other than a symbolic purpose and was probably intended to represent the primeval waters. Egyptian temples had a sacred lake which served the same purpose. It is more difficult to be certain of the cosmic meaning of the pillars referred to, but there is at least a strong possibility that they represented the foundations of the earth and the supports of the firmament. Some basis for this interpretation is found in the words of the psalmist who wrote that Yahweh 'built his sanctuary like the high heavens, like the earth, which he has founded for ever',[26] and by the fact that it was not uncommon to parallel the statement that Yahweh 'is in his holy temple' by the assertion that Yahweh's 'throne is in heaven'.[27] Attempts were made to adduce a very detailed correspondence, according to Dillistone, who states that 'in Jewish circles. . . the most elaborate schemes were worked out to show that the furniture, the dress of the priests, the vessels of the service, all corresponded to particular parts of the created order'.[28]

The idea is incorporated in the Byzantine architecture of early Christianity. Here the layout of iconographic symbols was clearly intended to represent the earth and the firmament, showing Christ *pantocrator* ruling the world from the celestial dome. With the development of Christian architecture in the west much of this symbolism was lost, to be replaced by one drawn primarily from historical events. Cosmic symbolism eventually ceased to be a principal theme of religious thinking there and tended to become the preserve of those outside the mainstream of tradition and to receive its renewals from contact with the orient. Once the symbolism of cosmic architecture was no longer understood, examples of it were dismissed as magical, its structures retained if they had any artistic value or abandoned if they served no aesthetic or functional purpose.

The architecture of world religion probably betrays a dichotomy between the cosmologically centred symbolism of those cultures in which myth is a living form and others in which religious symbolism is centred on history. Cosmic architecture is found scattered throughout the world, in Peru, China, Egypt and in India. When it is found, however, it derives from a period in which it was accompanied by a living cosmological myth. In the Hebrew culture the cosmic myth underwent such a transformation that the cosmic symbolism of its architecture now appears problematical. In classical Greece the connection between myth, ritual and architecture seems already to have been largely severed, and M. P. Nilsson consequently asserted that Greek myth was not translated into ritual.[29] But as Eliade points out, the Greek myths, although best known to us, do not provide the best grounds upon which to base judgments of myth, because they have already ceased to represent a living religious form of language and have been transformed into fictional epic poetry.[30] A cosmic architecture is found only when there is also present a structure of thinking in which cosmological myth provides the basis for a community's life.

These facts seem to suggest that symbolic architecture reflects the distinction which emerges with the development of world religion. In the east, the sense of immanent deity was retained from the age of myth, and nothing illustrates this more than the use of architectural symbolism based on the idea of a cosmic organism. Temple building was inclined to state the immanence of deity and the loss of the terrestial in the infinite represented respectively by the mountain temple with the principle of life within it and the staged tower suggesting a vertical ascent to worlds of increasing approximation to infinity. But in the near east and in the western world, the Hebraic-Christian tradition encouraged a sense of the utter transcendence of God on the one hand and a this-worldly concern on the other. God and man, heaven and earth were divided. This inhibited the expression of the cosmic totality in its architecture and ultimately resulted in western secularization, when the sacred dimension of human existence could find no other means of expression.

NOTES

1 See F. W. Dillistone, *Christianity and Communication*, Collins 1956, p. 32; H. Frankfort, *Ancient Egyptian Religion*, Harper and Row 1961, pp. 150–56.

2 Deut. 12.11.

3 Gen. 28.11–22.

4 Gen. 28.17.

5 Gen. 9.13.

6 See G. Coedes in: J. E. F. Gardiner (ed.), *Angkor*, Oxford University Press 1963, p. 46.

7 See R. E. Clements, *God and Temple*, p. 63, n. 4.

8 I Chron. 28.11 f.; Ezek. 40.

9 See G. K. Levy, *Gate of Horn*, Faber 1963, p. 170.

10 R. E. Clements, *op. cit.*, p. 3.

11 J. Mirsky, *Houses of God*, Constable 1965, p. 16; see also G. R. Levy, *Gate of Horn*, p. 169; A. Parrot, *The Tower of Babel*, SCM Press 1955, p. 64.

12 G. Lienhardt, *Divinity and Experience: The Religion of the Dinka*, Oxford University Press 1961, p. 32.

13 Quoted by G. Coedes, *op. cit.*, p. 43.

14 M. Eliade, *The Quest*, p. 79.

15 Coedes, *op. cit.*, pp. 44 f.

16 Coedes, *op. cit.* p. 46; cf. Parrot, *op. cit.*, p. 18.

17 *New Larousse Encyclopaedia of Mythology*, p. 184.

18 *New Larousse*, pp. 176 f.; J. Mirsky, *op. cit.*, p. 46; G. R. Levy, *op. cit.*, pp. 135, 177.

19 *New Larousse*, p. 184.

20 M. Eliade, *The Quest*, p. 79.

21 S. G. F. Brandon, *The Saviour God*, p. 24.

22 See E. Diez, *The Ancient Worlds of Asia*, Macdonald 1961.

23 J. Mirsky, *op. cit.*, p. 45.

24 The ziggurat of Babylon was the tomb of Marduk and a theophany mountain. See Levy, *op. cit.*, p. 95.

25 M. Eliade, *The Quest*, pp. 138–41.

26 Ps. 78.69, see B. S. Childs, *Myth and Reality in the Old Testament*, p. 86.

27 Ps. 11.4; cf. Pss. 14, 20, 76, 80.

28 F. W. Dillistone, *op. cit.*, p. 66; see also R. E. Clements, *op. cit.* p. 65.

29 M. P. Nilsson, *A History of Greek Religion*, Clarendon Press 1949[2].

30 M. Eliade, *The Quest*, p. 72.

9 Symbolism and Social Structure

SOCIETY AS A SYMBOLIC MICROCOSM

WE HAVE NEEDED on numerous occasions to take notice of
the fact that mythological man used himself as his ultimate
control model. He saw literally everything in the universe as
being analogous to himself. It seemed to him natural, therefore,
that there should be some sort of correspondence between
the structure of relationships in human society and that which
obtained in the cosmos at large. Thus much of his language
about the universe and the gods was not merely anthropomorphic but also social. The powers within the universe were understood to be related to one another and to man in ways
which manifested themselves within the complex structure of
human society.

This seems at first sight to be nothing more than a projection of man's experience on to cosmic reality. Indeed this idea
has lain at the root of much assessment of mythological language. From the point of view of mythological man, however,
this would have been a reversal of the truth. For him, human
society, like everything else, was the creation of divine action.
Consequently the prime analogate of such terms as father,
chief and king was sacred being. Their use of human beings
was only possible in a secondary or analogical sense. He thought
of human society not as providing an analogy for the divine
but as a projection out of the character of sacred being.
Social structures were symbolic media whereby a knowledge
of divine being was received. His reasons for thinking in this
way are not difficult to understand.

First, he assumed that everything that he discovered around him and with which he found himself involved derived directly from the power of the sacred. He experienced the cosmos as something given. It was already there when he arrived. This seemed to be true not only of such things as mountains, oceans and the seasons but also of basic social structures. He did not choose to have a mother, a father, a brother, a sister or a grandmother. A number of people surrounded him from birth to death, and with each one of them he had a specific relationship which was not of his making. The family structure therefore appeared to mythological man as being as much a manifestation of sacred power as everything else. It was given or ordained by God.

Second, it seemed that if these social structures were derived from sacred power, then they must participate in it and reveal something at least of its nature. In consequence he did not feel that he was making an analogy at all. God was to him not merely like a father or a mother, but was the fatherhood in his father and the motherhood in his mother. In the age of myth many things were held to provide a microcosmic reflection of the whole. Among these, pride of place appears to have been given to the complex pattern of human relationships. For mythological man, society reflected in miniature the cosmic reality.

Third, he regarded human society as an organic unity. Everyone was related to each other as limbs of one body. This is not hard to understand in view of the fact that many modern sociologists have found it convenient to use self-consciously the analogy in which a group is thought of as though it were a living organism. Its use made it possible for mythological man to see human society as an organ of cosmic life, as a vehicle for the divine in whose going forth into the universe he shared. An organic connection was thus both seen and experienced between the life of man in society and the cosmic life which pulsated through it.

We must now turn our attention to the way in which the experience of man as a member of society conceived as a microcosmic organism created the most fundamental language in which to speak of the sacred.

Many of the laws and customs with which ancient man surrounded the role of parenthood seem strange to us today. The use of capital punishment for what we regard as minor offences when committed against one's parents seem to us extremely harsh. In the earliest strands of Hebraic law, for example, men are not merely exhorted to honour their parents[1] but are warned that the punishment for striking or cursing one's father or mother is death.[2] When they died the reverential attitude of ancient man increased still further to produce what is referred to as ancestor worship. Underlying such attitudes it is not difficult to see the effect of the basic ideas already outlined.

As parents, men and women participate in the creative process and stand therefore in relation to their children as mediators of divine generative power. In the act of procreation they have passed on that life which has descended from primordial time and from the gods. In consequence, the ritual accompanying birth often included indications that the primeval act of creation was again taking place, as when one of the elders ceremonially breathed life into the new-born child as the deity had once done into the figures of clay moulded by his hands. The identification of parents with the divine source of all becomes most apparent in the funerary rites. The dead, as we have seen, were understood to have returned into the womb of the divine mother. In this process they have become one with the sacred and can then be given the names of deity, of Hathor or Osiris, and regarded as having attained to supernatural power and wisdom. It is not surprising, therefore, that men and women who had been bearers of the divine life as parents should after their death be accorded a veneration which was one with man's reverence for the sacred. In death they had become one with that source of life from which they themselves were descended and in the perpetuation of which they had participated.

In consequence of all this a language for deity emerged in

the most natural way. As the ancestral parents had passed on the divinely-given life which men enjoyed, it was appropriate to think of deity in terms of parenthood. The imagery arose directly out of human experience and created a mythological language as varied in its uses as the functions of parenthood from which it was derived.

The use of fatherhood as a description of deity appears to have been universal. The name used varies but the difference is usually only a matter of language. Among the Greeks the supreme deity was known as Zeus, 'the father of gods and men'. The Romans called the originating principle Jupiter. In India the creator was known as Djaus Pitar. All these divine names were designations of the originative creativity in terms of fatherhood. They were intended to be taken in an almost literal manner. Fatherhood as applied to God later came to have associations which were originally absent. In the teaching of Jesus, for example, the fatherhood of God denoted primarily a personal relationship of love and forgiveness. In the mythological period however the attribution of fatherhood to the supreme deity was understood in a virtually physical sense.

The originative creativity could also be thought of in terms of the primordial mother. Again, this appears to have been a universal phenomenon. In fact there is probably more direct evidence for the worship of the great mother than for any other religious representation in primitive times. This was perhaps because generative power was and is more easily associated with the mother than the father. Moreover, the symbolism of the father associated him especially with the sky and hence there was entailed a certain remoteness. The mother deity, however, was regularly associated with the earth and hence there was a sense of nearness and intimacy which gave the symbol greater evocative power. The role of deity as generative mother received an overwhelming number of characterizations. Even in one culture she was given many names to suggest her various functions. Thus in Mesopotamia she was *Ninsikil-la*, the virgin lady, as potential creativity. She was also *Nintu-ama-Kalamma* as 'the lady who gives birth' while her association with the earth, conceived as the cosmic mountain was portrayed in her name *Nin-hur-sa-ga* which meant 'the lady of the mountain'.[3]

The characterization of primordial deity in parental terminology was accompanied, as we might expect, in the dramatic narrative of myth by stories of birth. For this reason the creation myths were cosmogonies, stories of the birth of the world. Everything in creation comes out of the womb of primeval deity. A myth can often therefore be summarized in a genealogical tree.

The root of the tree arises out of the source of all being, the originative sacred. The first distinguishable descendents of that primordial being are the gods who are both the being and the power of being which men call sky, earth, rain, ocean and the like. Then come the vegetation deities, the gods of trees, corn and grass. The earth-mother can now give birth to the members of the animal kingdom who will feed on the food she has provided. At last man is born, a descendant, along with all other creatures, in the universe of the great God. The life which lay within him was derived from that same divine breath which blew on the waters of the primeval ocean so that the seminal egg within it would be born as the earth to become lush with vegetation and a paradise in which human society might flourish. The cosmogonic genealogy therefore linked man directly with the divine source of all being and indirectly with every living thing within the universe.

The symbolism of a cosmic genealogy has persisted throughout the development of religious language. It survived because it suggested that man was, in the whole of his being, dependent upon a sacred power in whose image he was made. Thus we find that although the scriptures of the Old and New Testaments avoid many of the devices used in mythology, they maintain the symbolism of the sacred genealogy. In the Old Testament the people of Israel are the children of God and in the New Testament Paul reminds his audience that both Greek and Jew know that men are 'God's offspring'.[4] The genealogy of Jesus as given in St Luke's gospel can perhaps be taken as an exemplification of all such thinking, for there Jesus's parentage is traced back through the royal line of Israel to Adam, 'the son of God'.[5]

Thus each man was placed within the whole as a child born ultimately of the creator. His existence as an individual, however, was always subordinate in mythological thinking to his participation in the community. Individualism is a relatively late phenomenon and probably results from the loss of that sense of identity with the whole of things which the organic model provided. Mythological man saw his life as one with that of the community. This produced some extraordinary practices from a modern point of view which is much more aware of individual independence than of mutual interdependence. It led, for example, to the custom of marrying outside the clan or tribe because members of the group were regarded as so closely related that marriage within it would constitute the crime of incest. The sense of oneness was so great that it was often held that the action of any one member involved all the rest in its consequences. Thus the New Caledonians declare a fool dead so that if he violates tribal taboos, he will not bring disaster upon the whole group.[6]

We find, therefore, that the individual was considered to be related to the divine source of all life through his parents and ancestors and also to be one with the whole tribe through which that same life flowed. Of these media of divine life, the tribe as an organic unit was often regarded as the most important. E. Durkheim was so struck by this fact, manifested in the identification of the clan totem with the sacred power worshipped by the clan, that he came to the conclusion that religious feeling was simply man's feeling for community and that the whole idea of deity was derived from a projection of the collective life of the clan.[7] Durkheim's thesis was well received for a time, but is no longer generally accepted because it is recognized that the phenomenon of totemism on which he rested much of his case has been far from universal and that there were other factors involved in the creation of religious practice and thought than merely sociological ones.

In consequence Evans-Pritchard remarked that 'it was Durkheim and not the savage who made society into a god'.[8] Society was for ancient man the medium whereby divine life was manifested at the human level, but what Durkheim tended to ignore was that the sacred was believed not merely to be immanent in the clan but also to transcend it.

THE ORGANIC PYRAMID OF SOCIETY

The elders of family and tribe occupied positions of outstanding importance. As participators in divine creative activity and destined to become gods they performed the function in a social context which was represented iconographically by the rainbow. The parental figure represented the point at which there was immediate contact between the divine and the human. In consequence we often find that the head of a household officiated at the family altar as a priest. It was through him that the divine life flowed into the social unit, and so he was like the serpent leaning down out of the sky into the world of men. Another way in which we could express this is to say that the parents formed the apex of the family pyramid. This is appropriate in view of the fact that the pyramid in mythology represented the organic mountain which was the mother of all life. We can speak of the mythological organization of society seen in this way as being that of a series of organic pyramids forming themselves into greater pyramids as families fitted into clans, clans into tribes, tribes into nations and nations into empires.

At first the family constituted the model for relationships in larger communities. The head of such a unit was therefore the patriarch or matriarch. The narratives of Genesis describe just such an organization. In Abraham, Isaac and Jacob we have the priestly ancestors of the Hebrew genealogy. They sacrificed as priestly mediators between God and their people and gave birth to a nation.

It is in the more developed social structure of the monarchy that we find the idea of a sacral society most fully expressed.

The families, clans and tribes looked up to the monarchy as the most complete human equivalent of the rainbow which connected earth with heaven. By the identification of the royal rulers with the essence of both deity and society, the gap between the heavenly and human realms was closed and society fully sacralized. To this end a number of symbolic devices were employed, each of which showed how different aspects of the sacred were thus incarnated within human society.

The king and queen were naturally associated respectively with the male and female symbols of deity. The king was often adorned with the symbols of the sun and referred to as the sun-king or as the son of the sun because the sun regularly represented the male principle within deity. The queen, on the other hand, was usually associated with the moon, which was the symbol of the female principle. Either one, however, could be understood to embody the plenitude of deity and consequently attract to themselves the symbols of both the male and female principles becoming the primal, androgynous being of the cosmogonic myth. The way in which this was done varied, of course, according as the society involved was patriarchal or matriarchal in structure. Whatever type of organization was used, however, the symbolic content had to be complete and in some way or other the monarchy had to incarnate all the essential symbolizations of the divine.

One of the ways in which the royal significance was shown forth was by the ascription of symbolic titles. The queen mother of the Ashanti in Africa was called the daughter of the moon. The rain-queen of the Lovedu was called 'the soil' in order to link her with the concept of mother-earth.[9] In such titles as these the royal rulers were identified as incarnations of the sacred among men.

On the other hand, the king or queen was also considered to be an embodiment of the people. Thus in Africa, Parrinder informs us, the king or chief is often understood to represent the mystical element in the life of the people.[10] The king is therefore able to act on behalf of the people as well as the gods and be in his person the bond between heaven and earth.

This unique position is achieved for the king in a number of ways. In Egypt the first king of the land was often said to have been the god Osiris himself. From him the Pharaoh was believed to have been descended by a mystical and unbroken tradition. Another way in which the Pharaoh's position was explained was to say that at his coronation he had been born again out of the throne which was identified with Isis. Once crowned he was no longer merely a human being but had become twice-born, and so as son of Isis an incarnate deity among his people. Frequently, therefore, it was possible simply to identify the king with representations of the sacred principle already present. In the far east the lingam pillar in the pyramid temple was understood to symbolize both the cosmic creator and the essence of the king. As an embodiment of the creative principle he could therefore be called 'the father and mother of all men' as in Egypt.[11] Lastly, we may note how among the Ashanti the significance of the 'son of the sun' is expressed by allowing him to claim that he is the centre of the world.[12] As the centre, whether as lingam pillar, pyramid mountain or maize-mother, the head of the state became fully the bond between heaven and earth.

In view of this, it is not surprising that the king usually takes to himself sacerdotal functions on his coronation. At that point he has become the great mediator between God and man. As a great high priest he can perform the role of the dragon-slayer in the annual re-enactment of the cosmogonic battle in the Babylonian New Year Festival or the Egyptian Osirian drama.[13] He can circle the boundaries of his kingdom to ensure the fertility of its earth. Although priestly duties may be distributed among many others, the full hierophantic ritual can only be accomplished by one who is himself both god and man.

The king is conceived as part of an order whose being is derived from cosmic reality. The usurpation of the throne by an illegitimate chief could therefore be understood as a violation of the cosmic order with consequences at all levels of human life. The death of the king was regarded as a particularly dangerous moment and the fact was often kept secret until the accession of the new king could be announced. Even to this day it is the custom in England to declare, 'The king is dead, long live the king'. The cosmic essence is unending, and no break therefore must be allowed to show in its symbolic representation in the monarchy. On his death the king was usually buried with considerable care in a manner which made his significance clear. The king's personal funerary temple was often the national temple. The corpse was placed in the primeval mountain and so replaced in the womb of being. The dead king had in a new sense now become a god. What was true of the king was also true of the humble commoner buried in his mound, but as the embodiment of the life of the nation the king had a special place. In his life he wore in Sumer and Egypt a royal headdress which designated his function and his final resting place. This was a replica of the sanctuary temple, a miniature ziggurat,[14] for in a sense the king was 'Great Mountain', as in fact he was called on his enthronement among the Swazi.

In order to show the nation as a microcosm of the eternal totality, the symbolism of religious architecture was extended in such a way as to place the seat of monarchical government within it. For this purpose the palace was identified with the centre of the cosmos and therefore also with the temple and the cosmic mountain. King, temple and mountain thus formed a single centre or place of theophany, of communication between God and man. In the Khmer civilization of Cambodia the king's capital was surrounded by the mountain walls and the moat of the primeval waters,[15] in order to suggest that the king ruled from the symbolic centre of the cosmos. In Babylon the palace was referred to as 'the Bond', i.e. between heaven and earth, between gods and men. At Mandalay in upper Burma, the eastern part of the palace which contained the audience room was said to stand at the centre of the world so that a meeting with the king was virtually equated with a theophany.

As the representative embodiment of the divine, the king was particularly believed to be the medium whereby the law of God was made available to men. So in addition to his role as a high priest, he also functioned as lawgiver and judge of men on God's behalf. The relationship between the king's promulgation of the nation's law and the will of God was shown to the people of Babylon in a picture in which the king Hammurabi receives the tablets of his newly formulated code from the sun-god. The true source of all law was understood to be God himself. The king was the means whereby it was passed on to the people by the man whom the Chinese called 'the son of heaven'. In this way the nation was understood to be a particular embodiment of the cosmos and the king would organize his rule so as to suggest this. Thus the government of ancient Burma structured its court and government officials on the basis of the symbolism of the four cardinal points. The ministers of the king acted on his behalf like the *lokapala* who guarded the four sides of mount Meru. The state then became a replica of the cosmos and was seen to be so by the use of the symbols which had been created out of the immediate experience of the world by primordial man.[16]

NOTES

1 Ex. 20.12.
2 Ex. 21.15, 17.
3 E. O. James, *The Ancient Gods*, p. 78.
4 Acts 17.29.
5 Luke 3.38.
6 E. A. Nida, *Customs, Culture and Christianity*, p. 146.
7 E. Durkheim, *The Elementary Forms of Religious Life*, Allen and Unwin 1915.
8 E. E. Evans-Pritchard, *Nuer Religion*, p. 313.
9 See E. J. and J. D. Krige, *The Realm of the Rain-Queen*, Oxford University Press 1960.
10 E. G. Parrinder, *African Traditional Religion*, p. 28.
11 E. O. James, *op. cit.*, p. 108.
12 E. G. Parrinder, *op. cit.*, p. 70.
13 S. H. Hooke, *Myth and Ritual*, Oxford University Press, 1933.
14 G. K. Levy, *Gate of Horn*, pp. 176 f.
15 *New Larousse*, p. 174.
16 See H. Frankfort, *Before Philosophy*, Penguin Books 1949.

F

PART THREE

Development and the Great Religions

10 Symbolism and Religious Experience

IN THE LAST three chapters we saw how certain basic patterns of symbolic language governed mythological culture. Although it was apparent that each culture possessed a symbol structure peculiar to itself, there was discernible nevertheless a common structure of language. In view of this it seems reasonable to suppose that underlying the whole there was a common type of response to the universe. This mythological appropriation of the cosmos deserves the title of primordial revelation because it appears to have been the basis on which all religious language was originally built.

We cannot, unfortunately, construct with any degree of certainty the nature of that experience. Its symbols have already become the archetypal images to which C. G. Jung refers when recorded history begins. We cannot see the myths in process of formulation, but must be content with studying them when they have already become the deposit of an ancient tradition. Even a study of contemporary archaic societies which are still dominated by mythological thinking does not help us much here for, even in these cases, there has clearly been a long history of oral tradition in which many of the originating perceptions have been lost.

Many attempts have been made to uncover the most primitive form of religion, and if they had been successful we should have a reliable guide to the nature of primordial revelation.

None of these essays in the origin of religion, however, have commanded unqualified assent. Theories based on fetishism, totemism and ancestor worship have been mooted only to suffer severely at the hands of critics.[1] It would seem that the mistake most frequently made was in looking for one simple and overriding explanation. The criticism usually made of these theories is that they were based upon phenomena restricted to one area and therefore unacceptable as the basis of a general understanding of man's early religious sense. If our study of symbolism so far has any validity we should expect primitive religion to have been of considerable variety and to have been capable of sustaining a number of apparently conflicting elements. The lesson we have learnt is that religious language is diverse and cannot be reduced to a simple, logical unity.

Nevertheless, beneath the bewildering variety it has been possible to discern a fundamental attitude, and there is now a considerable degree of unanimity about its nature.

It would seem obvious, in the first place, that the creation of religion and myth was possible because primitive man accepted the finite world as symbolic. He did not merely observe that objects existed in space but saw them as mediating that which was beyond themselves. Everything was understood to be a communicator. If this had not been so no mythological symbolism could have been created. Max Müller probably went too far when he asserted that a perception of the infinite accompanied each perception of the finite, but he nevertheless made an essential point. Even if the concept of infinity is wrongly attributed to primitive man, there can be no doubt that along with his perception of the finite world, he also received an intuition of that which was expressing itself through it.

The animistic theory of primitive religion as defined by E. B. Tylor holds that for early man each and every object in the finite world was at least potentially both alive and personal. On this there is much general agreement, and our study of mythological symbolism has reinforced this conclusion. No distinction was drawn between that which was alive and that which was dead, for in mythology death is continuously overcome. In consequence, the most ordinary events in life were charged with religious significance. Anything could be the means whereby some living power was expressing itself and relating itself to man. The whole universe was understood as a network of communication in which objects and events disclosed something which transcend themselves. Gathered up together, all these intuitions were creative of what is properly called religious perception. They suggested the reception of a beyond which communicated with man through the finite world.

Some have held, however, that there was a stage in the development of religion which preceded animism. An English missionary named Codrington came to the conclusion that primitive religion was made up merely of a belief in something which the Melanesians among whom he had lived called *mana*.[2] The word was very difficult to translate, but seemed to have its nearest equivalent in the word power. Others noted that there were parallels to this word and concept in the literature and faith of many archaic peoples. As a result it seemed to R. R. Marett that the 'taboo-mana formula' was 'a minimum definition of religion'.[3] Further exploration into the meaning of the word has led to the discovery that its use is almost unbounded. At first the assumption tended to be that what was referred to was being conceived in an impersonal manner and represented therefore a conceptualization at a lower stage of development than animism. It now seems evident, however, that the *mana* concept did not exclude the idea of personal agency. The term embraced everything which early man experienced as the other impinging on his life. As such, therefore, it does not represent an alternative to the animistic theory but places the latter in a fuller context of early religious language.

The idea of *mana* is particularly significant for us because it shows how the characteristics of symbolic language are to be found embedded in the very basis of primordial revelation.

It did not represent one element in experience but a multitude of intuitions. It is so wide in its connotation that it is virtually impossible to translate it without substituting long lists of possible equivalents. It denoted something in specific objects but also power in all things. On the one hand it was to be found in the most familiar objects and events, while on the other it was the basis for what Rudolf Otto called *The Idea of the Holy* or the numinous.[4]

These are but a few threads upon which to hang our knowledge of primordial revelation, but they are sufficient to show us that there was a common basis for the transition into the more specific types of religious experience which we find in documented history. The perception of the cosmos as full of a numinous power confronting man in various ways was to be the ground of religious experience down to our own day.

PATTERNS OF RELIGIOUS EXPERIENCE

Primordial revelation, as we have seen, was captured in a complex of symbolic formulations and rituals which perpetually re-created its power. Yet the construction of a mythological complex did not eliminate the need for personal religious experience. Rather it created the means whereby it could be continually appropriated by the community and the individual. This was essential if the symbols of myth were not to degenerate into the signs of superstition. Only if the symbolic perception of the cosmos could be constantly renewed would the life-expanding power of myth be retained. With this end in view, mythological culture provided rites of passage in which each individual was intended to take the primordial intuitions to himself and an annual cycle of ritual ceremonies in which the community could align itself with the cosmic working of numinous power and life. In these ways primordial revelation created its own means of self-perpetuation and an awareness of the universe as symbolic of personal life being passed on from one generation to another.

Even when religion had passed into more and more sophisticated phases of expression, we still find the ritual moment
one which is particularly likely to create a personal disclosure
of symbolic meaning. Within the framework provided by
religious ceremonial there could be a personal re-creation of
the primordial intuition, and also the perception of ever new
dimensions of significance. The prophet Isaiah's attainment of
a radically new understanding of primordial holiness was
attained during the hour of sacrifice. Within the context of a
familiar rite there was disclosed to him an ethical majesty
previously unknown.[5] St Paul is noted most for his experience
on the Damascus road, but that revelatory moment did not
receive its fulfilment of meaning until some weeks later when
he was in the temple at Jerusalem.[6] Korozumi Munetada, a
Shintoist of Japan, was only able to recover that enlargement
of his own spirit by a renewed communion with the living
power within the world in the context of his devotions to the
goddess Amaterasu.[7] These are only examples of a process
which has taken place universally throughout history.

Although the ritual forms of various societies have differed
greatly, they have given rise to experiences which are comparable. Even when religious perception is attained outside a
ritual context in the loneliness of the individual's personal
search for meaning, we can see that a basic pattern tends to
repeat itself. Comparative studies in the past have often been
too willing to think that all religious experience is of one kind,
but it is equally misleading to assume that there are no grounds
for comparison. A comparative study can show that underlying the creation or renewal of symbolic meaning there are
experiences which share fundamental elements.

Before attempting to isolate these elements we must note that
it is characteristic of such receptive or perceptive experiences
that the various elements tend to run into one another. Religious experience defies too precise analysis because it is a fluid
event in which everything seems to happen at once and the
transitory moments are hardly discernible. In the record of
such experiences it is inevitable that this should have certain

effects. On the one hand it accounts for the apparently suspicious fact that the same experience may be described in several different ways. There are several accounts of Paul's conversion experience and each one differs from the rest.[8] The change wrought in Paul probably took some time, as one account suggests, and yet to him it became clear that what was finally attained was already present in the very first moment in which he was overcome by the light of the Lord. On the other hand, time for reflection often obscures the original fluidity of the experience and a sequence of separate moments is stated in the interests of clarity. In such cases we must remember that what comes to us and what we must necessarily examine as a sequence is really no more than an isolation of elements which originally took place in the same kind of time as that in which we found the myths were located.

Bearing this in mind we can say that the basic sequence of religious experience seems to have three moments:

(i) The presence of an existential need.
(ii) The moment of disclosure or perception itself.
(iii) The embodiment of the experience in symbolic form.

The first element is required by logic even though it is often obscured and even unrecognized by the subject of the experience. The disclosure may appear to come 'out of the blue', but this merely denotes the transcendent quality of the event and the givenness of the result. No experience is conceivable which does not arise out of a question raised in the depths of the soul reflecting a psychic need hidden there. The second element is hardly discernible at all by itself, for while it may appear to last through an aeon of time, it is nevertheless a wisp which can barely be captured. The moment of perception, therefore, cannot really be separated from its symbolic formulation because the subject can never speak of his experience without the use of symbol.

In many ways the story of the Buddha's enlightenment is a classic example of the scheme we have outlined.

(i) The significant story of the Buddha began when the

ultimate question of the meaning of human life was presented to him for the first time in a way which struck at the depths of his being. He had been brought up in the luxury of a northern Indian palace. This had prevented any real awareness of the cruder aspects of life and of the suffering which prevailed beyond the walls of the palace garden. He was plunged into ontological anxiety by a journey through the town in which he saw the inescapable evidence of the transitory nature of life afflicted by disease, old age and death. The question of life had been raised for him in the presence of death. This discovery made him see the luxurious life to which he was accustomed in a new way. There had arisen a fundamental question which he had to answer and so he left the palace and began his search.

(ii) Having sought in vain for a satisfactory explanation from the ascetics and philosophers of his day, the Buddha began to meditate under a tree. Of what happened within him during that time we can know nothing apart from his subsequent symbolization of it. All we know is that the tree of his meditation became the tree of his enlightenment.

(iii) The forms in which the question of life and death had been presented to him and his own ontological anxiety coalesce into a symbolic complex of a spiritual battle. The sight of death on the road is given symbolic form when he feels himself confronted by Mara, the god of the underworld and the image of death. His moment of perception has already passed when he sees sexual love, seduction and infatuation as the daughters of Mara, and he has taken this truth into his own being when he is able to turn these fair maidens into hags overcome by age. The ability to symbolize the experience derives from the experience itself, for in a sense it provides its own forms of expression.

Our analysis of the Buddha's experience, does not of course, do justice to the complexity it clearly had or to the fact that it was part of an ongoing disclosure. The three elements we have isolated are often embedded in a more complex sequence in which they repeat themselves. A revelatory experience may and often does consist of a succession of disclosures which together form a total movement of the spirit. Within the whole, however, there seems to be what might be called a downward and an upward movement or an outward and a return journey. In the first phase there is the emergence and formulation of a need. This can be a complete experience in itself, in which case it is something like an unanswered prayer. The subject becomes aware of his own lack of symbolic meaning, enters into a disclosure experience in which this lack is experienced in its depth and power, and he is subsequently able to formulate his experience in symbolic terms. These terms are frequently those of boundless night, deep waters or unending desert. From the point of view of religious faith this is a case of arrested development, of failure to arrive at divine illumination. In the second phase the question is converted into an answer. The downward or outward movement merely raises and states the existential question while the upward or inward movement provides a response creative of integration within the subject as a result of the establishment of a harmonious relationship with the sacred beyond. The symbols of darkness give way to the creative symbols of light. In the perennial language of religion, the subject of such an experience is now said to have seen the light or to have been born anew.

In order to crystallize this fundamental dialectic in our minds we can set it out by extending our tabular analysis.

The Descent
   i. The presence of an existential need;
   ii. The moment of disclosure or perception of need;
   iii. The symbolization of ontological anxiety.

The Ascent
   i. The descent becomes the basis for further disclosure;
   ii. Creative disclosure or perception;
   iii. Symbolizations of integration and wholeness.

While this, too, is an over-simplification, its fundamental veracity is perhaps indicated by certain recurring features of religious experience and their symbols. Symbolic language is dualistic throughout and consists largely of contrasts between two realms: light and darkness, death and life, high and low. These symbols derive from the dialectic dualism of the cosmogonic myth. In the characterization of existential estrangement we can recognize a return to the primeval symbols of the deep ocean, the threatening chaos, the unfathomable absurdity. The same experience which created the myth of Tiamat is constantly re-experienced. In the creative integration of the second phase there appear the symbols of the victor. In the words of Dionysius, the darkness becomes translucent as though the sun-god has once more emerged from the womb of his death. The boundless desert becomes the infinity of the divine presence as life once more flows through to dispel death-producing anxiety. The voice of many waters loses its terror as it becomes the voice of the son of God.[9] From the dreadful silence of existential despair we move into 'the simple ground, the still desert, the simple silence' of Meister Eckhart's beatitude. Knowing that such is the result we can throw ourselves into the sea conscious that Leviathan has been transformed into the infinity of the divine presence.[10] As Cassirer remarks,[11] the formlessness with which the quest for the divine began is also where it ends but in images which have been transfigured. Finally, we should note that religious ritual has always recognized the necessity to provide for the reliving of precisely this dialectic. Perhaps the clearest example of this is in the Christian ritual in which the existential loneliness and despair expressed on Good Friday is countered by the triumphant assertion of life on Easter Sunday.

DISCLOSURE SIGNS AND PERCEPTION

Our brief analysis has shown us that those things which precipitate a revelatory experience often constitute the symbols in which it is formulated. The beginning and the end of religious experience exist in a dialectical relationship in which the first is transformed in its meaning. We can perceive in this a process in which something is seen in a new way. All the stages of religious experience are constituted by some kind of insight. The first of these is of that which may be called a disclosure sign.

A disclosure of any kind is only possible when something within a man's experience confronts him in such a way that a response is evoked within him. Objects and events which have the capacity to act in this way constitute disclosure signs. In so far as man is treated as a biological organism they would be referred to as signals, because in the language of science the sequence of events is merely one of presentation and conditioned response. On the other hand, we commonly use the term sign when we wish to indicate those things which tell us that something is about to happen. Thus we speak of the signs of spring meaning that certain sights suggest that the season of spring is beginning to come. Such signs act upon us as the signals to which the scientist refers. They immediately evoke responses in us and we begin to prepare ourselves mentally and emotionally for the birth of new life in all around us. In this context, therefore, a signal has become an evocative sign. When, however, objects and events are generative of a new understanding, it would seem best to refer to these as disclosure signs. The designation then suggests that they are signals in that they produce specific reactions in us, that they operate at the personal level of emotion and imagination or have symbolic potentiality, while it also indicates that something new appears to be given in the experience they create.

At first it may seem that the term sign is now being used in a different way from that outlined at the beginning of our study. The difference, however, is only one of role. The object or event which acts as a trigger of religious disclosure only functions in this way when it begins to take on the character of a symbol. While it remains as a sign it is merely designatory. It becomes symbolic through the dialectic of the disclosure experience. We have therefore in religious experience the basis of that transformation whereby the denotative sign of the cross became the evocative symbol of saving power. The change is effected by the experience. A number of examples will make this clear.

Mircea Eliade has used the example of the signs of spring in a way which illustrates their symbolic potentiality. He describes how branches, flowers and animals were sometimes carried in procession from house to house as a sign that 'spring has come'. He points out, however, that this ritual was not simply a kind of weather forecast. Embodied in the ritual these objects had been given another function. They were now intended to generate disclosure. The objects carried in procession were given symbolic value by the ritual which used them as representative of life and resurrection. Things which had been the originating disclosure signs on which the ritual was built were used within it in order to recreate the perception of ever-renewed life within the cosmos. They declare that the world is not dead, but that it constantly overcomes death. The ritual contained the fundamental assertion of the mythological mind and presented it in a symbolic complex which was able to function as a pattern of disclosure signs renewing the message of the myth. As soon as they began to evoke such understanding the signs had been transformed into symbols, and the observer had been caught up in the primeval cycle of cosmic existence.[12]

The symbolic power of a disclosure sign is, however, hidden until it is perceived with the inward eye. The signs which had such an impact upon the Buddha only operated in this way because they were personally perceived within himself. He did not merely see in them the particular but symbols of the universal. In consequence they reappear later charged with existential power.

I. T. Ramsey has particularly stressed the element of inner sight in the creation of disclosure and uses as his example the narrative in St John's gospel which tells how Peter and another disciple found the empty tomb. In this he traces three stages in the manner and quality of perception indicated by the use of three different Greek words. At first the disciples merely glanced casually into the tomb. This was followed by detailed scrutiny, which led to the third form of seeing which disclosed the truth to them.[13] A virtually identical sequence can be found in the story of Moses's experience at Horeb.[14] At first he merely notes that a bush is on fire, but then he turns aside from his journey to examine it more closely. This results shortly afterwards in a revelatory experience as he perceives the symbolic dimension of the sign. Fire has been used universally to denote sacred presence, but it did not have the power to mediate that which it represented until Moses could hear the voice of the Lord speaking to him through it.

These narratives illustrate the fact that disclosure is above all a way of seeing. We may suppose that others might have been present on either occasion without becoming aware of anything beyond the phenomenal facts. In this connection it may be noted that there has often been an illusion that if one had been born in the right place at the right time it would have been easy to have become a man of faith. More than one Christian hymn bewails the fact that the author was not born in Palestine when Jesus was alive so that he might have walked and talked with the Son of God. Yet in fact many did just these things, but did not perceive the Christ in the man from Nazareth.

In describing the moment of insight, a subject of a religious experience is often at a loss to know whether to speak of it as a revelation or a perception. Within the experience both appear as one. What does seem to be clear, however, is that a purely physical seeing does not produce the quality of revelation. The idiom of the Hebrew language seems to embody the ambiguity inherent in religious experience and to imply that the element of spiritual sight is essential. In his discussion of events in which a common sight comes to be invested with symbolic significance, Harry Buck reminds us that the Hebrew has no verb meaning 'to show'. In consequence it was necessary to get round this by saying that something was 'caused to be seen'. This may reflect an awareness of the fact that what can seem at first to be the result of human endeavour is often subsequently realized to be a gift to man from beyond himself. Moreover, a prophet is said both to 'see' and to be 'caused to see'. Buck suggests that we should translate such a sequence as

'I saw. . . and then I understood'.[15] In this way the idiom seems to have enshrined the essential development from mere sighting of phenomena to spiritual apprehension of significance. A phenomenon of language which has something in common with the Hebrew idiom noted by Buck is found among certain North American Indians and is interestingly described by Werner Müller.[16]

The ancient narratives of the Old Testament sometimes preferred to make the point in a more picturesque way. A story unique in that literature illustrates both the necessity for the eye of faith and for a sense of humour in the exegete. The book of Numbers tells us of a man called Balaam whose ass refuses to continue along the road despite the beatings administered by the rider. The reader is informed that the ass is behaving in this way because it can see an angel in the path to which Balaam is blind. Eventually the Lord opens Balaam's eyes and he, too, can see the angel. The writer of the narrative does not explain the significance of his story, of course, for fear of implying that the reader might be as stupid as Balaam thought his ass was.[17]

The same point is made in another narrative contained in the second book of Kings. This tells how the king of Syria sent his army to surround the city in which Elisha and his disciples were staying. One of Elisha's young men becomes very afraid but is told by his master that 'those who are with us are more than those who are with them'.[18] But the young man cannot see the hosts of the Lord until Elisha prays that his eyes may be opened. Then the disciple sees 'the mountain was full of horses and chariots of fire around about Elisha.'[19] Otto Eissfeldt finds it necessary to comment on the story by way of explanation and to point out that the vision discloses to the disciple 'insight into the higher reality surrounding man in the present'.[20] Something may be gained by such a paraphrase into modern terminology, but it is the biblical narrative which contains the evocative power.

These stories of Balaam and Elisha have a folk-tale quality about them and a kind of country wit which defies analysis and undue sophistication of thought. They move within the world of myth and symbol. If such language is to be understood in its depth, it must be done by our learning to think in its terms. Much is lost if we attempt to translate the imaginative language of faith into the abstract discourse of concepts.

ENCOUNTER LANGUAGE

In the ancient narratives of religion, revelatory experience is regularly described in terms which most of us no longer use. The seers of the ancient world are confronted by gods, angels and demons. This terminology is one which has been largely abandoned because we no longer move within the thought forms which created them. If we are to understand what lay behind the creation of such narratives we must uncover the secret of this encounter language. Only then will we be able to see these accounts as a meaningful description of disclosure.

The basis of encounter language lay, of course, in the outlook which held that the whole universe was personally alive. It followed that any revelation of reality must take the form of a personal confrontation. As, however, disclosure could vary considerably in depth, it followed that the language of encounter had to be adapted to provide for this. This was done by the simple expedient of speaking of men being confronted by a varying range of revelatory agencies.

In the mythological world this was accomplished by speaking of meetings between men and gods, some of which were more fully revelatory of the divine than others. As we saw these gods were accommodations of the ultimate reality to man, ways in which he perceived partial manifestations of the operation of cosmic life. In a world losing its mythological language and beginning to insist on the unity of the divine principle, the place of the gods was taken by beings to whom deity was not attributed. The encounter with God is therefore mediated in the biblical literature by angels, and this device is used skilfully to show that sequence of gradual illumination which characterizes disclosure experience.

Just as everything was potentially a god in the mythological world, so now anything in the universe could be spoken of as an angel. This was a way of saying that something carried out the will of the supreme God. The winds are called angels because they obey the will of the Lord.[21] Because the heavenly bodies simply express the will of Yahweh by the regularity of their movements, they too are angels.[22] The judges of Israel as administrators of the law of God function as angels.[23] As a prophet relaying the words of God to the people, John the Baptist is said to have been an angel.[24] An angel is in fact equivalent to an agency of God's will or the message in which it is embodied.

No ultimate distinction was therefore drawn between God and his angels, for the latter were merely accommodations of God in his appearance before men. An angel had no existence independent of God, as a flame has none apart from the fire out of which it emanates. The angels have no form except as some part of creation, as that through which God chooses to reveal himself. Yet although an angel and God were ultimately one, the distinction was not superfluous; it made it possible to indicate that angelophanies and theophanies represented two quite different depths of disclosure.

A number of incidents in the Old Testament stories illustrate this. In Gen. 16.7-14 we are told of an incident which takes place after Hagar, the handmaid of Abram, having been ill-treated by Sarah the lawful wife, has fled to the desert. There she is confronted by the angel of Yahweh, who advises her to return and promises that her child shall be the father of a great multitude. Here we have the familiar trait of a revelatory experience in that it comes as an answer to Hagar's anxiety and despair. The important point in this connection, however, is that the encounter with an angel turns out in v. 13 to be a confrontation with God. The transition marks the point at which Hagar recognizes that it was the Lord himself who had been communicating with her throughout. In the story contained in Gen. 18.1-22 the encounter begins as one between Abraham and three men. As various events take place, however, it becomes apparent to Abraham that he has to do directly with the Lord.[25]

From such narratives as these we can see that talk of meetings with angels is clearly a device to indicate that the recipient of the experience is not encountering God in his fullness but as through frosted glass or shadows. When the inner eye sees clearly, it is known that God himself has been present. This also gives rise to the peculiar language in which God is said to have been seen from behind: as we might say, the fullness of revelatory disclosure is only known in hindsight.

Another characteristic feature of disclosure experiences appears in narratives which tell of an encounter with angelic beings. The designation of something as angelic or caused by angelic power constitutes a recognition of it as a disclosure sign. This enables us to understand at least partially the meaning contained in those narratives which speak of miraculous events being caused by the operation of angelic power. The perception of an event as a miracle is equivalent in religious language to the assertion that it has been brought about by God. When the language of angels is employed, the event is naturally ascribed to angelic agency because this expresses the idea that something has mediated the action of God in a direct and personal manner. As an example of this we may cite the way in which some manuscripts of St John's gospel explain the healing properties of the pool of Bethesda. Some versions of the narrative merely state that people stayed by the pool in order to take advantage of the healing power of the waters when they were troubled. Many ancient manuscripts, however, explain that this troubling of the waters was caused by an angel of the Lord who went down to the pool at certain times.[26] We see from this how a story may be filled out with symbolic explanations by those for whom the healing capacity of the water in the pool was taken as a disclosure sign of God's personal activity. In the gospel of John, of course, this is a relatively unimportant point; the burden of the passage is to portray Christ as the presence of God's saving activity in its fullness.

We see, therefore, that talk of angels represents in biblical literature a partial disclosure of the presence of God, the apprehension of something as a sign of that presence and a recognition that a specifically religious disclosure is best described in the language of personal encounter.

VISIONS AND DREAMS

Encounters with angels are usually said to have taken place in visions. Such a description is apt, for we see that these experiences consist of a moment of unusual perceptivity. The recognition of an angel's presence indicates that the ordinary has taken on a revelatory quality which is extraordinary. It is truly a case of supernormal sight. Such a degree of awareness of the sacred calls for the use of a designation which sets it apart from everyday experiences.

The peculiar quality of the language used to describe visionary experiences derives from the fact that 'a real vision is always based upon ecstasy of one form or another'.[27] The word ecstasy means to be outside oneself. It denotes that kind of experience in which the limitations normally imposed are lifted. The language of the visionary is often mythological, for in ecstasy a prophet enters the space and time of the myths. Space is overcome so that the visionary is no longer limited by distance but can experience as though from outside space, even to the extent of becoming an observer of himself. Ezekiel can, in the picturesque language of his book, be lifted by the hair and transported across the desert to look down upon Jerusalem.[28] He is also freed from the prison of time and sees events in their wholeness to become a prophet of the future. Removed from the restriction of being enclosed within the physical, the ecstatic participates in some measure in God's perception. Freed from the objectifying rationality of finite thought, the universe comes alive with subjectivity for him and a life of true dialogue becomes possible. In such an experience, an encounter with angels who act like mythological deities becomes entirely comprehensible. In his ecstasy in the temple the prophet Isaiah quite naturally finds that the seraphim embroidered on the temple veil come alive, sing praises to God and even have physical contact with him. The ecstatic vision may be said to represent the most sensitive perception of the universe as personal confrontation between man and the sacred.

Visions epitomize those moments of total involvement in the world through myths and symbols which are our primary concern. They represent the fullest possible participation in cosmic life. Not suprisingly they often have the character of mythological drama.[29] In this connection it is perhaps worth noting that the vision of Ezekiel recorded in 43.12-17 appears to represent a recovery of mythological insight. In his vision Ezekiel sees the altar of the new Jerusalem in the shape of a ziggurat with three storeys and topped with four horns built on the summit of the holy mountain. A. Parrot suggests that this symbolism had been prompted by the prophet's observations in Babylon where he would have seen such a sight.[30] The Babylonian ziggurat had perhaps acted as a disclosure sign, giving rise to an experience in which the mythological symbolism of the cosmic mountain is recovered and put to fresh use. The temple of Israel's future would once again be the throne of the Almighty and the meeting place between heaven and earth.

We can understand something further of the nature of visions if we note that they are regarded in the biblical literature as interchangeable with dreams. Indeed, dreams are often referred to as night visions. This seems to be true also in the Koran, where the call of Muhammed is given both as a vision of the angel Gabriel 'on the uppermost horizon' and as a dream which came to him while asleep in a cave.

The identification is not surprising in view of the fact that dreams share with visions the capacity to abandon the limitations of normal experience. Both ignore the bounds of time and space. The dreamer, like the ecstatic, often has the sense of being a spectator of himself and of seeing everything from a new dimension. Above all there is a feeling in both of being totally involved so that one's very existence and meaning appears to be at stake. This being so, a dream must be regarded as at least a potential disclosure experience.

Psychologists tell us that dreams reproduce our experience and make us face problems which we would rather ignore. They thus possess the basic character which we noted as essential to disclosure. In dreams our existential needs take on symbolic form and precipitate a mental process in which we have to grapple with them. In the story of Peter's dream at Joppa we gain some idea of how this operates and how it receives its symbolic form from the fund of significant imageries provided by contemporary culture.[31]

When Peter went down to Joppa he had been wrestling with an angel of God for some time. Embedded in the teaching and example of Jesus his master was a negation of Jewish exclusivism, and yet neither he nor the rest of the Jerusalem church had been able to break free of the inherited isolationism of the Hebrew race. So he went to Joppa with a tension already present within him. While asleep on the roof top he has a dream in which a sheet is let down from heaven containing various animals which a Jew regarded as unclean and therefore forbidden. Nevertheless, a voice tells him that he must eat, for nothing which the Lord has made may be called unclean. Now it has often been noted that the dream does not seem to be directly relevant to the problem on hand. The issue which faces Peter immediately after the dream is concerned with the admission of the Gentiles into the Christian church. The dream, on the other hand, appears to deal with the question as to whether a Christian should continue to observe the Jewish dietary laws. One way of dealing with this is to assume that two different problems have been brought together in one narrative. The problem is much better solved, however, by observing the characteristics of symbolism than by looking for dislocations in the text. Peter's dream contains a symbolic drama and as such is not restricted in its application to any one issue. The symbolic imagery is derived from Hebrew custom. In his dream it represents the fundamental problem in Peter's mind, the admissibility of any kind of divisiveness in view of the teaching which he had accepted from Jesus. The dream acts as a disclosure experience in that it shows Peter that a command is laid upon him. The dream by itself, however, does not have the ability to revolutionize Peter's whole outlook and way of life. Afterwards he goes with some messengers sent by a Gentile, Cornelius, somewhat unwillingly. The revelation contained in the dream is only accepted by Peter when it is reinforced by a further disclosure experience in which he becomes aware that God's Spirit has been given to the Gentiles in his presence.

At one time the acceptance by men of dreams as revelatory events was simply scorned as being beneath modern man's contempt. The development of psychology has, however, substantially altered the estimation of dreams in the post-rationalistic world of the twentieth century. It has been established beyond doubt that dreams are important as revelations of the depths within the human psyche. It has also become clear to many that we cannot dismiss such knowledge as being merely that of the individual. If we keep purely within scientific terms of reference, of course, it is appropriate to restrict comment on dreams to their place within human history and experience. The way is open, however, once again to see dreams as being capable of disclosure not only about those to whom they come but also about the realm of subjective existence in which as human beings we are involved. The possibility that dreams may be a voice of God, moreover, is made easier by knowledge of the fact that those who have been able to approach nearest to God have constantly affirmed that a knowledge of God only came to them accompanied by a greater knowledge of themselves. The secular psychiatrist may not, therefore, be pursuing a line very different from that of the ancient prophets when he enables a patient to find a meaningful life by listening to the words spoken from the subconscious.

Personal disclosure experiences, the language of which we have attempted to elucidate in part, do not take place in a vacuum however. The story of Peter's dream demonstrates very clearly that the symbolic formulations of a man's culture not only dominate the manner in which his revelatory experience will be couched but can help or hinder progression towards deeper understanding. For most people, for a very long time, the symbolic structure within which they have placed their own experience has been provided by one of the great religions and to a consideration of these we must now turn.

NOTES

1 E. E. Evans-Pritchard, *Theories of Primitive Religion*, Clarendon Press 1965.

2 R. H. Codrington, *The Melanesians: Studies in their Anthropology and Folklore*, Clarendon Press, 1891.

3 Quoted E. Cassirer, *Language and Myth*, Harper and Row 1946, p. 64.

4 R. Otto, *The Idea of the Holy*, Oxford University Press 1923.

5 Isa. 6.5.

6 Acts 22.17–21.

7 W. E. Hocking, *Living Religions and a World Faith*, Allen and Unwin 1940, p. 39.

8 Acts 9, 22, 26; cf. Gal. 1.11–17.

9 Rev. 1.15.

10 See the imagery used by Niffari, a Muslim mystic, given and discussed by A. Huxley, *The Perennial Philosophy*, Chatto and Windus 1946, pp. 240 f.

11 E. Cassirer, *Language and Myth*, p. 74.

12 M. Eliade, *Patterns of Comparative Religion*, pp. 412 f., 426 f.

13 I. T. Ramsey, *Christian Discourse*, pp. 1–3.

14 Ex. 3.2 ff.

15 H. Buck, *People of the Lord*, Macmillan 1966, p. 189.

16 Werner Müller, 'The "Passivity" of Language and the Experience of Nature', in: J. M. Kitagawa and C. H. Lang (eds.), *Myths and Symbols*, University of Chicago Press 1969.

17 Num. 22.21–35.

18 II Kings 6.16.

19 II Kings 6.17.

20 O. Eissfeldt, *The Old Testament. An Introduction*, Basil Blackwell 1966, p. 54.

21 Ps. 104.4.

22 Ps. 33.6; 147.4; Jer. 8.2.

23 Ex. 21.6; 22.8.

24 Mark 1.2.

25 Gen. 19.1–21; 21.17–19; 22.11–18; 31.11–13; 32.24–30; Ex. 3.2–6; Josh. 5.13–16; Judg. 2.1–5; 6.11–14; 13.2–23. See the discussion of these and other passages in G. A. F. Knight, *A Christian Theology of the Old Testament*, SCM Press 1964, pp. 65–83.

26 John 5.2–9 and variants.

27 J. Lindblom, *Prophecy in Ancient Israel*, Basil Blackwell 1962, p. 107; cf. Eissfeldt, *op. cit.*, p. 77.

28 Ezek. 8.3.

29 E.g. Isa. 21; Ezek. 8–11.

30 A. Parrot, *The Tower of Babel*, p. 34.

31 Acts 10.9–16.

11 Classic Revelations

JUST AS THERE are moments of discovery in the life of the individual, so also we can detect episodes in history in which a people become the recipients of revelatory experience. These are aptly named classic revelations, for they are the communal experiences which give rise to the great religions of the world.[1] In these movements we find the same elements already noted as essential in individual disclosures but on a much larger scale. They arise out of the deepest needs of a whole people and focus on a particular point in history the quality of which all subsequent ages attempt to perpetuate in various symbolic forms. The details of the dialectic are even less easy to determine than they are in the case of individuals, for the number of factors involved are multiplied many times, but their fundamental character appears to be much the same.

It is noteworthy that many of the world's great religions came into being at about the same time. It is as though a massive revelatory experience took place in which large parts of humanity were involved. Karl Jaspers refers to this period of history as the axial age and suggests a date somewhere about 800 BC as the point at which it can be seen clearly to have begun and 500 BC as the date at which the originative forces had largely passed from the stage of history.[2] During that time there arose a succession of revolutionary leaders who transformed the lives of millions of people in various parts of the civilized world. In Palestine the great prophets of Israel appeared. In Persia Zarathustra began to teach. In China Confucius and the first Taoist leaders emerged. In India the period saw the writing of the Upanishads, the beginning of the Buddhist movement and the birth of the Jina. In Greece it was the time when the first stirrings of that new thinking were taking place which would become the foundation for western philosophy and science. It seems as though a large part of the world was undergoing a spiritual renewal. The ultimate questions were being asked again and new formulations made in answer to them. The axial age thus constituted a major break with the past and from that time onwards those who had not taken part in it or been taken up by the movements it produced came to be regarded as not merely backward but barbarous.

Two of the world's great religions, of course, began much later than the axial age. Christianity did not come into being until some five centuries later, while Islam did not emerge for a further six centuries. In different ways these two religions illustrate the way in which major revelatory experiences have taken place since the axial age.

Christianity derived from one of the religions produced by the axial age at a time when there was a widespread necessity for renewal. Classic revelations have a character in one respect very different from individual disclosures. Because they affect the lives of so many people they are formulated in a symbol system which becomes increasingly complex with the passage of time. The symbols generated by the originative events begin to lose their power because there has been no personal participation in the experience which gave them birth. In this kind of situation there is always need for rediscovery. The rise of Christianity represented just such a renewal of creative faith-language. In the process of rediscovery, entirely new elements came into being but even these were expressed largely in the language provided by the classic revelation out of which Christianity arose.

Islam, on the other hand, seems to represent a religious movement among a people who had been largely untouched by the movements stemming from the axial age. Before Muhammed the people of Arabia appear to have been living in a mythological culture. There had been some contact with both Judaism and Christianity, at least on the part of Muhammed himself, but it appears to have been with a somewhat debased form of the two faiths. Consequently Muhammed saw himself as a true heir and purifier of the Hebraic-Christian tradition. To the people of Arabia, however, it was a belated participation in the axial age.

Within the situation created by this period there was room and necessity for constant development. Sometimes this took place slowly and almost imperceptibly, but also on occasions in sudden bursts of reactivation. In the case of Christianity the new wine burst forth from the old bottles of Judaism. In Arabia a thread leading back into the distant past suddenly brought a backward people into the arena of the great religions of mankind.

THE COLLAPSE AND RENEWAL OF RELIGION

The causes of classic revelations would seem to be extremely diverse, but they could hardly have arisen if there had not been present on a fairly large scale a need for new religious insight. While a symbol system is functioning well, the prophet has little chance of success. When the formulations of a bygone age no longer speak there is a basis for the success of new movements. In times of spiritual distress a new religious leader can be accepted and new ways of living tried out.

The history of religion, therefore, seems to be punctuated by periods of symbolic disintegration followed by religious renewal. Joachim Wach wrote that a new faith often appears when there is a 'protest against and rejection of the traditional cult'.[3] Such a rejection is only possible, however, when that cult is no longer the bearer of meaning. The symbol complex of a previous age must become otiose before any real need arises for a new one. The failure of past formulations sets the stage for new revelation which is often in essence a recovery of understanding. The chequered history of world religion presents a picture much like the temperature chart of a patient who is now hot and now cold. As each movement loses its original vitality and becomes a dead legacy there is invariably a reaction which contains the basis for new creative advance.

The emergence of Gautama Buddha as a great religious leader was assisted by the fact that for a large number of people the Brahminism of the day had ceased to be a meaningful context in which to live. The success of Buddhism east of India was assured by the presence of spiritual voids left by the erosion of indigenous religion.

The success of Christianity in the Graeco-Roman world is at least partly explained by the fact that contemporary culture was in urgent need of a new gospel. That world had long ago lost the symbolic value of its own myths and yet no great faith had arisen to take their place. There was an eagerness, therefore, to find something which would replace the gods now laughed to scorn and the cold comfort of the philosophical schools.

Men and women listened to the words of Martin Luther and John Calvin because the medieval understanding of life had collapsed under the impact of the new learning. The iconoclasm which marked the reformation period was only possible because the icons had become meaningless idolatry to a large number of people. There was once again a fervent search for the meaning of human life at a time when the cultural patterns of the past had collapsed.

Yet while the presence of a great need can explain the success of a religious movement, it does not necessarily tell us anything about the way in which an answer comes about. Joachim Wach guardedly remarks that 'it is generally agreed that the emergence of a great new religious faith is one of the inexplicable mysteries which have accompanied the ascent of man and bears the most convincing testimony to the contingency and spontaneity of his spiritual history'.[4] Wach is clearly not prepared to admit that the classic religions are also classic revelations. To speak of 'contingency and spontaneity' pretends to give an explanation while admitting that there is none. The words merely restate the fact that the birth of religious faith appears as an 'inexplicable mystery'. The preparation for a new faith is readily explained, its arrival is not.

The history of religions school which flourished early in the twentieth century made the mistake of thinking that when it had shown that the world was ripe for the message of a resurrected Christ, it had also accounted for that message. But if the words of the Christian kerygma had merely been derived from what was already present, there would have been no disclosure. It would only have been a repetition of a well-known song to a worn-out audience. As we shall see, the great religions of the world divided into two basic types. One spoke of its classic insight as having been attained by man, while the other held that it was revealed by God. What they all agreed upon was that their faiths were not the accidental products of fortuitous history. Both theistic and atheistic religions have regarded the impersonal empiricism of scientific history as inadequate to all the facts. The language which could do justice to the birth of classic religion was necessarily for them the participator language of faith and not the observer language of science.

CLASSIC REVELATION AND MYTHOLOGY

The classic religions were born out of the corpse of mythology. They rejected a symbol system already thousands of years old because in its decline it no longer answered to the full spiritual needs of the people. On the other hand, a complete break with mythology was impossible, for in it was enshrined an accumulated wisdom which could not be merely dismissed. Consequently, we find that mythological thought is rejected with great enthusiasm at one point in history only to appear again at a later point more powerful than ever. The originating impetus of a classic revelation always seems to have been a reaction against an outworn mythological structure and this is evident in various ways.

The literature produced during the creative period of classic movements is regularly one from which mythological elements have been deliberately excluded or transformed. Confucius was noted largely for his work in gathering together the literature of his people's past, but in doing this he carefully purged it of their heritage of mythology.[5] Similarly Jains and Buddhists rejected the Vedic mythology of the land in which they were born. The deliberate elimination of mythological elements from early Hebrew literature is equally apparent.

A rejection of mythology is most evident in the denial of mythological deities. This appears to have taken two forms.

In one type of tradition there was a denial of ultimate deity along with the rejection of personal imagery, and religions which belong to this tradition are often classed as monistic for this reason.[6] In Buddhism, for example, the gods as such are not denied but they are no longer seen as mediations of an ultimate and personal being. The Buddhist understood the spirits to need enlightenment in the same way that man does. Their mythological role as mediators of the supreme reality was therefore lost.

In the other type of religion the gods of myth disappear altogether, or so it seems at first. The Hebraic narratives which derive from myth are carefully expunged of all deities except Yahweh, although there are relics of plurality in the language. Muhammed's attack on the Christian concept of the Trinity was clearly aimed at what was considered to be mythological deification. For some reason unknown to us he believed that it represented the characteristic trinity of mythology: a divine father, a cosmic mother and a sacred child. But the loss of the mythological gods in this tradition was mostly a matter of name. They were replaced by angels. The mythological concept of the gods as accommodations of ultimate truth was retained under a new terminology. Thus in Hebraism the gods became the angelic agencies of Yahweh. Zarathustra replaced the gods with the Amesha Spentas of the one Ahura Mazda. The Koran retained the angels of the Bible and added the jinn, the indigenous mythological spirits of Arabia, ranking them between angels and men. The mythological gods of other peoples often became the evil counterpart of the angelic, the demons. So in early Christianity the gods of pagan Greece and Rome were regarded as demons.

An attack upon mythology inevitably involved a rejection of its cultic manifestations. The Old Testament prophets not only attacked the mythological culture of the Phoenicians and Canaanites but were also extremely critical of the sacrificial system operating among their own people. Sacrifice was in fact often the object of attack by the leaders of the axial age. The opposition of Akhnaton of Egypt and Zarathustra of Persia to blood sacrifice was typical of the spirit abroad at that time. Mythological society usually maintained a professional priesthood as part of its sacral structure. Many of the great religions, however, were initiated by men who stood aside from the priesthood. A Moses became the leader rather than an Aaron. The hierophantic structure of society was therefore usually opposed by movements which had their initial impetus within a lay reaction. Consequently society was desacralized, the divinity of kings removed and the hierarchical division of men and women into castes severely criticized or ignored.

Desacralization was, of course, accompanied by secularization. Zarathustra showed a real concern for the peasantry and their cattle. The Old Testament prophets spent much of their time attacking the injustice of the law courts. Confucianism was almost totally concerned with political and moral behaviour, largely ignoring the ultimate religious concerns of theology. The elimination of the gods left the world free to be secular so that the work of man had value in its own right and not merely as a reflection of an eternal order. In place of mythology we often find religions of inwardness, of ethics and social concern.

Yet secularization left the world devoid of any clear, ultimate meaning. The classic revelations were therefore usually overtaken by mythology before long. After a period of desacralization there was a resurgence of mythological power. In ancient Greece the philosophers laughed the gods to scorn but they reappeared shortly afterwards in the eruption of the mystery religions. As the native gods had been lost mythological gods were imported from elsewhere. The humanism of

Taoism was overtaken by mythology. The magi of Persia turned the Amesha Spentas of Zarathustra into the Immortal Holy Ones. In Islam the development of the Shi'a doctrine of the Imam or divinely appointed ruler, with superhuman qualities descended from Adam through Muhammed, shows the same resurgence of mythology at a later time. The Imam doctrine revived the primal man concept. Like the divine Bodhissatvas developed in Buddhism, especially in Tibet, the Imam was held to cast no shadow and to be incapable of physical harm. Some even held the Imam to be an incarnation of deity. The revival of Shintoism in Japan recaptured a native mythology after a period of invasion by Buddhism and Christianity. This produced a resacralization phenomenal in the twentieth century with an overt divinization of the emperor.

The mythological cycle appears within the development of religion in a dialectic of rejection and recovery.

PERCEPTION AND REVELATION

The reader must at times have felt uneasy at the attempt to treat all the great religions as though there were no fundamental differences between them. It is necessary at this point to redress the balance at least to the extent of noting that the description of originating insight is given in two quite different ways.

Some faiths, Buddhism, Confucianism, Taoism and Jainism among them, have described their disclosures as being the result of human effort. It is not inappropriate to speak of these as gnosis religions, for the basic idea embedded in their language is of the attainment of a spiritual knowledge and within the history of Christianity such language is primarily represented by the gnostic movement which flourished in the early church for a time. The term also serves to include movements which were simply philosophical such as those in ancient Greece. An attempt must be made to note its distinctive features.

(*a*) The language employed is primarily that of the intellect, although the knowledge of which it speaks is often mystical. A number of characteristic words appear regularly, understanding, enlightenment and perception being typical. Metaphor tends to give way to simile. Whereas revelatory experience seems to charge something with symbolic meaning, gnosis experience creates a language indicative of the intellectual search for adequate expressions. In the Buddhist scriptures, for example, an attempt is made to convey some idea of Nirvana to the mind by self-conscious analogies in which the number of positive characteristics are precisely given. 'Nirvana', it is written, 'shares one quality with the lotus, two with water, three with medicine, ten with space, three with the wishing jewel and five with a mountain peak.'[7]

(*b*) Emphasis is placed upon the human effort involved in the attainment of insight. The founder of Jainism is referred to as the victor, not in the sense this would have in a mythological context, but by virtue of his having discovered the nature of being. Similarly, the Buddha is one who attained enlightenment rather than one who received a revelation. The scriptures which were created as a result of his efforts are full, therefore, of such words as striving, seeing, understanding and following the path. In both Yoga and Buddhism a detailed programme of study and meditation is given so that the climb towards understanding may be pursued successfully.

This gives rise to a characteristic symbolism which is conveniently set out by Anders Nygren in his study of *Agape and Eros*.[8] He notes the appearance in the writings of Gregory of Nyssa of those symbols which he regards as typical of the eros motif: the heavenly ladder by which the mystical ascent is made, the wings of the soul which carry the mind aloft, the mountain up which the would-be victor must climb, the arrow of thought which finds out its target, the flame which restlessly attempts to reach the heights of understanding and the chain of love whose links carry one to a sight of the unutterable beauty. Indicative of the whole is the central symbol of Buddhism, the Bo-tree, whose leaves are flame-shaped like the blue ethereal flame which is said to appear on the head of a yogin in *samadhi*, the final state of enlightenment.[9] Nygren notes that these same symbols can be modified for use of revelatory experience and for this reason they have been stated here in the form in which they naturally appear as descriptions of gnosis experience.

(*c*) As the symbols just given imply, there is a flight from the world of sense and this in turn contributed to a characteristic terminology. Again Buddhism provides obvious examples. Rather than finding the world immanent with deity as in mythological thinking, the Buddha taught the ultimate un-reality of the world from which man must escape. Thus there was created a language of not-this, not-that. The soul is compared to a chariot which is unreal apart from its wheels, axle, pole and body. Equally unreal are all other things and so the imagery of illusion, dream, phantom, mist, cloud, foam, bubble, mirage. The only substance is that created by the illusion of the mind which can hold man in a bondage symbolized by the weary wheel of existence.

(*d*) Finally, we find a complete lack of the language of encounter. The ultimate discovered is at most impersonal being or principle. There is a total negation of mythology's anthropomorphism. The gnostic is not one to whom a word is spoken, but one who discovers that there can be no word. All idea of God may be discarded as in Buddhism, or impersonal-ized and virtually ignored as in Confucianism. Not surprisingly, therefore, the imagery is frequently derived from the realm of the inanimate. Nirvana, for example, in the quotation already given is described in terms which rely on anything but a reference to personal being.

When we turn to Judaism, Zoroastrianism, Christianity and Islam, on the other hand, we find a constant claim to revelatory experience. Whereas the mystic or philosopher is typical of the gnosis religions, here we meet the prophet who proclaims, 'Thus saith the Lord'. This has produced a quite different pattern of language.

(*a*) The most obvious difference we discover is that the revelatory religions speak of man as being the passive recipient. Spiritual insight is not attained but given. The language of

ascent is replaced by the language of descent. Yahweh descends
on Mount Sinai and comes down to be incarnated in Jesus of
Nazareth. The prophets of Israel are seized by the presence of
the Lord. Pseudo-Justin illustrates the language of total passivity when he compares the action of the Holy Spirit on the
human soul to the way in which a plectrum plays upon the
strings of a musical instrument. Athenagoras similarly speaks
of the breath of God blowing divine music through the human
flutes he chose as his instruments.[10] Muhammed understood
himself to be a tool in the hands of Allah. The typical characterizations of men in relation to God therefore are those of apostle,
servant and prophet.

(*b*) A complementary language for God speaks of him as
king, lord, master, lawgiver, judge and potter. Perhaps the
clearest expression of passivity language is found in Islam where
the mosque is literally a place of prostration. Islam itself
means total submission, and Allah is above all things the
omnipotent one.

(*c*) Yet despite a language indicating the passivity of man
and the totality of divine power, the terminology of encounter
is not lost. Man is not obliterated, but drawn into a dialogue.
The omnipotent deity of Islam is also the compassionate and
merciful one. The Hebrew was not only the servant of Yahweh
but also called to be a bride and a son.

The distinction between the two traditions, however, is
never absolute. Even Buddhism resorted to the language of
revelation to describe the nature of the insight mediated by the
Buddha while Islam gave birth to a lively mystical movement.
Both types of language tend to appear in all world faiths. In
this we can perhaps see that at the root of the ambivalence of
all religious symbolism there lies the ambivalent nature of the
experiences which give rise to it. The moment of disclosure
may be stated anthropocentrically or theocentrically, but the
truth is best captured in the language of paradox typified by
the words found in the *Theologia Germanica* which speak of
'pure submission to the eternal Goodness, in the perfect freedom
of fervent love.'

THE SYMBOLISM OF THE BEGINNING

The great religions came into being at a particular point in history. This has had important results for the way in which their language has been structured. The symbol complex has tended to gather round the originative point in time and to derive its strength from it.

The most obvious feature about the time of the beginnings is the importance of individual persons. Each of the great religions looks back to a specific founder. Sometimes historical research makes it doubtful if the purported founder ever lived, in the case of Lao-Tse and Zarathustra for example, but their symbolic importance is never in doubt. This interest in particular individuals is in marked contrast with the age of myth which had been one of regular anonymity. No names ever appear in mythological material because the individual had been swallowed up in a collectivist culture. As soon as the axial age dawns, however, the anonymity of ancient texts like the Vedas and the Book of the Dead give way to the autographed works of individuals. The importance of the founder can hardly be explained if we do not see in him a substitute for the symbolic centre of mythology.

This led to a growing body of material purporting to tell of the originative event and its central character. The whole of Hebrew law was attributed to Moses, although the total corpus was clearly created out of a number of law reforms. In other religions, too, there has been a tendency to attribute a large body of literature to the cultic founder. Because the originating prophet was accepted as the bond between heaven and earth, the whole of subsequent revelation in the derivative religion was attributable to him. He it was through whom the truth had been given, the law revealed and the vision of the sacred vouchsafed. While there had been development subsequently, this was always seen as merely an extension of what was implicit in the first revelatory moment. There was, therefore, no attempt at deception, but rather an acceptance of the principle that all were dependent on that one ladder which had been placed between heaven and earth.

The way in which the link with the sacred was expressed varied from one religion to another, but there was an intention, which seems to have become more intense as the historical gap from the time of the beginnings increased, to assert the fullness of the original revelation. The most direct way in which this could be stated was to speak of incarnation. This appears naturally in Christianity because it asserted the sacramental character of creation. In Hinduism the god Vishnu is held to have appeared on earth to enlighten mankind on a number of occasions in a variety of forms or *avatars*. This type of language is also used where we would least expect it. The development of Buddhist thought eventually turned the teacher who had found the truth into one who had been born for the sole purpose of revealing his message to mankind. In consequence, the language of incarnation was developed to express the idea of the Buddha's birth as part of a planned revelatory sequence. The Buddha is said to have entered the womb of queen Maya as a white elephant when she was impregnated in her right side by its tusk. In this way the superhuman quality of the Buddha is shown to be the result not of a subsequent enlightening meditation but as something already attained before his birth. Moreover he is made to be the originator of his own birth, for it is a deliberate act of compassion on the part of one already entitled to escape the mortal coils of this life. It is not, of course, intended to suggest that Christianity, Hinduism and Buddhism are all making exactly the same statements, but they all use a common device of symbolic language whereby the point can be made that an extraordinary revelation was vouchsafed by speaking of its being incarnated or embodied in some person within historical existence.

The time of the beginnings is also characterized by an abundance of miracles. When men have been most conscious of the impact of the beyond upon their lives, they have invariably spoken of many miraculous events having taken place.

The question of miracle has vexed theologians for decades

and the issue is too complex to be discussed here. Still, one or two vital points bearing on the nature of religious language must be made. A miraculous event can only appear as such to those who have spiritual eyes with which to see. In the scriptures the symbols of religious language have to perform the function of those spiritual eyes for those who were not and could not be present to perceive the act of God. The language of miracle therefore acts as a substitute for the disclosure signs in the event itself, and when appropriated by the spirit assumes its potential power for faith.

It is also worth noting that miracle stories are not all of one kind. In addition to those just referred to which are actual events having a religious significance for the eye of faith, there are also narratives which are purely symbolic and have no reference to an actual event. One example must suffice. According to Matthew 27.45, the sun became dark at the moment of Jesus's death. This is most unlikely to have been a physical fact as the Passover was celebrated at the full moon. On the other hand, the symbolic significance of the reference is so rich that after attempting to explain it one wishes that it were possible simply with the author of the passage to rely on a fund of symbolic tradition. We are immediately reminded for example of the Egyptian idea of the sun as the eye of Ra, the eclipse of which plunges mankind into the darkness of the primeval chaos. Around this basic sun-symbolism there was a wealth of ideas on which the author could rely. The reader less well acquainted with the possible overtones conveyed can only be advised to consult such a work as that by Jacquetta Hawkes entitled *Man and the Sun*.[11] In applying this complex of ideas to the moment of Christ's crucifixion the author gave the clearest possible indications of what he perceived to be the meaning of that event.

Even when an incident is inserted for purely symbolic purposes, however, there is an intention to assert that it refers to something real in the nature of the event. The presence of symbol in narratives of the miraculous was intended to be coterminous with the activity of the power symbolized. These narratives tell not merely of the emergence of ideas but of real events the truth about which can only be spoken of in terms of symbols. The time in which symbols can be created is also the time when spiritual power is available. While much of the writing surrounding the inception of the classic religions is so full of miraculous symbolism that we can hardly discern the historical events which gave rise to it, we must nevertheless accept that such a profusion of symbolic representation indicates that men experienced a power other than themselves on a scale which they felt was unprecedented.

The time of the beginnings, therefore, constitutes a focus of a religion's symbol structure. The historical moment replaces the primordial events to which the myths look back and works within the symbol-complex in much the same way.

Anyone living within a classic religion is always looking back to the time of miracles and saints as mythological man remembered when God walked with men in the garden. Whenever the language of one of these religions loses its power it is reactivated by a return to the beginning. For this reason there is always a vast amount of historical research into the originating period.

Even the sites associated with the beginnings take on symbolic power. Benares is revered as the spot on which Vishnu first placed his foot. The site of the Bo tree and of Christ's crucifixion contend with one another for supremacy in world symbolism. Alongside research into documentary evidence there is added the work of the archaeologist whose location of the sacred sites has more than an academic interest to those whose meaning is found within the complex of events associated with them.

All this concern is often due to the feeling that the power has gone away, the prophets no longer speak and miracles are never seen. Just as the myths spoke of a time when man had been cast out of the garden, so here we find that subsequent ages feel that it was only at the beginning that the power of divine truth was present with man. Often this loss of the sacred is given symbolic form. The patriarchs of the Old Testament

G*

are said to have lived for hundreds of years. It has often been suggested that some obsolete means of calculation was being used, but it is far more likely that it represents a sense that the age of Methuselah was one in which the sacred power was present. The Jains hold that the first tirthankara was 2,000 cubits high and lived for 8,400,000 years. We should not see in this either a more obscure system of measurement nor a more fantastic imagination, but an indication of the quality which the Jain was prepared to acknowledge. The attribution of enormous height and longevity of life are not unusual ways of representing the presence of superhuman essence. This is but one more way of stating that the presence of the sacred among men has become comparatively tenuous, an attitude which is summed up in the idea of devolution which appears in Hinduism, Buddhism and Jainism. Within each, there is a tradition that the world has been steadily shrinking.[12] By this it is clearly intended to assert that mankind has become steadily poverty-stricken in spirit. The proclamation of a concomitant physical shrinkage, however, is probably the result of a phenomenon common in the history of religious language, the literalization of symbolism.

Once a classic revelation has established itself, it assumes an archetypal role in the lives of those within its influence. When an individual undergoes a revelatory experience, there is a need for an appropriate symbolic expression. The great religions provide the language needed by the individual and the context within which it can be placed. In this way the individual is integrated into the whole and linked with the power manifested at the time of the beginnings.

NOTES

1 J. Macquarrie, *Principles of Christian Theology*, SCM Press 1966, pp. 130 f., refers to these as primordial or classic revelations. In the present book the first of these terms has been reserved for the revelatory experiences which created mythological religion.

2 See A. C. Bouquet, *The Christian Faith and Non-Christian Religions*, Nisbet 1958, pp. 47, 56, 405.

3 J. Wach, *The Sociology of Religion*, University of Chicago Press 1962, p. 307.

4 *Op. cit.*, p. 307.

5 H. Ringgren and A. V. Strom, *Religions of Mankind*, Oliver and Boyd 1967, p. 393.

6 E.g. by D. W. Gundry, *Religions*, Macmillan 1958.

7 *Buddhist Scriptures*, Penguin Books 1969, p. 157.

8 A. Nygren, *Agape and Eros*, SPCK 1953, p. 221.

9 See F. Spiegelberg, *Living Religions of the World*, Thames and Hudson 1957, p. 235.

10 See E. Hatch, *The Influence of Greek Ideas and Usages upon the Christian Church*, Williams and Norgate 1898, pp. 51, 72.

11 The Cresset Press 1962.

12 See Spiegelberg, *op. cit.*, p. 67.

12 *The Hebrews and their History*

As WE HAVE seen, the Hebrew people shared in the remarkable transformation of the axial age. They call for special consideration for two reasons. First, they are of special interest to the Christian reader because they laid the foundation of his distinctive religious language. Second, they gave birth to a sense of history which has been a decisive influence on the development of western thought.

It is not intended to suggest that the Hebrews were entirely alone in thinking that events might constitute a history. There were clearly intuitions that events formed themselves into a meaningful sequence elsewhere. The Hebrews, however, seem to have been the first people to perceive this in such a radical way that they transformed their whole manner of life in accordance with it.

In the life of an individual we found that all kinds of objects and events could trigger off a new understanding. Similarly, certain events can take on the character of symbolic signs and act as signals to call forth a people's response to the meaning of their existence as a community. This was pre-eminently true in the case of the Hebrews. They became the people of a book which was a record of historical events. It told of a succession of moments in which they had seen the hand of God.

Although a great many events were perceived as specially significant by the Hebrew people, one event in particular stood out from the rest. This was the exodus from Egypt. This was seen not as part of a cycle of existence but as a once-for-all event. The Hebrews asserted that nothing had ever been the same for them since that moment. In the Old Testament, therefore, the exodus represents the appearance of an entirely new point of view, that events took place in a time sequence and there was a history which was always pregnant with that which was novel and unrepeatable.

It is extremely difficult to determine to what extent this was understood at the time of the exodus. We can only be certain that at some time subsequently it came to be seen as a moment of unclassifiable importance. In the narrative recollection of that event its significance is given clear symbolic form. As P. L. Berger expresses it, the Hebrews understood that at that point in time they had made a radical break with the cosmic order as seen in the myths represented by the fleshpots of Egypt.[1] The taunt made to Moses that he had brought them out of slavery in Egypt only to die in the desert may be taken as symbolic of the first sense of fear at having given up the security provided by the prison of the mythological world.

Mythological culture did not suddenly disappear, but a prophetic tradition was created by which its power was increasingly diminished. The prophetic movement was so far successful that the literature of the Old Testament is dominated not by the idea of cyclic repetition but by certain events which were held to mediate disclosure of God's ongoing concern. Just as they understood a sequence of actions to communicate an awareness of another's subjectivity, so they saw the sequence which is history to mediate the self-disclosure of God. History was in consequence a confrontation between them and God, a persons-to-person encounter. Events were understood as the speaking voice of the divine Thou. Their historical writing is throughout subjective because they allowed themselves to enter into a dialogue with the living God of history.

This was only possible because they saw events in a certain way. For events to become triggers of disclosure they had to be seen with the eye of faith. In the terminology of a German theologian, Martin Kähler, *Historie* had to become *Geschichte*. The bare facts of history had to be understood as personally meaningful. More than this, history for the Hebrews became *Heilsgeschichte*, a story of the acts of God. Consequently the ordinary sequence of historical events was lit up for them with the light of the divine presence and mediated God's concern for his people.

THE SYMBOLIC EXPRESSION OF HISTORICAL DISCLOSURE

If the disclosure value of history experienced was to be portrayed, it was necessary to present it in such a way that its revelatory character would be manifest. The prophets and writers of Hebrew history achieved this by a transformation of mythological imageries. They did not discard a heritage which had given meaning to their lives in the past. They were concerned to add a new dimension of understanding rather than to start afresh.

The primodial myths were retained. Their stories of creation were placed at the opening of their scriptures. They were seen now, however, as the beginning of a story which was still going on. The creation was the first of many events and not merely an eternally repeated event. Hebrew history starts with what had been myth, but it is changed so as to be hardly recognizable as myth because the drama is now part of historical time. The primordial events had initiated a history. As Eliade puts it, the Hebrew God was not merely the 'creator of archetypal gestures'[2] but a God who was the creator of new events. Their classic revelation had turned the Hebrews from the worship of nature to the Living God of history.

The creation myth was seen not only as the beginning of history but also as containing an interpretative principle for the understanding of subsequent history. On many occasions the Hebrews felt that the cosmogonic struggle was being repeated in the events of their national life.

The exodus event was taken as such a close parallel to the act of creation that it is often impossible to separate the mythological from the historical elements in passages such as Psalm 74 which speak of it.[3] In this event the Hebrew believed that the God of creation had once again overcome the forces of destruction. The leviathan of the myth had once again been destroyed. In the manner of symbolic myth, the dragon of chaos was seen as active in more than one form during the exodus. As the oppressor of Israel, the nation of Egypt was identified with Rahab.[4] The serpent is also present in its primordial form as the waters of the Red Sea and the victor of the creation myth parts the monster in twain so that dry land may appear upon which the Hebrews can cross to safety.[5]

As a political force hostile to Israel, Egypt is frequently seen as the mythical Rahab.[6] In this way there was expressed an assurance that such power is doomed to eventual destruction. Typical is Ezekiel's characterization of Pharaoh Hophra as 'the great dragon that lies in the midst of his streams', who is destined to be fished out of its waters and fed to the 'beasts of the earth and to the birds of the air'.[7] In such terms did prophetic Judaism assert that Yahweh was not merely a power in nature but also in the political and military scene.

Isaiah 14 is an especially useful example of the use of mythological material in the interpretation of a historical event. At the time at which the chapter was written the power threatening Israel was Babylon, whom the author identifies with the mythical rebel, Helel, the son of Dawn, who challenged the chief god, Elyon of Mount Zaphon, in the Phoenician myth. Mythological material is here used to create a taunt against the king of Babylon who had said: 'I will ascend to heaven; above the stars of God I will set my throne on high; I will sit on the mount of assembly in the far north; I will ascend above the heights of the clouds, I will make myself like the Most High.'[8] Isaiah here sees the king of Babylon acting out a fundamental motif in the mythological cycle. The imperial pretensions of Babylon are said to be like those of a lesser god attempting to usurp the throne of the high god. The myths taught that everything has its proper place and the Hebrew story-teller loved to show that false exaltations of the human spirit were always doomed to disaster. Whenever man left his proper place as one who was to look up to the Lord, he is cast down. So the king of Babylon had eventually been laid in the grave where 'maggots are the bed' and worms the covering.[9]

Myths had always been archetypal narratives, but as used by the Hebrews they were given an added dimension. Their relevance was no longer restricted to the cycle of natural events. They were used to express a faith in the lord of history who, they believed, would always be triumphant over the beast from the sea whatever form he might take.[10]

The significance of history was also portrayed in symbolic models. These were often derived from a basic mythological symbol. Its cosmic dimension, however, was replaced by a historical and social meaning. These symbolic models were used to show how a sequence of historical events constituted a meaningful relationship and disclosed the subjective dimension of history. Several models were used for this purpose, but one which will serve to exemplify the whole is that of the vine.

The vine was a familiar feature of the Palestinian landscape and played an important part in the life of the people. Much of their livelihood was dependent on the vine and few things gave the Hebrew greater pleasure than a good vintage. A good season for the vine meant a good year for the people. It also came to symbolize peace, for in time of war the vineyards were neglected and often destroyed. The vine, therefore, possessed the essential characteristics required of a good symbol. It had numerous evocative associations and could thus be used by the prophets with great effect.

In Psalm 80 the model is set out in some detail. This psalm was probably written at the time of the downfall of the kingdoms of Israel and Judah and the psalmist looks back over the history of Israel down to his own day. He tells his audience that Yahweh once took a precious vine out of Egypt and planted it in Canaan where the ground had been carefully prepared to receive it. In the new soil the vine had prospered and become so great that 'the mountains were covered with its shade, the mighty cedars with its branches'.[11] It sent its roots deep into the earth where they spread out to the Mediterranean on one side and to the Jordan on the other. After this period of growth and prosperity, however, the walls built to protect the great vine had been destroyed. Marauders and wild beasts ravaged its fruit. In this situation the psalmist calls upon the Lord of Israel to restore his vineyard to its former glory.

Our example shows how the model was frequently used. The vineyard is made to represent the Israelite nation, and the fortunes of the vine reflect the political history of the people. As used in this psalm the nation is pictured as a purely passive recipient of Yahweh's care and the enemy's insults, because the psalmist wished to stress the dependence of Israel on her Lord. The model could also be used, however, in a way which assigned an active role to the Hebrew people. For this purpose the vine is personified so that it can represent the nation and be held responsible for its own actions. Thus Jeremiah claimed on behalf of Yahweh that his choice vine of pure seed had 'turned degenerate and become a wild vine'.[12] In the eyes of the prophets this degeneracy was constituted by the worship of Baal, the god of nature mythology, and a desertion of Yahweh, the Lord of history. Consequently Hosea claimed that the more prosperous Israel became, the more worship was paid to Baal, for 'the more his fruit increased, the more altars he built'.[13] The prophets believed, moreover, that such false worship was always accompanied by social injustice. The fruit which the owner of the vineyard looked for was justice and righteousness, but instead it had been bloodshed and despair.[14] The real despoilers of the vineyard were in Isaiah's eyes the elders and princes of the people who had heaped up treasure in their own houses by 'grinding the faces of the poor'.[15]

From this example it can be seen how the cosmic tree could be historicized. The tree ceases to be a replica of the cosmos and becomes an analogy for the people of Israel and their history.

The effects of the new historical sensitivity were various. The mythological view had penetrated every aspect of life. It was therefore inevitable that any disturbance of the mythological basis would have many repercussions. The Hebrew had perceived history as pre-eminently important and this had made him rethink his myths. It also made him rethink everything which depended on the myths. This of course was a process which took a long time, for ideas can change more rapidly than the liturgical, social and personal structures which are dependent on them.

The ritual traditions of the Hebrews were gradually but radically transformed. Whereas Israel had previously shared a ritual life based upon and interpretative of the cycle of nature, now it began to understand its rites in terms of history. What had previously been a participation in the creative round of the seasons now became a sacramental re-enactment of decisive events. The nature-myth culture had based all its ritual festivals on the rhythm of the heavenly bodies, of the flock, the crops and man himself. The Hebrews did not abandon these but added a new dimension to them. They turned them into celebrations of those moments in their history when the hand of God had been manifest. The festivals continued to betray their ancient ancestry, but as the prophetic sense of history became stronger this background was gradually eliminated so that it is often difficult to get back beyond the historical significance of a festival.

As the originative disclosure the exodus took pride of place in the new ritual year. The celebration of the Passover was carefully explained to the young Jew as a memorial of the triumphant escape from Egypt. Many of the features of the Passover ritual had existed prior to that event. A spring festival had celebrated the new birth of nature. The grain harvest had been celebrated by rites which included the removal of the old leaven. A number of elements from these earlier festivals found a place in the Passover rites, but their restyling by a historical consciousness was such that the origin of particular customs are the subject of lively debate. The Hebrew wished to make his greatest ritual event a time for remembering the birth of his nation at the hand of God. The symbolism of new birth therefore was given an entirely new meaning.

Other nature rituals were similarly treated. The feast held at the end of the grain harvest was given a double significance by linking it both with the covenant made with Noah and with the giving of the law on Mount Sinai. The autumnal festival of ingathering or tabernacles was drawn into the exodus complex by interpreting the booths as a reminder of the tents in which the Israelites had lived in the wilderness. It is quite likely that this festival celebrated the victory of Yahweh over the destructive waters if Hab. 3 and Psalm 29 were used liturgically at this time of year as some scholars believe. The Ninth of Ab with its distinctive feature of lamentation may well have had an origin in rites for the death of Tammuz, a vegetation god, but this was overshadowed and then obliterated by turning the festival into a lamentation for the destruction of the Temple and of Jerusalem by Nebuchadnezzar in 586 BC. Later the ceremony was given added point by another destruction of the centre of Judaism by the Roman commander, Titus, in AD 70. The complete round of the ritual year, however, assured the Jew that the living God was always active in history to save as well as to judge.

The rejection of mythological ideas necessarily involved a denial of sacral kingship and with it the old view of human society as a microcosm of the total divine-human structure. It is likely that in the early days of Israel the monarchy was regarded in a mythological way, although the evidence provided by a literature edited at a time subsequent to the rejection of the sacral monarchy is indecisive.[16] Nevertheless, there are certainly relics of the concept left in the language employed. The king is frequently said to sit upon the throne of Yahweh[17] and he can be said to act on behalf of Yahweh as lord of the sea.[18] Nevertheless, it is clear that the classic revelation of Judaism left no room ultimately for a sacral kingship. The prophets fought against the idea and the nation finally abandoned it. But such an important element in the religious understanding of the age of myth could not be merely discarded. The sacral monarchy was displaced rather than eliminated and new forms of symbolic language came into being as a result.

The language which had once been formulated to express the role of the king was now applied to Yahweh exclusively. The old sacral kingship left a legacy to the prophets of Israel in the form of a model in which they could speak of the king of creation. Zion was regarded as his capital and the temple as his palace wherein his throne was located.[19] The psalms which may once have been used to celebrate the coronation of a Hebrew king were now used to declare the lordship of Yahweh over all creation.[20] To Jerusalem and its temple the people came in state procession to have an audience with the great king of all the earth.[21] In this way the sacral kingship was replaced by a theocratic ideal which completely altered the role of the king in Israelite society.

One of the most important effects of the rejection of sacral kingship in Israel was to create a view of political structure which made revolution possible. As a mere tool of God rather than as an embodiment of the divine in human life, the king was no longer regarded as absolute. He was required to submit to the law of a greater king. He could be overthrown whenever the prophetic consciousness became aware of a disjunction between the rule of the king and the will of Yahweh. As God and king were not identified even in principle, they could be opposed the one to the other. The prophet was able to stand before the king and utter words of condemnation on behalf of the God of Israel. The developing ethical consciousness which was so much part of the distinctive prophetic religion of Israel meant that the prophets usually confronted the king as representatives of the people in their demand for justice. As a result the Israelites produced a somewhat unstable monarchy, especially in the northern kingdom, in which the prophets were responsible for a number of political revolutions which swept away the king when he was unwilling to conform to the advancing standards of the Israelite conscience. The static society founded on myth was therefore exchanged for a constantly changing, revolutionary society of history. In this the Hebrew paved the way for the purely secular conception of the state which has developed in western thought and for the idea that the state must be subordinate to the ethical consciousness of the people.

Another shift in language resulted from the rejection of the sacral monarchy. The erosion of the ancient cosmic symbolism at the behest of historical sensitivity included a rejection of the idea that the king and his spouse could represent the bisexuality of the cosmic principle. The female element in the concept of deity was almost totally abandoned and the Hebrew God was conceived as severely masculine and denied any female counterpart. There was a retention of a female consort for Yahweh among the Jews in Egypt but this never entered the mainstream of Hebraic development. The queen, therefore, played no sacral role in Israel. The feminine element had been intimately associated with the religion of nature and the mythological fertility cults which the prophets opposed, so it was destroyed in the process of ridding Israel of the worship of Baal. But it was not ousted without trace. As with everything else, the Hebrew transformed rather than destroyed. As the king no longer played a sacral role, there was no place for a sacral queen. The sole king was Yahweh himself. His feminine counterpart, his wife, was henceforth Israel. The nation took over the role of the consort and this gave rise to a persistent imagery in which Israel is seen as the wife of Yahweh. In this way the static or cyclic concept of the sexual principle gave way to a dynamic and historical perspective. The history of Israel was seen as the story of a relationship between the heavenly husband, Yahweh, and his terrestial spouse, Israel. Here, too, the Hebrew had secularized the mythological concept. The sacral queen had become the lay community of Israel.

The secularization of Hebrew society was not without its disadvantages. The immanentism characteristic of mythological thinking had given men and women a sense of the nearness of God. The divine was seen as impinging upon them in every part of the sacred ritual and the sacral society. The revolution brought about by the prophets swept away many of the media of divine presence and asserted a radical transcendentalism. Yahweh became a God who was wholly other and consequently the people often experienced a sense of being cut off from the sacred springs of life. The difficulty experienced by many of the people is evident from the fact that the prophetic movement had to wage a constant war upon the mythological culture to which the Israelites frequently resorted. The secularization of society had left a void which was often felt most acutely. It enabled a major advance in the development of social justice, but at a cost of a great increase in ontological anxiety.

On the personal level the historicization of myth, the transformation of its ritual and the secularization of society had profound consequences. The individual was no longer caught up into the eternity mediated by the myth but placed specifically in time and made aware of his historical contingency. When everything was seen fulfilled in the eternal cycle of existence, the individual found his meaning by absorption into the divine. This approach to human fulfilment was now broken. He was still a member of the community but that community was no longer sacral. He was told that his meaning was to be found in the history of his people but this did not allow for any means of individual, personal fulfilment such as had been provided for by identification with deity in the funerary rites.

Hebraic secularization had forfeited the mythological provision for immortality. In Egypt the Hebrews had been among a people who possessed a very highly developed mythological symbolism of immortality, but prophetic Hebraism turned them away from this culture. The attraction of mythological eternity clearly lingered in Israel and was probably one of the major reasons why there was a constant retreat from Zion to the high places of Canaan. The mythological symbols mediated a participation in the eternal life of deity, with the result that the prophets were often ignored and men were found conversing with the dead in the manner of the old rites. The prophets were eventually successful and the Hebrew was then forced to face the contingency of both history and his own being. He retained a belief in Sheol, in a continuance of a shadowy life beyond the grave, but he had lost the richness embedded in the mythological symbolism of immortality. The singer of Israel, therefore, is constantly confronted with his own finitude in the face of which he makes a plaintive cry to a God whose transcendence seems to have removed him from the world of men. He may still acknowledge the presence of God in every place, but the symbolism which had given substance to this had gone.

We find, therefore, that prophetic teaching was so concerned with the discovery of history as a dialogue between a secular society and a transcendent God that a void had been left for the individual. He begins to experience the agony of loneliness. As always, however, the appearance of anxiety is but the prelude to new discovery. A new symbolism was born out of need. The answer for Israel had to be found in terms of the sense of history which had become its dominating passion.

ESCHATOLOGICAL MYTHOLOGY

As history was being taken seriously as an ongoing concern, it was inevitable that the Hebrews should ultimately have created an eschatology. This developed slowly, for the implications of replacing the mythological view of time as cyclic by a linear concept of history were not immediately apparent. They were only forced upon the Hebrew consciousness by the existential void which was created by the abandonment of mythological culture. Yet with the realization that it was no longer possible to think of man's time being eternally fulfilled in mythological time, it was necessary to consider how the fulfilment of man might take place from within the new historical perspective. In response the Hebrew looked to the future. If history was a movement through time in which the new and the unique could appear, the answer to man's ontological anxiety could be found in the future which was yet to be. A history which had a beginning and a development must also have an end, a point at which it was fulfilled and attained its meaning.

As the end lay in the future, it was impossible to speak of it in other than symbolic terms. It was still the unknown which could only be dimly perceived. As the Hebrews had been prepared to make use of mythological symbolism to speak of the genesis of history and of its development, it is not surprising that they should have found it appropriate to use the same imagery to speak of the coming eschaton. The cosmogonic myth, therefore, was used to create a symbolic picture of the way in which the meaning of history would be revealed at its fulfilment. It seemed logical to assume that the creative power which had brought the world into being and maintained it against the forces of destruction should finally be completely triumphant. We find, then, that as the myth had spoken of Yahweh overcoming the dragon of the abyss at the time of creation, so it could now speak of the eschaton as an ultimate victory for the slayer of serpents. The contingency of history with its resulting ontological anxiety was thus overcome. The eternal would take over the temporal and time would be redeemed when Yahweh took history entirely to himself. In the last days the divine dragon slayer will be finally victorious over all his enemies both cosmic and historical. So in Isaiah 2.2–4 the myth of the cosmic Zion is transformed into an eschatological event. The world will become paradisal and all the nations will come to the garden on the cosmic mountain of Zion from whose temple the river will flow.[22] 'In that day the Lord with his hard and great and strong sword will punish Leviathan the fleeing serpent, Leviathan the twisting serpent, and he will slay the dragon that is in the sea.'[23]

If the individual was to find a personal fulfilment, it had to be within the context of such a vision, and so there emerged, somewhat late in Hebraic development, the idea of resurrection. Secular history necessitated the symbolism of resurrection as a counterpart to the eternity offered in the mythological cycle. The form which this took was determined by historical understanding. The dead would enter the eternity of God by an awakening from the sleep of death, to participate in the fulfilment of history. In this way the tears and travail of human life could once again be seen to make sense after the historical view had been adopted. Yahweh would achieve a victory over man's finitude and slay the dragon of ontological annihilation.

The secularization of history had been so drastic, however, that at first the dead were understood to be resurrected in order to take part in a new terrestial kingdom rather than in a noumenal dimension which would take over history and translate it into something entirely new. In consequence we hear of a new kingdom which sounds sometimes like the reestablishment of the lost sacral society. The place of the sacral king is taken by the messiah, who will reign for a specified period of time. For an attempt to create a complete synthesis of historical and mythological time we have to turn to the New Testament.

NOTES

1 Ex. 16.3; P. L. Berger, *op. cit.*, pp. 115 f.
2 M. Eliade, *Cosmos and History*, Harper and Row 1959, p. 104 (a reprint of *The Myth of the Eternal Return*).
3 F. F. Bruce, 'Our God and Saviour', in: S. G. F. Brandon (ed.), *The Saviour God*, pp. 51–66.
4 Isa. 51.9 f.
5 Pss. 66.6; 77.16–19; 78.13; 106.9; Isa. 51.10.
6 Pss. 87.4; 89.8–10; Isa. 30.7.
7 Ezek. 29.3, 5.
8 Isa. 14. 13 f.
9 Isa. 14.11.
10 See Dan. 7.
11 Ps. 80.10.
12 Jer. 2.21.
13 Hos. 10.1.
14 Isa. 5.7.
15 Isa. 3.15.
16 For discussions of the role of sacral kingship in Israel see A. R. Johnson, *Sacral Kingship in Ancient Israel*, University of Wales Press 1955; S. Mowinckel, *He That Cometh*, Basil Blackwell 1954; H. Ringgren, *The*

Messiah in the Old Testament, SCM Press 1956; H. Ringgren, *Israelite Religion*, SPCK 1966, pp. 220 ff.

17 I Chron. 28.5; 29.23; II Chron. 9.8.
18 Ps. 89.25; cf. Ps. 72.8 ff.
19 Ps. 48.2; Isa 6.1.
20 Ps. 29.10.
21 Pss. 5.2; 47; 68.24.
22 Ezek. 47.1 ff.; Zech 14.8.
23 Isa. 27.1.

13 Types and Antitypes

CHRISTIANITY began its life as a sect of Judaism. Jesus himself remained within the orbit of Judaism and directed his teaching specifically at his own people, being reluctant throughout his ministry to go beyond the confines of his native culture. His disciples followed his example and appear at first to have seen their work simply as a rejuvenation of Judaism. They centred their lives on Jerusalem, attended the temple there and maintained among themselves the customs and rites of Judaism. Although there was inherent in their new-found faith that which would tear them apart from Judaism, this does not at first appear to have been realized. In consequence, the symbolic language of Christianity at its birth was that of Judaism.

That which was new in the faith and understanding of the disciples of Jesus was first of all expressed within the framework of language provided by Judaism. As W. Pannenberg would express it, the new and the unique could only have meaning when appropriated within a context or tradition already possessed.[1] Judaism thus gave the Christian a frame of reference within which he could locate his new-found insight. We find, therefore, that the same symbolic complexes appear in the New Testament which had already been formulated within the Old Testament. The symbols which had become so meaningful to the Jew were taken over by the Christian as part of his heritage. Within the New Testament we find frequent references to such common Hebraic symbols as the bride, the tree, the servant and the son of man.

In particular, we find that the pattern models of historical disclosure used in the Old Testament were taken over. In this way the men of the New Testament were able to relate their experience to a language already built to cope with a revelation of God in history. In order to make room for the new events which were taking place the Christian merely had to extend the pattern models which were his birthright. One of the clearest examples of this is the way in which the model of the vine was adopted and put to new uses.

Jesus himself made use of the imagery of the vine in his parable of the wicked husbandmen.[2] His story was built up of elements already very familiar to his audience. In fact Jesus clearly relied upon this, so that his parable would need no explanation but be able to point clearly to his intended message. God is still, as in the Old Testament, the owner of a vineyard which is Israel; the Hebrew people remain the cultivators of the vineyard who are expected to ensure a good crop of righteousness and mercy as their yield to the Lord. But Jesus used this familiar theme in order to introduce a new element. He suggests in a manner typical of the Old Testament prophets that a critical moment has arrived in the relationship between the husbandmen and the owner. He reminds them that the servants of the lord of the vineyard have been frequently mishandled and even killed. Now they were confronted by the son of the owner. At this point the parable, again in a manner typical of prophetic practice, goes beyond the present moment to anticipate what is about to happen. A forecast is made both of the killing of the son and of the inevitable judgment which this will bring forth from the lord of the vineyard. The parable thus makes use of a familiar theme to draw out the significance of the contemporary situation. Like a Jonah before Nineveh, Jesus confronts the Jews of Jerusalem and gives them the opportunity of repentance now that they can see from his parable where their actions are taking them.

Yet while Jesus's parable is couched in familiar terms, it contains something which has the seed from which a quite new language will be created. He has asserted that the decisive moment has arrived in the history of Israel. From the very beginning of his ministry he had asserted that the time of Israel was nearing its end for the kingdom of God was already impinging upon it. The new era predicted by the prophets was already coming into being. The Christian community created by this teaching therefore did not merely see itself as a later moment in the history of the Hebrew people, but as the end of Hebrew history in the sense that there can be no further story when the climax has arrived. The Christian believed that in Christ the Old Testament story had been fulfilled. The church constituted a New Israel and this meant that the church was both the legitimate heir of Judaism while at the same time displacing it by a radical transformation.

Here lies the source of that tension and paradox which manifests itself throughout early Christian literature. In the time of its completion, the history of Israel had taken an entirely unexpected turn. The end, when it came, had not taken the form in which the tradition of the past had envisaged it. John the Baptist preached a messianic message, but did not find in Jesus the kind of messiah he had anticipated.[3] Thousands thronged around the man from Nazareth but only a comparatively small number of them saw in him the fulfilment of Old Testament hopes. The difference between the expectation and the fulfilment was so great that the Christian found the most expressive prophecies of Jesus in passages which had never been regarded as messianic at all. Jesus had taught that the messiah was truly a servant and one who must suffer and die. This was a startlingly new idea, which necessitated an entire rethinking of accepted religious concepts. When the new age spoken of by the prophets dawned, it was seen to fulfill the prophecies in strange ways, and this strangeness meant that the Christian faith had to assert both a fulfilment of the past and the emergence of something entirely new. Christianity had burst from the womb of its birth. New became the key-word of the new faith. A new aeon had begun in which men participated by a new birth into a new Israel which would find its fulfilment in a new Jerusalem.[4]

Most of all, a new language was required, fresh forms of expression in which to capture the massive disclosure which had taken place. Because Christianity saw itself as the actualization of all the hopes and ideas of the past, it created the distinctive language of fulfilment which is called typology.

TYPOLOGICAL INTERPRETATION

The idea of the church as born out of a new understanding of the Old Testament is typified for us in a story in the gospel of St Luke. The author tells of two disciples who walked from Jerusalem to Emmaus after the crucifixion of Jesus. On their journey they are joined by a stranger whom they subsequently perceive to have been the Christ. They then remember how he 'interpreted to them in all the scriptures the things concerning himself'.[5] The story seems to represent that point in the experience of the resurrected Christ in which the scriptures were seen in a new way. There had begun that process whereby the Christian was able to find Christ everywhere in the Old Testament. Christian typology had been born.

The root of typological interpretation lay in the strict linear understanding of history bequeathed by the Hebrew revelation. This made it possible for the disciples to understand that one event could fulfil another. One set of events could be seen to have a correspondence with another at a different time, and on a linear understanding of history this would not merely be a repetition but part of an ongoing movement. As history went forward, on the Hebrew view its meaning became clearer as the purpose of God was more fully worked out. Typology thus sees an event in the past as pointing towards and being completed or fulfilled in another event. The first of these is usually known as the type and the latter as the antitype. The type had its own reality at a certain point in history, but its full meaning was not known until the antitype appeared. The type, therefore, is sometimes described as being like a shadow, while the antitype constitutes the appearance of that which cast the shadow long ago. What had been perceived only dimly at one point in time becomes clear at another.[6]

Typological interpretation in the New Testament was made easy by the fact that the Hebrew had already created a certain understanding of history by seeing it as symbolic. The events which were now seen as types of the Christ-event, therefore, were events which had already been understood as pointing beyond themselves to a higher reality. The Christian needed only to add a further dimension to the Old Testament symbols which he did by declaring that what they had merely hinted at was now fact. Typology, therefore, in its fundamental essence declares that the age of symbols has been replaced by an age of actualities.

TYPOLOGY AND CHRISTOLOGY

The early development of thought about the man from Nazareth is reflected in a succession of titles which were applied to him. He was successively called rabbi, prophet, the messiah, son of God, etc. In each of these we can see how categories already known within Judaism were used in an attempt to portray the significance that he had for the disciples. From the very beginning, therefore, christology was largely a matter of typological interpretation. This was the form in which the disciples cast a developing sense of the meaning of Jesus. As the titles develop, we can see how they find it necessary to become more and more ambitious. The purely human categories with which they begin gradually give way to those which are superhuman and eventually to titles which suggest divinity itself.

This development is, of course, obscured in the gospels because they were written when the christology of the church had been formulated. In the light of their later understanding, it seemed obvious that Jesus had always been the true king of Israel, the divine son of God and the saviour of mankind. When the gospels of Matthew and Luke were written, it was already possible to show this in the symbolism of the birth narratives. Even before his birth, it is known what the child will become and what at a later date he will be known to be. In the manger he is recognized as the king and saviour of the world. These were convictions which had been arrived at by an ongoing process of disclosure. They were provoked by the observation of events in Jesus's life. Hence the importance attached in the gospels to the disclosure signs with which they saw his ministry punctuated. As each parable precipitated insight and one event after another took on the character of the miraculous, the revelation of Jesus's meaning became increasingly clear to them and was captured in the symbols produced by a typological understanding of the Old Testament. He was compared with various Old Testament characters, credited with fulfilling the role of a number of key offices in Israel and finally with being the antitype for all the prophecies in which the highest hopes of Judaism had been cast.

The Old Testament character who was most frequently seen as a type of Jesus was not unnaturally Moses. As Moses had been the focal point for the symbolic complex of Israel, it was inevitable that he should be the primary type in relation to which the work of Jesus as the focal point of Christian understanding should be seen. Moses had been important as the one in whom and through whom the significant events creative of Israel had been accomplished. Jesus was now seen as the one in whom and through whom the new Israel was created. This meant that the comparison was not simply made between Moses and Jesus, but between the two complexes of events which had been determined by them.

The Christ-event therefore was seen as a new exodus event. Like Moses, Jesus had been saved from a massacre of the innocent young. He, too, had come up from Egypt,[7] spent in miniature a period of time in the wilderness and finally come among his own people in the land God had given them.[8] He provides bread and water as Moses had done in the desert.[9] Like Moses, Jesus ascended the Mount, was transfigured in the presence of God and delivered the Word which had been

revealed to him.[10] Jesus also sends out his seventy elders to
announce his message to the people.[11] As Moses had held up
the brazen serpent, so Jesus saves his people by being raised
up with arms outstretched on a cross.[12] The identification
of Jesus with the promise that one like Moses should come[13]
is explicitly made in Acts 3.22 f.; 7.37; but even apart from
these references it would be clear that the manner in which
we are told about Jesus has been moulded in the symbolic
model derived from the Moses tradition.[14]

Although the exodus tradition was dominant, other comparisons were also made. Jesus was, in particular, likened to
Elijah who was to come before the end, according to the
prophecy contained in Mal. 4.5.[15] Some of the miracle stories
of Jesus have a distinct similarity to those attributed to Elijah,
and in the narrative of the ascension of Jesus there is an echo
of the fiery prophet's translation.[16] Jesus is also compared to
Jacob, and his character as the antitype is made clear in John
4.12 ff., for the water he gives does not run dry like that from
the well of the patriarch. His birth is heralded by a Magnificat
which recalls the Song of Hannah,[17] for this is the new Samuel
who continuously answers to the call of the Lord. His name is
a variant of Joshua and, like the hero of the conquest of Canaan,
Jesus is a saviour of his people, for that was the meaning of
the name.[18] He is even the antitype of the strange enigmatic
figure of Melchizedek[19] and the rock in the wilderness from
whence came the saving grace of God.[20] As befits one who
summarizes in himself everything that the symbolism the of
Old Testament had pointed to he can be the antitype both of
the recipients of divine revelation and of the forms which it
took in the experience of Israel.

The disciples saw in Jesus everything which their tradition
taught them as significant. In this man they recognized that
which had been with the Hebrew people throughout their
history. The story of Jesus was in fact seen as a recapitulation
of the whole revelation of God in the history of Israel. The New
Testament declared that in the man from Nazareth everything that had revealed the God of history was seen again

H

gathered into one person and manifested with a clarity previously unknown.

As the fulfilment of Israel, Jesus was more than Israel had ever been and this because he was the messiah and the promised son of man. The prophets had given rise to the idea that a son of David would come to bring justice to the burdened Hebrew race. In calling Jesus the messiah or Christ, the disciples claimed that this time had come. The messiah concept was one of an age of fulfilment, and so the statement that the kingdom had come was accompanied by the assertion that the prophecies had been fulfilled. The Moses and Elijah identifications gave way to an ascription of messiahship to Jesus, the highest category which Judaism provided. As the messiah, Jesus was seen as the one in whom the saving activity of Israel's God was incarnated on earth.

Typology is thus the natural result of a sense that the eschatological hopes of Israel have been realized. Within the framework of thought which sees history as moving purposefully forward, it is clear that the ultimate meaning of history is more and more manifest as the climax approaches. Just as we understand increasingly the intimations of a film or play as it nears its finale, so it was felt that the meaning previously seen but dimly in history was now made clear. Within the New Testament there was the feeling that the curtain had gone up on the final act, and consequently they now saw what the play had been all about.

The climax when it came, however, was not an unambiguous end. The appearance of the messiah meant for the Christian that history up to that point had reached its finale. On the other hand it was also the first moment in a new drama, the opening of a new aeon which pointed forward to its own eschaton. As the king and shepherd of his people, the messiah had in Jesus become the reality towards which the sacral kingship had once pointed, but when he had come to his capital to woo his bride, he had been enthroned on a cross. That event, therefore, did not complete the sequence of history for the Christian. The enthronement of Christ in the resurrection and ascension was not manifested yet on the stage of history. Only in faith was Psalm 110 known to have been fulfilled. While in Jesus the past had been completed, there remained a future in which the lordship of Christ would be established on earth.

Typology had made of Jesus the centre from which everything came into its proper perspective both in the present and in the past and in the future.

CHRIST AS THE CENTRE

The spatial symbolism of the centre found its place in Christianity as it did later in Islam. In addition to being antitypal, many events in Christ's life are associated with the cosmic mountain. The one in fact inevitably brought in the other by association. When Jesus is made in Matthew's gospel to give his new law from the mount, there is both a fulfilment of the Sinai revelation in view, and underlying this, the symbolism of the mountain as the place of God's disclosure to man. The motif appears on several occasions. The narrative opens with a story of temptation in which Christ formulates his message in confrontation with the Devil and in reliance on the word of God, appropriately located on a mountain. The moment of disclosure to the disciples of Jesus's nature and mission takes place on the mount of Transfiguration. At the summit of the mountain they see him converse with the saints of the past. His crucifixion was later held to have taken place upon a hill, and Calvary became the focal mountain for much Christian theology, because at this moment above all it came to be held that God had revealed himself to man. Finally the ascension is said to have taken place on the mount of Olives in such a way that the symbolism of the summit as the point of meeting between man and God is clearly shown. His ascension from this point implies a moment in which the two worlds of mythology are joined.

As Christianity spread abroad, it looked backwards to the point of origin. Just as the Jew turned his eyes back towards the centre which was Zion, so now the Christian turned towards that Zion which was Calvary. The eastward orientation of the altar, the cultic mountain, is hardly explicable apart from something more than a desire to remember a geographical location. Similarly, the Muslim lays his prayer mat on the ground and prostrates himself towards the revelatory centre of Mecca. It is noteworthy that in Christianity those movements which have wished to demythologize their faith have regarded the eastward orientation as dispensable.

On the other hand, Christianity sees another centre than the mythological. The symbolism of space is joined by that of time. Of far more importance than the place of Christ was the time of Christ. Jesus as the Christ was the centre of history.[21] The typological symbolism of Christianity made everything that had happened before that time point towards it and find its fulfilment in it. It also saw that event as determinative for everything which was to follow. After such a once-for-all event nothing would ever be the same again. As the major event in history, it was held to have radically altered the whole shape of that history. The Christ event was the symbolic centre, the point from which everything else received its meaning. The Christian's perspective on history was from that moment in time determined by the cross.

MYTHOLOGICAL TYPOLOGY

With the notion of Christ as the centre we have already entered the realm of mythology. When we see a tradition growing up that the Calvary cross had stood on the same spot as the tree in the garden of Eden, we realize that joined to the historical perspectives of the Old Testament there had been added the symbolism of mythology. This was possible and necessary because mythological categories were still very much alive in the Graeco-Roman world. If Christianity was to present a complete message, therefore, it had to be couched in the language of mythology as well as of history. Only in this way could the Christian relate his understanding to the world in which he lived. The beginnings of Christian painting illustrate this for us in the clearest way. The first portrayals of Christ in Christian art showed him in the likeness of the primary mythological figures of the Hellenistic world. This was done because it was believed that in Christ the ideas and hopes enshrined in the myths had been actualized. In the birth of Jesus the Egyptian Christians naturally saw the historicization of the myth in which the divine mother of Egypt, the queenly Isis, had suckled the infant Horus. The day of Mithras, the sun-god, became the day of Christmas and Eostre became Easter. In his confrontation with the intelligentsia of the day, Clement of Alexandria inevitably pointed out that, for the Christian, Christ was the true Orpheus whose music drew all men to him and who suffered a cruel death so that he might go down into hell in order to recover and save his bride, the church. Christ was therefore not merely the antitype of historical characters and notions but also of the archetypal forms which were present in the mythological complex. Moreover, this was not a feature which was introduced as the historical moment of Jesus receded into the dim past. Mythological typology appears in the New Testament itself.

Of the New Testament use of mythological typology we can only give a broad outline in order to note examples of the way in which key mythological archetypes were employed in order to bring out the cosmic significance of the historical Christ-event.

First of all it is helpful to note that the church dealt with the Christ-event in a way similar to that in which the Hebrews had dealt with the exodus event. The Hebrews had seen in the escape from Egypt the work of the God of creation and a re-enactment of the mythological portrayal of the cosmogonic process. The Christians did exactly this with the life, death and resurrection of Christ. This meant that the Christ-event was understood to be a new cosmogony, a rebirth of creation. Throughout the New Testament, therefore, we find that the world is being made anew. 'Therefore, if any one is in Christ, he is a new creation; the old has passed away, behold, the new has come.'[22]

In turn, it followed that the agent in this creative process could only be adequately described as cosmogonic deity. If that same creativity was present in Jesus the Christ which had given birth to the cosmos, it was entirely appropriate to the New Testament Christian to identify his Lord with that creativity. So Paul asserts that 'in him all things were created, in heaven and on earth'.[23]

In going thus far in the delineation of the role of Christ, the Christian had applied to Jesus what the Hebrews had previously reserved to Yahweh. It is one of the striking characteristics of New Testament language that it dares to use the symbolic language created to designate the actions of Yahweh of Jesus. If comparisons had merely been made with Old Testament saints, the Christian church might have remained within the Judaic fold. The attribution of deity to Jesus as the Christ, however, constituted a claim with which the non-Christian Jew could not compromise.

Although the New Testament handles mythological symbolism in an entirely new way, it is nevertheless possible to see how the great cosmogonic myth appears and how the architectural, organic and anthropomorphic models still serve to articulate it.

The cosmogonic myth underlies much of the language of the gospels. As Yahweh had slain Leviathan, so Christ triumphs over Satan. The *Theos victor* becomes the *Christus victor* so well described by Gustaf Aulen.[24] A recognition of the mythological value of many of the references in the gospels makes clear what would otherwise be obscure. The ministry of Jesus opens with his own baptism in which he descends into the waters of the Jordan and arises out of them as the son of God, the bearer of new life. This is immediately followed by the temptation narrative in which Jesus is confronted by the devil who is to be his adversary throughout his ministry. He heals the sick who have been bound by Satan, drives out the demons or agencies of Satan from the human bodies they have taken to themselves and raises men from the grip of the lord of death. Many of the so-called nature miracles show in familiar symbolic terms this continual victory over the old dragon of the sea. When his disciples are threatened by a storm on the sea of Galilee, Jesus speaks to the sea as though it were a personal agency. As has so often been remarked, he appears to exorcize the sea, to rebuke the demon of the storm as Yahweh had once rebuked the Red Sea. On releasing the Gadarene demoniac from the devils who had plagued him, he suffers them to return to their symbolic home in the sea into which they fall dramatically off the cliff. His triumph over the Satan of the deep, however, is most clearly indicated in his ability to walk upon the waters and to give his disciples similar power, for commissioned by him they are able to tread upon serpents. The success of the disciples on their missionary tour means for Jesus that Satan has fallen as lightning out of the heaven in which, like the king of Babylon, he had installed himself. Finally, his death becomes a conquest of Satanic power, which Matthew's gospel indicates in a typical mythological manner by recording how the prisons of the dead are broken open so that the dead rise and walk about.

The architectural model provided, as always, the setting in which the cosmogonic victory could be portrayed. The life of Jesus of Nazareth is given a cosmological dimension and significance by its use. His birth becomes a descent from heaven to earth, his death a further descent into the underworld and his resurrection and ascension a return to heaven where he is exalted above the earth and above the heavens.[25]

The organic model finds a natural place in the teaching of Jesus. In addition to using the tree imagery in the manner of the Old Testament prophets of Israel, Jesus also, according to John's gospel, applied it to himself. In John 15 Jesus is the vine of which the disciples are the branches who depend entirely on being part of him for the new life which brings forth good fruit. In this way Jesus becomes the cosmic tree which is the source of universal life. It is not surprising, there-fore, to find in the book of Acts that the cross is referred to as a tree,[26] for in this way a linguistic association is made between the tree as a source of life and the cosmogonic sacrifice which makes this possible. Also associated with the tree in mythology was the well from which the rivers of the world flowed. So Jesus by implication is the well from which he offers to give the woman of Samaria the waters of life. Again there may be allusion to this mythological motif in the reference to the fact that, at his death, blood and water flowed from his side, water being frequently that which is provided by the blood of the slain anthropos. This, however, has already introduced the anthropomorphic model.

The idea that God's power had become incarnate in Jesus as the Christ made the use of the anthropomorphic model more appropriate than any other. The architectural model appears so little because the temple representing the cosmological house has become his body. Jesus is seen as the antitype, therefore, of the primal man out of whose being all life came. As the source of life, Paul tells us that Jesus is the body of which each Christian is a member. He is also the head of that body which is the church made up of the bodies which are living temples.[27] Jesus is in fact the New Adam. Paul explicitly tells us that Adam was a type of the coming one, although in this case the antitype does not fulfil so much as reverse what had been done by the type. 'For as in Adam all die, so also in Christ shall all be made alive.'[28] In Paul's mind, therefore, the first Adam no longer constituted a symbol of life but of death and this because for him the second Adam alone symbolized true life.

To become a member of this body, a man had to be born again, as Jesus explained to Nicodemus.[29] This meant a death to the old life and a new beginning. Baptism was regularly understood to symbolize a descent into the grave and a rebirth into the new body of the new creation.[30] As Osiris had been the mythological archetype with whom the Egyptian was ritually identified in his death, so in baptism the Christian became one with Christ, for in that rite the death and resurrection of Christ was re-enacted.[31] Christ as the new Adam had been, like the first Adam, the first-born of the creative act.[32] But he is also the creator who breathes into the first men the breath of life.[33]

The newborn man lives off the body of the son of man of which he is at the same time a part. It is the flesh of Christ which is the bread of life and only by partaking of his flesh and blood can a man participate in the life of the new world.[34] In John 7.38 Jesus makes reference to an unknown scripture which speaks of rivers of living water flowing from the heart of the belly. This may be a popular paraphrase of Old Testament language in several places. In any case it reflects precisely a mythological use of the anthropomorphic model.

Yet the new body of the second Adam is not like the body of the primal man. 1 Cor 15.45 ff. insists that the new creation is of the spirit and not of the flesh. The language of mythology may have been used, but it is put to an entirely new purpose which paradoxically implied the end of all myth and symbol.

ANTITYPE AND ARCHETYPE

As the fulfilment of mythological and historical types, Jesus, strictly speaking, had brought an end to all symbolism. By virtue of being the centre, he was in himself Jacob's ladder, the manifestation of God and so the way to the Father, the gate into the other world and guardian of the sheepfold. This can be best illustrated by seeing how Jesus renders the angelic mediation of God obsolete.

At first Jesus himself had been understood merely as a messenger or angel, a partial manifestation of God and his will. Ultimately, however, it was asserted that in him dwelt the fullness of the divine pleroma,[35] and the perception of his angelic nature gave way to an acknowledgment that God himself was present. This meant that there could really be no further room for talk of angels in Christianity. The language of mythological symbolism was used to set forth its end. In Gal 3.19 Paul says that the angels had given the law to the Hebrews and it had become a kind of bondage and a

H*

barrier between God and man. Christ, however, had removed this barrier. He had triumphed over the angels and been placed higher than they.[36] The angels had been regarded as mediators in prayer, but Christ teaches his disciples that they have direct access to God as father. The folk-angels, too, are made obsolete, for in Christ all men are one, and the partial manifestation of the sacred in particularist nationalism has been obliterated by the removal of the barrier of languages at Pentecost, languages which were held to have had an angelic origin. The angels had fallen like Satan at the coming of Christ.[38]

Yet the angels continued to play a part in Christian language after the Christ-event. Christianity had to exist in a strange tension. On the one hand, the type had been fulfilled and the new age had dawned. The Christian lived in the age of the antitype. Their eschatological hopes had been realized. On the other hand, the end was not yet. There was still an un-fulfilled typology which waited for the eschaton. Only the first fruits had been gathered. Only in Christ had the end taken place. For the Christian, therefore, an eschaton still lay in the future. He lived in the present as though it were the end and in the present as looking towards the end. He lived immediately in the noumenal presence of God, but still he did not yet see him face to face. It is this tension which gave rise to the peculiar paradoxes of the New Testament and to the variety with which its message could be stated. It led to a stress now on one element, now on another. Some have built their religion on the present reality in metaphysical, mystical or existential terms. Others have asserted the move-ment within secular history towards a kingdom of God on earth, have been millenarian and looked forward in a total denial of the present. The New Testament provided the basis for both points of view. On the one hand, it asserted a realiza-tion in the present, on the other antitypal fulfilment became the basis for the forward-looking symbolism of eschatology. The incarnation mediated the quality of the end in the present in the Christian's actual existence, while his ritual served to remind him of a future yet to be fulfilled. In the eucharist he remembered the antitypal sacrifice which was at the same time an archetype of the Christian's future translation into the body of his resurrection.

While Jesus was held to have rent the veil between God and man by his passion and resurrection, a ritual was found to be a necessary ingredient of Christian practice. Although the old ritual had been fulfilled, a new ritual came to take its place. The very centre of the cultus, the temple, was regarded as having been rendered obsolete by the Christ-event. By his death he had rent in twain the veil which divided God from man and created a temple out of the living flesh of his own body and that of his disciples. Nevertheless the symbolism of Jesus as the new temple was worked out in two quite different ways.

On the one hand, the concept of the temple was existentialized. In the temple of flesh, which was the church, the offerings presented to God were spiritual sacrifices. A practical concern shown for the needs of others constituted a fragrant offering such as Christ himself had given to God in a temple created by a spiritual worship which offered up human bodies to be dwelling places of the Spirit.[39]

On the other hand, the new temple is that which is the body of the resurrected and ascended Christ, and which is not manifested in history until the eschatological day of the Lord. The appearance of the antitype in flesh and spirit appeared to leave no room for further ritual practice, but the antitype which was Christ was also an archetype of that which was yet to be. The existentialization of the temple and its ritual did not do away with the necessity for a cultic drama. This remained necessary both to give symbolic expression and sacramental enjoyment of the existential reality and also to show forth the body of Christ as the archetype of that which was to come. Thus although the sacrifice on the cross had fulfilled the Passover ritual, the eucharist came into being as a sacramental participation in the feast with the Lord which still lay in the future. The full actualization of ritual typology can only be realized when the tabernacles of the flesh are put off in exchange for the eternal habitations of eschatological fulfilment.[40]

From the way in which New Testament thought developed in its thinking about the temple, we can see that it continued that process of interiorization of history and mythology which had been begun by the prophets of Israel. Of the many other examples of this which could be considered it is appropriate to speak by way of illustration of one which was central to the development of Christian symbolism and theology. Mythologically, Yahweh had been seen as the saviour from the ontological forces of destruction. He was the God who maintained the Hebrew in a life poised over the prison of death. By historicizing this idea, the Old Testament had seen Yahweh also as the one who had redeemed them from the slavery of Egypt. Moses, therefore, could fittingly be termed the redeemer of Israel[14] as the one through whom Yahweh had acted. The prophets of Israel had added to this complex of thought a further dimension. For them, Yahweh was not only the lord of life and a saviour from national annihilation but also one who called Israel out of the pit of iniquity. The prophets had thus already ethicized the concept of redemption. In the New Testament the historicism of the Old Testament use of redemption language is abandoned, for the inherent universalism of Christ's teaching ultimately left no room for the particularist or nationalist concept of Israel. It did, however, maintain the other two elements in the Hebraic use of redemption terminology. Christ is presented as the one who ransoms the soul of man from a devil who is both the lord of death and the deceiving tempter. The early Christian church retained, therefore, the two elements in the symbolism of redemption which spoke to the interior being of man. By the resurrection the ontological anxiety of the Christian had been overcome, leaving him free to pursue the new life of love in imitation of his archetypal lord.

The extent to which the New Testament had interiorized and ethicized the symbols of mythology and history in its prophetic fervour is indicated by the fact that on many occasions, movements within the church have been able to make out a good case for the proposition that faith is entirely a matter of the inner man. Sometimes one of the elements has been stressed to the exclusion of the others. At one time Christianity seemed to become simply a means whereby a man could face death with equanimity. At other times Christian faith has been identified with a purely inward disposition of good will and love. The fullness of the New Testament faith, however, is only present when both are accepted and the language known to indicate something more than a frame of mind. The message of and about Christ asserts that the present enjoyment of faith and love is unreal apart from their actualization. Love must be incarnated in the Christian's active concern and involvement in the secular world of God's creation in the knowledge that the faith which does not fear death is but a foretaste of its transcendence in that eschatological exaltation of a man to be with the lord of all life.

While there was still history to run, the types which had pointed to the future could only be fulfilled proleptically[42] by one whose life and death was but an archetype of the end. Christ had only as it were given a trailer to the film which was to follow, a preview of the drama to be enacted. As the archetypal figure, Christ had revealed the nature of the end and given the Christian confidence in facing what would otherwise have been an unknown future. Yet despite the incarnation of the eschatological truth in flesh and blood, that future could only be described in the symbolism of a Christianized mythology.

This found its classic expression in the book of Revelation, without which the New Testament would have lacked a fully integrated picture-symbolism of the end to which it looked. In the Apocalypse the eschatological intimations scattered throughout the New Testament are brought together to form an architectonic description of the end in terms of the cosmogonic myth. Here the Christus Victor theme achieves its fullest mythological expression. The cosmogonic struggle reaches its climax as Michael and his angels contend with the dragon and cast it down from the heaven to which the beast has exalted itself. On earth it pursues the child-bearer and seeks to drown her in the flood of waters from its mouth but the earth swallows up the threatening flood. The beast, which has power and authority over the dragon, emerges from the sea and wages war on the saints of God until a final battle takes place at Armageddon. Then the dragon is overcome and bound for a thousand years in the prison of the abyss, after which it is released only to be flung into the lake of fire and brimstone. As a result of the eschatological battle the sea is no more and the garden of Eden is re-established as the New Jerusalem in the midst of which is located the tree, the throne of God and the lamb from which come the waters of life.[43] The complex symbolism of the book of Revelation has given commentators much difficulty, but the basic story outlined above is easily recognized as a version of the cosmogonic myth the multivalence of whose symbols is responsible for the variety of interpretation.

As the Christian church moved out into the Gentile world, however, such historicization of mythology in an eschatological vision became increasingly difficult to maintain. In the Graeco-Roman world the background to most thought was provided by a mythology revived in the mystery religions and a philosophy which was equally lacking in a sense of history. Although the Christian missionaries were remarkably successful in bequeathing a Jewish history book to their Gentile converts, it nevertheless remained a book which represented an alien culture. The eschatology born of a linear understanding of history was largely lost, and in its place a Christianized mythology was ontologized with the aid of tools provided by the philosophers of Greece.

NOTES

1 W. Pannenberg, in: James M. Robinson and John B. Cobb Jr, *Theology as History*, Harper and Row 1967.

2 Mark 12.1–9.
3 Matt. 11.2 f.
4 Mark 1.27; 2.21 f.; 14.24; 16.17; Acts 17.19 ff.; II Cor. 5.17; II Peter 3.13.
5 Luke 24.27.
6 See G. W. H. Lampe and K. J. Woollcombe, *Essays on Typology*, SCM Press 1957; J. D. Smart, *The Interpretation of Scripture*, SCM Press 1961, pp. 93–133.
7 Matt. 2.14 f.
8 Matt. 4.2.
9 Ex. 16; Mark 8; John 6; cf. I Cor. 10. 1 ff.
10 Mark 9.2 ff.; cf. Ex. 24.15–18; 34.29 ff.
11 Luke 10; cf. Num. 11.16–30.
12 John 3.14; cf. Num. 21.8 f.
13 Deut. 18.15 f.
14 I Cor. 5.7 f.; 10.1 ff.; Heb. 3.7 ff.; Jude 5.
15 Mark 8.28.
16 E.g. Luke 7.11–17, cf. I Kings 17.17–24 and II Kings 4.32–37; Acts 1.9 ff., cf. II Kings 2.11.
17 Luke 1.46–55; cf. I Sam. 2.1–10.
18 Matt. 1.21; cf. Heb. 4.8.
19 Heb. 5.6, 10; 6.20; 7.1 ff.; cf. Gen. 14.18; Ps. 110.4.
20 I Cor. 10.4; cf. Num. 26.8 ff.
21 See O. Cullmann, *Christ and Time*, SCM Press 1951.
22 II Cor. 5.17.
23 Col. 1.16.
24 G. Aulen, *Christus Victor*, SPCK 1931.
25 E.g. Eph. 4.10.
26 Acts 5.30; 10.39; 13.29.
27 Rom. 12.5; I Cor. 3.16; Eph. 1.23; 2.21; Col. 2.19.
28 I Cor. 15.22; cf. v. 45 and Rom. 5.14.
29 John 3.3 ff.
30 Rom. 6.3–9; Col. 2.20.
31 S. G. F. Brandon, *Man and His Destiny in the Great Religions*, pp. 37 f.
32 Col. 1.8.
33 John 20.22; cf. Acts 2.2 ff.
34 John 6.48 ff.
35 Col. 1.19.
36 Rom. 8.38; Heb. 2.2; I Peter 3.22.
37 Eph. 1.21 f.
38 II Peter 2.4; Jude 6.
39 Rom. 12.1; Eph. 5.2; Phil. 4.18; I Peter 2.5.
40 Luke 16.9; II Cor. 5.1–5.
41 Acts 7.35.
42 Luke 22.16–18.
43 Rev. 12.7 ff.; 12.13 ff.; 16.13 ff.; 20.1 ff.; 21.1; 22.1 ff.

PART FOUR

The Erosion of Symbolism in Western Thought

14 The Ontological Models of Philosophy

CONFRONTATION AND REFLECTION

IN ADDITION to the symbolic language of religious experience, there have grown up other kinds of language which derive from it but which have taken on a distinctive character of their own. These other languages are born of reflection rather than of confrontation. It is appropriate, therefore, to classify them broadly as philosophic, although as western thought developed there emerged out of philosophy various disciplines which were to become largely autonomous sciences. The symbols and myths of religious language had come out of man's direct confrontation with the world as subjective being, his immediate response to it and his involvement in it. Religious language had been essentially an I–Thou language. As a philosopher, however, man reflected on his experience, attempted to analyse it and place it within a logical frame of reference. What had previously presented itself to him as personal encounter then became the object of his thinking. The change was thus fundamentally from subjective appropriation of the world to an objective rationalization. Instead of a man conceiving himself as a subject in a world of subjects, in reflection upon the world he came to deny the subjectivity of everything except at first himself, because he had adopted the stance of an observer. What had previously, therefore, been immediately apprehended in symbolic forms was now subjected to a rational analysis which was fundamentally an objectifying procedure.

Such a change did not, of course, happen suddenly but over a considerable period of time. We can, however, discern the beginnings of the process in the emergence of Greek philosophy. In the classic literature of Greece we can see the change taking place. In the tradition which lay behind the Iliad of Homer and the poems of Hesiod we can catch a glimpse of the mythological age. In the writings of the philosophers themselves we can still see the influence of mythological patterns of thought. This is exemplified by the use of myths by Plato and the way in which the Pythagorean school combined a breakthrough in mathematics with a way of thinking which was clearly mythological. Nevertheless, a real change was taking place. While it would be incorrect to imply that mythological man did not reflect upon his experience, the Hellenistic philosophers present us with reflective writing which bids fair to overwhelm its basis in actual experience even in the mystical philosophy of neoplatonism.

The effect of rational reflection upon experience is of particular importance to us. The influence of the change on the development of Christianity can be studied by a comparison between the New Testament and late patristic writing. The New Testament was fundamentally symbolic and mythological, but this gave way in the patristic period to a language of propositional theology which has it first culmination in the Athanasian creed. In the appendix to this it is asserted that salvation depends, not upon encounter with the living God, but upon the acceptance of the propositional statements of belief which it contains. This development was largely the result of the creation of an apologetic with which the church could meet the Graeco-Roman world. To this end the experiences and the resultant symbols of the Christ-event were integrated into a system of thought with the aid of models derived from Greek philosophy. The Christian entered the arena of philosophical argument and perforce had to use its conceptual tools. The impassioned insight of immediate impact was replaced by a reasoned analysis. Faith was turned into propositional belief embodied in credal formula.

The change which had taken place in the use of language is illuminated for us by the distinction drawn by J. A. Hutchinson between 'first-order' or faith statements and 'second-order' or theological statements.[1] The first type of language is that of symbol and myth, of immediate encounter, while the second is the result of bringing these statements into a system of concepts. The same distinction is noted by Gerardus van der Leeuw,[2] who distinguishes between religion as the primordial experience of power and theology which emerges from the constant reflection of rational man. Under the impact of Greek philosophy, therefore, we have to recognize a fundamental change in the character of religious language.

On the other hand, it is important to note that this change did not constitute a complete break with the past. Symbols which had once been vital did not simply disappear. They remained in the depths of the psyche. Consequently they constantly took new forms at the conscious level. The symbolic models of the age of myth turn up again in the philosophical systems of the western world transformed into ontological models. The myth of the cosmic giant and its corresponding anthropomorphic model appear in a new guise as the mind and body model of Hellenistic and Christian thought. The living stage scenery of mythology and its architectural model reappear in a systematic scale of being. Mythological symbolism was thus responsible for two basic motifs which for a long time dominated western philosophy. They are used, however, for a new purpose. Whereas symbolic models were primarily intended to relate man meaningfully to the universe, ontological philosophy attempted to describe the nature of the universe in itself. In place of the question, 'How do I fit into the scheme of things?' ontology asked of everything, 'What is it?'

THE ONTOLOGIZATION OF THE ANTHROPOMORPHIC MODEL

The emergence of ontological forms of thought proceeded gradually. There arose numerous schools of thought, movements and counter-movements which obscure the basic tendencies. But if we restrict ourselves to a consideration of particular features it is possible to see a development which illuminates something of the character of the whole. First of all we can note how the anthropomorphic model was ontologized. This appears to have taken place in three stages.[3]

(i) The first phase in the philosophical use of the model was still firmly rooted in mythological thought. It is found in the Greek writers previous to Socrates. There it was taken for granted that the universe was a living body, self-moving and instinct with mind. As man had body, life and mind so the universe was held to possess matter, motion and order. As in mythology, man was still the microcosm of the macrocosm. On the other hand, the analogy of man for the cosmos has ceased to be purely mythological in that it has been subjected to careful analysis. Man is no longer seen as one but as a mixture of three elements. The cosmos is now being studied as an object with analogies which are becoming increasingly self-conscious. Thales, for example (c. 630–545 BC), was attempting to describe the universe when he spoke of it as an animal. When he went further and spoke of the cosmic organism having lesser organisms within it, each with souls of their own, he was consciously subjecting man himself to objective rationalization. He saw man both as an independent soul and as part of the whole. The mythological basis of his thought remains clear. He spoke of the earth as floating on water as in the myth and held that water to be alive. The transition towards philosophical conceptualization is, however, evident in that his purpose seems to have been primarily the construction of a cosmological hypothesis.[4]

The symbolic and philosophical uses of the model at this stage are very close indeed. They differ only in their object. When the model is allowed the freedom of symbolic ambivalence it is unlikely that ontological statement is a primary motif. But when it is used in argument, it is probably the basis of ontological conceptualization. This can perhaps be made clear by a comparison of two New Testament passages. The epistle to the Ephesians contains a passage which refers to the 'one God and Father of us all, who is above all and through all and in all'.[5] Taken in isolation, parts of this statement appear to be philosophical. They suggest the transcendence and immanence of deity. On closer examination, however, it becomes clear that it is intended primarily as a symbolic statement. It is a declaration of faith and appeals to existential experience. The body to which reference is made is the body created by the Christ-event, one which emerges out of history. The passage asserts that the God of creation is not exterior to creation but immanent within it and lord of its history. This expression of faith is possible only in the context of the fact that the author is 'a prisoner for the Lord' and the purpose of the statement is to encourage his readers 'to lead a life worthy of the calling' which they have received in Christ.[6] In so far as the passage makes use of the model derived from the analogy of man, it does so for existential and not philosophical purposes.

In Acts 17 we have a very different use of the model. In Athens, Paul came into contact with the intelligentsia of the region in which he was carrying out his missionary work. Here he has to speak with Epicurean and Stoic philosophers. Faced with this situation Paul has to abandon the employment of symbolic, faith statements for argumentative propositions. He takes an inscription which he has noticed, 'To an unknown God', as the text of a sermon. The sermon is not truly kerygmatic, however, but argumentative apologetic. He attempts to align himself with his philosophic audience by denouncing the popular rituals and shrines. He tries to show that he is one with them in this. Moreover, he appeals to one of their own poets, Aratus, who had written that 'in him we live and move and have our being', and accepts the imagery which spoke of men as 'offspring' of God.[7] Thus Paul makes use of the anthropomorphic model in an attempt to find a common ground with men who had accepted the model for their own thinking. The validity of the model is no longer based upon personal encounter with God in the midst of life but upon an appeal to rationality. The model is not being used for the expression of personal experience, but as a suitable analogy for characterizing the nature of reality. It is an ontological usage.

Paul appears to have regretted this sortie into philosophical dialogue. He returned to the preaching of the kerygma and refused to know anything but Christ and him crucified. The necessity to find common ground with the academic world of the day, however, and the attractiveness of the model for discursive purposes led others to follow Paul's lead at Athens. When typological fulfilment could not be a basis for dialogue, it was perhaps inevitable that ontological categories should take its place. As Christianity moved further into the intellectual world of the day and as that world invaded the church itself, the philosophical defence of Christianity became more and more urgent. The model, therefore, tends to appear as a useful apologetic from time to time. We find it in Athanasius[8] and in Tatian.[9] It finds a classic expression in Origen of Alexandria who wrote, 'I am of the opinion that the whole world ought to be regarded as some huge and immense animal, which is held together by the power and reason of God, as by one soul'.[10]

This form of the model tended to be abandoned as time went on, but reappeared especially when there was a revival of Hellenistic modes of thought. In Nicholas of Cusa, for example, the renaissance delight in ancient Greece found expression in a return to the idea of nature as being ensouled with deity. 'Nature', he wrote, 'is an organism whose soul is God and whose organs are the infinite multitude of persons who live and move and exist in him.'[11] It is significant that Nicholas of Cusa makes use of the one point in Paul's thinking in which he spoke the language of the Greek philosophers.

(ii) The second stage in the development of the model is denoted, according to R. G. Collingwood, by a division of the parts. In place of the intelligent, ensouled body which was envisaged in the first use of the model, the mind, soul and body came to be understood as distinct entities. What had been seen at first as merely different aspects of one whole were now seen as distinct components. Anaxagoras anticipated the new view by asserting that Nous or mind was not mixed with matter but an independent source of motion. The philosophers from Socrates onwards tended to assert the absolute transcendence of mind over the body. The idealistic philosophy of the Platonic tradition which paved the way for the philosophical realism of the Middle Ages taught the independent existence of the mind apart from matter. It created therefore a radical dualism between the world of the mind or spirit and the world of matter. Moreover, the Platonic tradition tended to oppose the two elements to one another. Mind and body were placed at opposite ends of a short but decisive scale of being, life occupying an ambiguous place between the two.

Again the New Testament reflects the transition which was taking place. There are numerous passages which stress the unity of man as ensouled body. There are others, however, which suggest a dichotomy between the flesh and the spirit.

The effects of this divisive conceptualization were of considerable importance and can hardly be overstressed. The dualism inherent in the new use of the model meant that it was difficult to see an ontological equivalent to the rainbow staircase of mythology. The divine and the human worlds were seen as two distinct and essentially different entities. This meant that Christian theology would have to state an ontological impossibility. What was incompatible had to be joined in some way, and fundamental philosophical presuppositions now made this a hopeless task. The results can be seen best by taking three major examples.

Because the philosophy inherited from Greece attempted to give an analysis of the whole of being, theologians had perforce either to see God as an ontological category or to claim that he was outside the ontological structure. Both alternatives appear to have been followed at one time or another. The second alternative, which claimed that God was beyond the categories of being and non-being, was really a return to mythological insistence on the impossibility of the conceptualization of deity. The object of philosophy, however, was to provide a system of thought which would be totally embracing and therefore this argument necessarily suggested that the rational thinking of philosophy was being abandoned. So in the interests of philosophical completeness it was more common to attempt to see God as an ontological entity. Not unnaturally, deity was then identified with the mind in the model. God was not to be a mind immanent in the world but in the new divisive concept of the model he was to be a mind totally transcending the world. Typical was Aristotle's idea of God as thought thinking about itself. This tradition was inherited by Christian theology and became a fundamental postulate in the scholastic period. Theologians, of course, supplemented such ideas with others but the analogy of mind as a separate entity was dominant.

Once God had either been placed outside the ontological structure or identified with the separate reality of mind, it became impossible to see any way in which God and the world could be related to one another. In no sense could it now be allowed that the creation constituted the body of God. Theology was safeguarded from what became the horror of pantheism, but failed to find any basis on which a real relationship between God and the world could be stated. Cosmologically the model created a dichotomy between earth and heaven, natural and supernatural. It created the illusion of two worlds and led to insoluble problems as to how they could be related to one another. Any act of God within the world could only be conceived as a vertical intrusion from another and quite different realm of being, and for this the model could not now make provision. God's activity in the world required a metaphysical miracle. The question of God's relationship with the world was therefore to be a central question right down to our own day, because a radical transcendence of God derived existentially from the Old Testament had been translated into ontological immutability.

In the patristic period the battle was fought primarily in terms of christology. Once deity was radically opposed to flesh, the idea that God should become man became inconceivable. The translation of the birth of Jesus from the Father of heaven into a doctrine of incarnation involved the assertion of the logically impossible. The battle was fought out at the Council of Nicaea in which Athanasius, who was prepared to use the first phase form of the model, maintained that the transcendent divine could have a vehicle in the human. Those who denied or wished to modify the doctrine of incarnation based their thinking on the philosophical transcendence of Plato's idealism. The Council of Nicaea could only outlaw what it regarded as a heresy of exaggerated transcendentalism by using an ontological statement itself. The fathers at the Council, therefore, included the first metaphysical proposition in a creed and asserted that Christ was 'of one substance with the Father'. They did this unwillingly. They desired to restrict themselves to biblical phraseology, but had to accept the inevitable although they knew that ontological language could not capture the truth of symbolic statement. The christological problem was never solved. After further prolonged argument, the Council of Chalcedon asserted the presence of deity and humanity in Christ in their completeness but made no real attempt to show how two irreconcilables could have been brought together.

Finally, on the practical and devotional levels, philosophical ontology created a similarly impossible situation. As the earthly and the spiritual life were seen as radically different, man was placed in the strange position of denying his humanity in order to gain his spirituality. It led to the growth of asceticism and world-denial and to the acceptance of man's inability to know God in the flesh. The angels ceased to appear and man no longer walked with God in the garden. The disclosure of God in the world was replaced by transcendental mysticism. Alternatively, it meant that the spiritual had to be denied in order to be human. The church tried to maintain its sacramental doctrine of the embodiment of the divine in the things of the world, but against the background of doctrine framed in ontological rather than in kerygmatic, symbolic and mythological terms, it was virtually impossible to succeed.

Ontologism slammed the door on personal relationship with God. Once God had been defined as pure thought or pure actuality, the possibility of personal relationship with God tended to be excluded. Aristotle's God cannot even know the persons within the world because he has no body through which to be aware of them. God himself was, moreover, qualified to such an extent that he came to seem unreal. The negative characteristics in the anthropomorphic model were ultimately stressed to such an extent that its usability was destroyed. God had become so totally other that men were rendered spiritually speechless.

While the anthropomorphic model had been used symbolically, it could function for the purposes of religious existence. As a philosophical idea, however, it quickly became irrelevant to religion. Charles Hartshorne therefore noted that although the mind–body analogy has been seen to be intellectually useful, it has not been prominent in the language of religion.[12] Moreover, the transcendence of the divine mind made it possible in the end to dispense with the concept altogether; this is what appears to have happened when we move to the third stage.

(iii) The dichotomy established by philosophic idealism was eventually abandoned and an attempt made to return to a unified concept of nature. The world was then again seen as an animate organism and deity as mind within it. In Girolamo Cardano (1501–76) there is a hint of what is to follow. God is not allowed to be a free and independent agent, but one who acts under necessity. Deity is reduced to an operative force obeying a law in the being of things. As such an immanent law, however, God was merely a component within nature. The result was a simple hylozoism in which matter was seen as instinct with life and complete in itself. The full story of the organic model from which the concept of deity had been removed was not told until the emergence of evolutionary theory in the nineteenth century, to which we must turn in the next chapter.

THE SCALE OF BEING

Accompanying the mind–body model throughout the period dominated by Greek philosophy we find another model which was so closely related to it that it is sometimes difficult to disentangle them. This was the scale-of-being model which to some extent developed out of the consequences of the mind–body model. The latter had distinguished between mind and matter, placing them in opposition to one another. Another way of stating the relationship between mind and matter was to place them at either end of a scale or ladder of being. Today a materialistic mentality is inclined to see mind as a product of matter, but in the long period to which we refer the reverse was generally accepted as true. Matter or creation was radically subordinated to mind, which was regarded as the originating principle of creation.

The way in which the philosophers understood the relationship between mind and matter is shown to us in their use of two analogies, one likening creation to the work of an architect and the other seeing creation as an emanation from the divine mind in a manner similar to the diffusion of light. The use of these two analogies laid the foundation on which the scale-of-being model was raised.

Because the universe was being understood now as a rational system, it is not surprising that it should have been conceived as created in a way similar to that in which an architect might proceed. First he would construct a picturing model in his mind. He would then commit his ideas to paper as drawings and plans. He might well go further and construct a scale model of the building to be erected. Finally he would bring the building into existence. To a number of philosophers this seemed to offer an excellent analogy for a new conception of creation based on the supremacy and primacy of mind.

We find it employed in late Judaism under the influence of Hellenism and also in the patristic theology of Christianity.

In this use of the analogy, creation was understood first to have been conceived within the mind of the creator. The reason of the creator was commonly referred to as the *logos*, an ambiguous word which could play a significant role in the application of the analogy. The picturing model in the mind of the creator was called the *logos endiathetos*, and was both the reason of God and the plan which had formed within his mind. When the plan was put into operation, it was as though the idea had gone forth out of the mind of the creator. This was known, therefore, as the *logos prophorikos*. The *logos* had now become the active, creative principle of the Godhead. In one sense this corresponded to the scale model or plans drawn up by the architect, but this scale model was credited with creative power in itself. When the cosmos set forth in the scale model had come into being, the work of the *logos* had not been completed. The *logos* was then understood to be immanent in creation as the sustaining power of rationality and order. As a rational creature, man was believed to share in the *logos* in a special way. This was expressed by saying that he possessed within him the *logos spermatikos* or the seed of the divine mind.[13]

Such an impressive analogy naturally found a large place in the development of thought. It played an important role in early Christian thinking because it provided a way in which the cosmic role of Christ could be understood. It enabled the theologian to give philosophical expression to the religious apprehension of Jesus as the son of God. In consequence we find Christ spoken of as having been with God the Father from all eternity, and as having been begotten or gone forth as creative word both in the creation of the old cosmos and the new. It also provided an apt way of expressing the immanence of Christ in the believer. In this analogy Christ was as close to a man as his own thought. The imagery of the *logos* was later abandoned, however, as it became apparent that a philosophical use of the analogy entailed such a radical subordinationism that the full deity of the son of God was endangered.

The second dominant analogy was that of the diffusion of light from the sun. At its source in the sun, light appears to be one with the sun. It also emanates from the sun and travels away from its source. The further the rays of light are from the sun, the weaker they become, and there is finally a limit to this diffusion and an area which is dark, untouched by the sun's rays. This was seen as an ideal complementary model to that of the architect, for light is at first within the source and also a power flowing out of it. It had, however, some advantages lacking in the architect analogy. As an ontological model the sun represented the plenitude of being, while the darkness beyond the rays of the sun symbolized the absence of being. The differences which appear in the cosmos could be explained as the result of a varying degree of participation in being, just as some things were more fully illuminated than others in the analogy. Moreover, for the purpose of the analogy, at least, the rays of the sun were thought of as simply descending, so that it was possible to see in this the scale of being. At the top of the ladder of being was the sun as the source of being; at the bottom of the ladder was the depth of darkness which was non-being.

The use of light as an analogy for deity had frequently figured in the religious symbolism of the world. It had played an important part in the New Testament writings, especially in the Johannine books, where Christ was called the light of the world which the world could not put out and the Christian was described as one who walked in the light of his Lord. There is, however, a change when we find it used in the Nicene creed. Here Christ is confessed to be 'God of God, Light of Light, Very God of Very God' along with the assertion that he was 'of one substance with the Father'. In such a context the imagery of the divine light now approximated at least to the use of light as an analogy for a doctrine of metaphysical emanationism. An imagery which had been symbolically powerful was now considered to be philosophically and theologically apt. This is but one example of the way in which ancient symbol complexes were given a new life as metaphysical models.

In a number of ways, the scale-of-being model took over from the architectural model of mythology. The 'spaces' of mythology became the 'levels' of ontology. We see the parentage of the various points on the scale in the worlds of the architectural model. The threefold division of being into mind, life and matter reflects the three-storeyed universe of mythology. The heavenly sky became the realm of ideas or mind but this was itself often divided up. John Pico della Mirandola, for example, spoke of there being three worlds. The highest level of being was the super-celestial world inhabited by angels. The middle level was occupied by the celestial world of the planets. The lowest was the infra-lunar world of brutes and men.[14] At a number of points we can see how the architectural model of mythology was transformed into metaphysical philosophy.

In the architectural model the supreme deity was sometimes seen as the inhabitant of the highest place and also as transcending all space. In the ontological version we find that God was also conceived in two ways. In some systems God was held to be the plenitude of being and therefore within the scale of being, although at its summit or source. On the other hand, it was argued that God was beyond the categories of being and non-being. In other words, it was held that God could not be conceived as a metaphysical entity at all. Mirandola, like many philosophical theologians, was forced to assert that God was beyond being while at the same time the source of all being and possessed of the perfections of all beings. Here we see the difficulties which ontological thought contrived. In mythological symbolism it was possible to make paradoxical statements, but in the discursive logic of ontology it was necessary to be specific. In consequence it became necessary to fit God into the system or to assert that he had no place in contemporary thinking. Thus the scale-of-being model was no more successful in philosophy than the mind-body model had been. Neither achieved a satisfactory integration of the sacred into a system of thought.

At the other end of the scale was the absence of light. This immediately suggests the symbolism of the primeval dragon living in the dark waters. There is not merely a co-incident symbolism but a real connection between the two ideas. As mind or light at its source represented the fullness of being, so the other end of the ladder reached down into the depths of non-being. Tommaso Campanella, along with many others, held that as one descends through the scale there is a diminishing element of being and an increase in the measure of non-being until one finally reaches a total absence of being. Mythology had seen the earth as maintained over the threat of destruction represented by the engulfing flood. In the ontological version the creation is maintained against the threat of non-being.

The ontological scale of being implied an evaluation. Being and value were equated, and so the top of the scale enjoyed maximum value while the bottom of the scale represented a total absence of value. In consequence it was possible to attempt a solution to the problem of evil by suggesting that it was not created by God but merely represented an absence of God's creative activity. Being was, however, always reaching down and attempting to overcome the absence of being. Thus a metaphysical dualism of being and non-being replaced the mythological dualism of the victor and the dragon.

Midway between the highest and lowest realms was man. The radical dichotomy propounded by the mind-body model was to some extent overcome in the scale-of-being model. As a possessor of both mind and body and as one who enjoyed being always under the threat of dissolution, man was able to serve as an ontological equivalent of the rainbow or bridge between the opposing realms. Man as a microcosm had within himself both the elements, which were divided cosmically. The scale of being posited a gradation suggested by its use of emanation analogies, and so it did not entail the total dualism and opposition of the mind–body model. As man was held to

I

occupy a place in the middle of the ladder of being, therefore he could link both realms; he both gazed upwards to the heaven of being and cast anxious glances down at the hell of non-being.

The role of man as the centre and bond of the universe was expressed in a variety of ways and by a number of philosophers. At the very centre of the Christian faith was the idea that Jesus had constituted the bond between God and man, the way to the Father, and united within himself the divided realms of the cosmos. What was true of Christ according to accepted doctrine a number of philosophers held to be true of man as such. Thus Heinrich Cornelius von Nettesheim (1486–1535) held that man was the ontological link between the three worlds, terrestial, heavenly and spiritual, and hence the means whereby the universe was harmonized. Paracelsus (1493–1541) said that man had three bodies – physical, astral and immortal – corresponding respectively to the terrestial, astral and sidereal worlds. So it was held that man, by virtue of his participation in all levels of being, formed the link between them.

The idea of various levels of being proved a fruitful way of dealing with those realities which the myths had designated as lesser gods. Under the impact of strict monotheism, the gods of myth had been renamed angels. As angels, the function of the mythological gods was stated with clarity; they were mediations of the word of God to man. In the ontological version the strength of a revelation indicated a certain level of being. God himself was the fullness of being. A revelation of God's word, an angelic mediation, must always be partial, but nevertheless a participation in the plenitude of being which was God. The angels, therefore, as a result of ontological thinking, were organized into ranks of being according to their closeness to or participation in the source of all being. The period thus gave rise to a number of angelologies. The most famous of these was one produced as early as the sixth century by Pseudo-Dionysius. He arranged the order of being in accordance with the classes of society in the court of

Byzantium, dividing the angelic powers into three hierarchies of nine choirs:

Seraphim	Cherubim	Thrones
Dominations	Virtues	Powers
Principalities	Archangels	Angels

The work of Pseudo-Dionysius became determinative for Byzantine art and ultimately authoritative in the west both iconographically and theologically.

Thus 'the idea of a hierarchy of levels of reality from matter, through organisms, animals and man, up to pure spirits' which was 'a leading feature both of Aristotelianism and of the Platonic tradition',[15] transformed the architectural model of mythology into a structure which J. Huizinga aptly called 'a cathedral of ideas.'[16] A system of thought had been created which satisfied intellectuals as an adequate basis for philosophy for many hundreds of years. There were, however, considerable losses.

It was a step backwards in the sense that it produced a conception of the cosmos as a static reality. Thought was dominated by the vertical conception of the scale of being. In this respect ontology was at one with mythology, for both failed to take the horizontal dimension seriously, neglecting the ongoing movement of history which had been the major strength of the biblical perspective and its language. In place of the eschatological orientation of the New Testament, metaphysical speculation had given man a view of the universe as an eternally static reality.

A static view of the cosmos inevitably suggested that society should be an unchangeable structure. As with myth, so with ontology, man's conceptualizations were embodied in his social system. In the medieval period, therefore, there grew up a fully integrated structure which was believed to be divinely sanctioned because an exact copy of the levels of being which philosophy had formulated. The assertion of a correspondence between society and cosmic reality meant that no progress towards a kingdom of God was either possible or conceivable.

The kingdom was already present. Salvation became a matter purely of the soul, which must fly away from the body up into the heaven of God.

The ambivalence of symbolic language had been discarded by many for the clarity of systematic philosophy, but the fruit of this was a destructive tension. Taken as propositional statements of a metaphysical kind, the assertions of religious experience lost much of their content and what was left no longer carried self-authenticating authority but could only be validated at the bar of that reason which had been exalted to the highest metaphysical category and to an exclusive tool in the pursuit of knowledge.

Finally, the ontologization of mythological models led to a division between theologian and believer. The abstractions of philosophy were beyond the majority of people and so there grew up a distinction between simple faith and the expertise of the theologian. The first was symbolic and the latter onto-ogical. The two became impatient with one another. The man who had found the sacred in his own experience thought the abstractions of theology both irrelevant and impertinent. The discussion of deity as though God could be an object of man's rational manipulations seemed to him to be no less than blasphemous. On the other hand, the philosopher of religion became impatient with what appeared to be the naïveties of the believer because his symbolism was not reducible to systematic thought. The tension, of course, often existed in one and the same person, producing a kind of spiritual schizo-phrenia. The God of encounter and the absolute of philosophy are not the same. Invariably one is destroyed by the other. Either faith rejects philosophy as unnecessary, if not pernicious, or philosophy discards the symbols of faith as mere primitivism.

NOTES

1 J. A. Hutchinson, *Language and Faith: Studies in Sign, Symbol and Meaning* Westminster Press 1963.

2 J. D. Bettis, introducing *Religion in Essence and Manifestation* in J. D. Bettis (ed.), *Phenomenology of Religion*, SCM Press 1969, pp. 53f.

3 See R. G. Collingwood, *The Idea of Nature*, Clarendon Press 1945; D. S. Wallace-Hadrill, *The Greek Patristic View of Nature*, Manchester University Press 1968.

4 R. S. Brumbaugh, *The Philosophers of Greece*, p. 16.

5 Eph. 4.6.

6 Eph. 4.1.

7 Acts 17.28.

8 *De Incarn.* xli.

9 *Orat. ad Graec.* xii.

10 *De princ.* ii 1.3.

11 Quoted in A. M. Fairbairn, *The Philosophy of the Christian Religion*, Hodder and Stoughton 1902, p. 102.

12 C. Hartshorne, 'The God of Religion and the God of Philosophy', in *Talk of God*, Royal Institute of Philosophy Lectures Vol. 2, Macmillan 1969, p. 155.

13 Cf. H. Frankfort's remarks on the idea of Ptah's thought in Memphite theology, *Ancient Egyptian Religion*, pp. 20 ff.

14 F. Copleston, S.J., *A History of Philosophy*, Doubleday 1963, Vol. III. 2, pp. 17 ff.

15 *Op. cit.*, p. 48.

16 J. Huizinga, *The Waning of the Middle Ages*, Penguin Books 1955, p. 204.

15 *The Desacralization of the World*

To THE MAN of the twentieth century, the age of myth is regarded as one in which men personified a dead universe so that they might talk with the creations of their imagination. The fact that modern man is inclined to see mythological culture in this way tells us very little about primitive man, but a great deal about the way in which man today has been taught to see the world. For him there is no subjectivity in the cosmos such as mythological man saw. He is the heir to a process which has largely been successful in desacralizing the world by first impersonalizing it. This has cut him off not only from the world of myth but also from much of the language of the great religions.

The roots of this attitude lie in the transformation which overtook western society in the period of the Reformation and the Renaissance. At that time novel approaches to the world came into being. They did not at first seem to be destructive of religion. The period was one of intense religious fervour, of rediscovery and of evocative symbolizations. Nevertheless, there were embedded in these events directions of thought which would call in question and ultimately destroy the symbolic apprehension of the world.

The Reformation was to a great extent a process of de-symbolization and found its natural expression in iconoclasm. It was a time of the breaking of symbols. The sacraments of the church were reduced in Protestantism from seven to two. The development of sacramental thought had moved in the direction of universalization. The multitude of sacramental acts suggested that the whole of life mediated the transcendent meaning of the cosmos. The reduction of the sacraments on the other hand implied a withdrawal. The broad vision in which acts of God were seen all around in a multiplicity of miracles was curtailed. The vast array of mediators provided for man in the Middle Ages between God and man were removed. The invocation of the saints, the veneration of the Virgin Mary and prayers for the dead were condemned. The superfluity of altars was replaced by a single rude table. Even the few channels of grace which were allowed to remain were often bereft of symbolic formulation. The churches which had been microcosmic temples of salvation history became bare-walled rooms. The altar which had been adorned to bring out its significance as a cosmic calvary was deprived of its symbolic dress and often became merely a place to remember a link there had once been on earth between man and God. It is hardly surprising that Max Weber should have referred to the reformation as a period of disenchantment.

The Reformation undoubtedly made a justified revolt against symbols which had become signs and against sacraments which had become magic. Protestants eradicated the lumber of literalized symbolism in order to make room for a living faith of the most personal kind. Catholicism set about recovering the symbolic dimension of the sign system which it insisted on retaining. The Counter-Reformation was singularly successful in finding men and women who were able to perceive the divine wind breathing symbolic life into the things of sense. Protestantism had chosen the hard road of almost total rediscovery. It had begun again and needed time. History, however, was speeding up and the basis of a non-religious appropriation of the world being rapidly laid. Before a new sacralization could take place, modern man under Protestantism was left with a natural world devoid of any clear means of being the revelation of the sacred.

The theologians of Protestantism, moreover, provided formulations which gave intellectual authority to the declaration that God had been separated from the world. Calvinists asserted the total transcendence of God and the total depravity of man so that the infinite could never be contained within the finite. Lutheranism, although it maintained the capacity of things of earth to be a vehicle of the divine, nevertheless handed over the world of men to the secular arm.

The loss of symbolic sensitivity is reflected graphically in the history of European art. In the days of the icon, the human features and creaturely dress were vehicles of the transcendent. As we approach the reformation period there appears a movement towards naturalistic portrayal which was to destroy the capacity of painting to be symbolic of the eternal. In Giotto and others there began a concern to show nature and man as they appeared in themselves and so to eliminate the symbolic devices which had previously dominated painting. Not surprisingly, Catholicism's recovery of symbolism was accompanied by the mystical art of El Greco. Protestantism, on the other hand, was ultimately left with the artistic reconstructions of the man Jesus in paintings which often said much about the human plight but little about the divine answer. Art itself finally rejected the pursuit of the natural and engaged in a violent search for renewed symbolism. It is perhaps noteworthy in the present context that renewal has been sought by many in the rediscovery of the artistic activity of mythological and symbolic man as preserved from ancient times and in archaic societies.[1]

The Renaissance was in many respects a rediscovery of Greek humanism. Nevertheless, the revival of interest in classical Greece did not lead to a recovery of the idea of the universe as an ensouled, intelligent organism. Rather it had as its father the later Greek division between mind and body and as its mother the exaggerated transcendentalism of the new theology. God was therefore conceived as extra-cosmic mind imposing his will upon the world. The model of the anthropomorphic organism had little life left in it. At the beginning of the seventeenth century Francis Bacon was still speaking of a magnet being drawn upwards by a piece of iron as 'forsaking its natural affection' for the earth, but this was merely a relic in word patterns of an imagery which had ceased to be symbolically powerful. The natural world of the new age needed a new model in which to express the nature of a desacralized world. This was found with the invention of the clock.

THE MECHANISTIC MODEL

The mechanistic model had been introduced in ancient Greece by Anaximenes, but it was given little attention until the sixteenth century. By that time the printing-press, the windmill and the pump had been invented. The machine age had dawned. Because machines came to play such a large part in the lives of men, it was inevitable that they should furnish a model for cosmological speculation. Galileo Galilei linked two interests with significant results. He became interested in the swinging lamp in the cathedral of Pisa and noted that each swing occupied the same period of time no matter how long the pendulum might be. He also discovered that objects of different weights fell at the same rate by dropping them from Pisa's leaning tower. To this interest, which was to produce the pendulum clock, Galileo added another. He made a telescope and observed the heavens, applying to his observations his growing awareness of mechanics. Galileo had moved in a direction of thought which was to see the universe as a vast mechanism, a universe which seemed to be complete in itself.

The work of Galileo was furthered by Isaac Newton, for whom nature was an intricate law-abiding machine and predictable in every detail. Newton held that this mechanism was the work of an intelligent and purposeful mind which was exterior to it. God was for Newton, therefore, an artisan and a maintenance mechanic who adjusted the system from time to time. These adjustments seemed necessary because

I*

Newton had not found any other satisfactory explanation for certain phenomena.

Pierre Laplace was able to eliminate any necessity for a divine mechanic. For him creation was a self-regulating mechanism. The mechanistic model had led, as was inevitable, to a denial of deity. The adoption of the model in the first place had been possible by holding that God was totally outside the mechanism. This meant, then, that the universe could be examined without reference to God, that is, without reference to any subjective dimension of reality. God thus ceased for Laplace to be a necessary hypothesis. Newton had laid the foundation for this denial by positing a God who was no more than a lord of the gaps in his knowledge. The gaps steadily disappeared, the mechanism seen as completely autonomous and all subjectivity, including God, removed from the universe.

In view of the tragic existential consequences of the adoption of the model it is necessary to see clearly why it was so readily adopted. J. S. Haldane gives us a sound scientific reason for the replacement of the organic model by the mechanical. He wrote that vitalism 'was useless as a means of explaining phenomena or suggesting definite paths of investigation, and was even blocking further progress. The mechanistic theory, on the other hand, suggested at every point clear and intelligible working hypotheses for further investigation.'[2] The model was widely adopted because it was fundamentally simple, yet could enable men to describe and anticipate events which could be calculated mathematically. Above all it enabled man both mentally and practically to manipulate the world in which he lived. He discovered that if he treated the world as a mechanism, then he himself could take over the role of God and become himself the great designer.

The mechanistic theory was used first in astronomy and physics. The new tool enabled these sciences to become so successful, however, that it was but a short time before it was taken over by those working in other fields of study.

The application of the machine model to biology was largely

the work of the nineteenth century. The distinctive qualities
of life seemed to make the analogy inappropriate at first, but
this hesitation to explain the phenomenon of life in terms of
something which lacked this quality was eventually overcome.
Biology was then successfully subordinated to physics and
chemistry. An even more unpromising field for the application
of the model was in the study of human society and development. The age of science, however, was not prepared to leave
any area of study outside the model's còmpetence and so the
new discipline of sociology was created. This was achieved
when Spencer, Hobbes, Rousseau and Comte found ways of
applying the machine model to the form and development of
social structures. Auguste Comte significantly described the
new science as 'social physics'. Finally the model was applied
in an assault on the citadel of subjectivity, the human mind.
As this, too, became an object of scientific description, the
freedom man experienced existentially disappeared in a
language of conditioning, repression and obsession. Descartes
and Freud were so successful in turning the self into an object
that man became 'the ghost in the machine'. The application
of the machine model to the study of man was eventually
carried to its inevitable conclusion in the science of cyber-
netics which makes a comparative study between man and
such machines as the electronic brain. The computer is placed
alongside the human mind which conceived and created it
and a comparison made which no longer seems strange. A
man's memory can now be thought of as being like the
computer's store of information, his intellect like the arithmetic
unit which manipulates a store of facts and his will merely
analogous to the control unit which supervises the operation
of the machine.

THE MECHANISTIC MODEL AND
RELIGIOUS LANGUAGE

No analogy developed into a control model has had such
a disastrous effect upon religion as that of the machine. Its

use led (as we have seen) not only to the elimination of God but also to a denial of any real subjective existence in man. It is the most outstanding example of an observer model, and as such leaves no room for a man's personal involvement either with the universe at large or, logically at least, with his fellow men. It embodies, therefore, a total negation of all that for which religion stands and in the period when it was most used created that diametrical opposition between science and religion from which we are only now beginning to recover.

The inherent power of the model to destroy religious faith and erode religious language has not always been recognized. Sometimes theologians have turned a blind eye to the presence, from the religious point of view, of overwhelming negative characteristics in the model in order to attempt a dialogue with science in its own language. Others have been genuinely impressed by the model and felt it could be safely used when supported by other genuine religious models. In their day William Paley and Joseph Butler wrote works based on the use of the model which became for a time textbooks of Christian apologetics. They have been abandoned now, however, because it is clear that even if they had been successful they would only have succeeded in retaining the clockmaker-deity of Galileo which has little relevance for religious insight. Nevertheless, the vision of the world as a great machine has continued to have its effect upon the theological language of philosophers and scientists. Collingwood, for example, referred to God as the 'architect or engineer' of the universe[3] and Sir James Jeans is well known for his description of God as the Great Mathematician. Such language, however, could even less than the mind–body model provide a basis for religious life even if, as Alan Richardson remarks, the marvel of the cosmic machine must always raise the question of its creator.

The assessment of the symbolic importance of the model depends, however, not on the logical adequacy of theological formulations based upon it but on the loss and gain with regard to man's subjective appropriation of meaning in the universe.

Hume expressed the new model with an admiration bordering on religious intensity. 'Look round the world: contemplate the whole and every part of it: you will find it to be nothing but one great machine, subdivided into an infinite number of lesser machines, which again admit of subdivisions, to a degree beyond what human senses and faculties can trace and explain. All these various machines, and even their most minute parts, are adjusted to each other with an accuracy, which ravishes into admiration all men, who have ever contemplated them.'[4] There is in such a description a hint of that wonder with which the Hebrew psalmists gazed at the regularity of the heavens. It was therefore possible for the machine to become evocative for man and to raise his spirit.

On the other hand it was capable of attaining a sinister significance. Carlyle, for example, wrote that the world had come to be regarded 'as an old eight-day clock made many thousand years ago, and still ticking on, but dead as brass which the maker at most sat looking at, in a distant, singular, and now plainly incredible manner'.[5] For Carlyle man had placed himself in the existential dilemma of being a caring self in a metallic and uncaring universe. This he had achieved by the simple expedient of choosing a particular analogy which he allowed to dominate his whole attitude toward the world and his own life. Strangely, however, the complex of ideas surrounding the use of the machine model suggests a revival of certain basic human experiences which were once captured in mythological terms. This may indicate that whatever changes take place in man's intellectual development, he is unable to escape those fundamental human intuitions which originally gave birth to the symbolic formulations of myth.

Alongside the model of the machine there grew up the idea of a law of nature inherent in things which reminds one forcibly of the Egyptian concept of *Ma'at* and the Indian idea of *Rita*. Both expressed man's awareness of order in the cosmos. Although the language of science operated with a different terminology, the law of nature was at one time credited with exactly the same kind of ontological reality which once made of it a god in the ancient world. As in the age of myth, the symbolic significance of the universal law was ambivalent. On the one hand, it created a sense of well-being, while on the other it promoted a feeling of disquiet, of being gripped by forces acting in a quite impersonal manner. This ambivalence is hardly surprising. It is a repetition of the experience which led to the Greek of ancient times being both grateful for the security which a doctrine of fate offered and also afraid of the irreversible inevitability in which man was swallowed up. In the despair of modern man as he faces the world perhaps the latter reaction has been predominant, and the mechanistic model may have reincarnated the more disagreeable aspects of that thinking which created the concept of karma in Hinduism and of a fate determined by the heavenly powers in astrology.

The mechanistic model created a deistic concept of an original clockwinder who has no further contact with the world. A similar idea had once been expressed by saying that the creator, High God, had gone far away. The later absence of any God hypothesis, moreover, reminds one of the fact that for all practical purposes the existence of a Brahma or Shang-Ti was often forgotten.

The tragedy inherent in the use of the model, however, was not so much in the removal theoretically or practically of the High God himself but in the fact that it made it impossible to recognize any of his accommodations. The model taught that the world is one of objects. It eliminated the animism which was a basis for perceptions of confrontation with the Thou of the universe in the subjective significance of man's cosmic environment. Because purposefulness, either human or cosmic was ruled out, man was unable to encounter the universe as one in which like meets like. He was turned into a spectator of that which was alien to himself.

It is not surprising that there should have been a revolt against the model both in religion and outside it. Teilhard de Chardin represents a typical religious reaction to the treatment of man in mechanistic theory. In his book on *Man's Place in Nature*,[6] for example, he objects to the dismissal of man's consciousness as an epiphenomenon. This device which is used when something does not fit into the prevailing analogy is compared by de Chardin with the way in which radium was treated because the physicists at first did not have a place for it in the system. Existentialism in the twentieth-century has been a massive protest against the dehumanization of man by the machine, whether in the form of science, politics, morals or theology.

Even the apparently cold reason of science, therefore, has important symbolic dimensions. The current philosophical rejection of the mechanistic model perhaps reflects, not merely a recognition of its intellectual inadequacy in physics, biology and psychology, but also its emotional inadequacy as a controlling view. In practice, however, it is still maintained, especially by the younger sciences of psychology and sociology, because without a model of some kind, they could not be sciences and no other model has yet appeared to be currently respectable.

NOTES

1 See A. C. Bridge, *Images of God*, Hodder and Stoughton 1960; E. Newton and W. Neill, *The Christian Faith in Art*, Hodder and Stoughton 1966.

2 J. S. Haldane, *Life and Mechanism*, quoted by A. S. Pringle-Pattison, *The Idea of God*, Clarendon Press 1917, p. 71.

3 R. G. Collingwood, *The Idea of Nature*, p. 32.

4 D. Hume, *Dialogues concerning Natural Religion*, Part II, quoted in: N. Smart (ed.), *Historical Selections in the Philosophy of Religion*, SCM Press 1962, p. 207.

5 *Sartor Resartus*, Book 3, ch. 3.

6 P. Teilhard de Chardin, *Man's Place in Nature*, Collins 1966, pp. 17 f.

16 The Contemporary Crisis

THE COLLAPSE OF SYMBOLISM

AT THE PRESENT time we are undergoing a major crisis in
the development of symbolic language. A change has taken
place in our time such that the language in which man's
perception of the sacred was previously couched has become
for many people impossible to understand. With the loss of
such understanding there has been inevitably a loss for many
people of the faith and meaning which it expressed.

We have already seen some of the causes for this. Mythological culture ceased to have all-embracing power after
the axial age. The classic religions demythologized. Myth was
transformed by the Hebrews into history and by the Greeks
into philosophy. It continued to exercise a potent influence
at the popular level but lost its support among the leaders of
intellectual life.

Protestant iconoclasm and the revival of Greek humanism
reasserted the secularization of the classic religions. This was
followed by the use of a mechanistic model which turned a
living cosmos into a dead machine. The mechanistic theory
is now rejected as a piece of discredited ontology, but its
symbolic power remains so that the universe is still a thing to
be used and manipulated. Man remains in the metallic world
created by a demythologized imagination. He struggles
with the loss of metaphysical speculation and tries to construct
a purely functional philosophy. His real difficulty, however,
is that he cannot now find an adequate and self-authenticating
symbol. He lacks a picture which will enable him to participate

in the world and must remain a mere observer of its detached machinations.

In consequence man has been overtaken by the death of God. This has taken place because the angels have been destroyed. If we remember that an angel is a communicating sign, something which has the power to become symbolic of the sacred, we see how in the modern period the citadel of God was first attacked by skirmishes in which the angelic guardians of the ultimate disclosures were eliminated.

The height of symbolic power is epitomized by the ability of men to attribute a multitude of names to the sacred. Polyonymous deity indicates that there are many ways in which the divine may be known. Isis was virtually everything in man's world when she could be given ten thousand names. Under monotheism the equivalent polyphony was the choir of angels. When this polyphony is silenced, the avenues to knowledge of God have been narrowed. Monotheism has usually been regarded as the high-spot in the history of religious development because it suggests the unity of the cosmos which the rationalizing mind requires. It is possible, however, to see it in another way as the point at which little is known of God. To name is to have knowledge. To name God is to have angelic knowledge. To have only one name for God suggests the absence of the complementary images which symbolic language requires in order to speak of that which is ultimately beyond all language. When the angels have been silenced, there are no communicators even of partial divine knowledge.

The death of the angels took place in western thought when neither nature nor history any longer spoke of transcendent meaning to man. The heirs of Protestant iconoclasm have reflected the predicament of modern man and imported it into theology. In several movements of modern theology, neo-orthodoxy, existentialism and linguistic theology in particular, the death of the angels has been declared. God has been said to be incognito in nature and history. Consequently the immanence of the sacred has been denied in order to guarantee its transcendence. As William Hamilton has pointed out, however, it is but a short step from an absent God to none at all.[1] The natural result of the death of the angels is the death of God himself. The God about whom Rudolf Bultmann could say nothing must become the one who is not there in Paul van Buren.

This tragic development could not have taken place unless the symbolic language of religion had first been rendered mute. This has come about through the literalization of symbols.

Symbolic language is created out of immediate experience and attempts to preserve that experience for future ages. Without a constant renewal through present experience, however, symbols become signs, ritual turns into magic and models are transformed into cosmology.

The prophets of the Old Testament had to attack a literal understanding of the presence of God in the temple at Jerusalem because many had lost their understanding of the symbolic centre.[2] The symbolic words of Jesus were frequently taken in a literal manner so that the power of his message was lost. The disciples imagine that they are free from the leaven of the Pharisees because they have no bread in the boat,[3] Nicodemus wonders how a man can re-enter his mother's womb to be born again,[4] and the woman of Samaria can only remark that the Lord has no bucket when offered the water of life.[5] The Roman empire became nominally Christian under the Emperor Constantine, but the imperial grasp of Christian truth appeared doubtful when he forbade the branding of a man upon his face because he was made in the image of God. In the history of Christian thought, the symbolic models of religion have frequently been turned into the theories of theology so that perceptive men like Thomas Carlyle were unable to stomach a doctrine of atonement which appeared to be in direct opposition to the moral sense which Christianity itself had done so much to encourage.

In the ancient world a literal understanding created the concept of magical ritual because the loss of symbolic meaning meant that everything had to be done in accordance with texts which had become collections of esoteric signs. In the modern world, however, it has often led to scientific allegorization. Those who have kept the scriptures in which the symbols of the past were enshrined have attempted to defend them by making them consonant with current scientific theory. This has, of course, been going on for centuries. The Aristotelian-Ptolemaic theory of the universe was read back into scripture during the Middle Ages. In an even more self-consciously scientific age it has been seen necessary by some to harmonize evolutionary theory with the order of events in Genesis. The location of the garden of Eden has been discussed and the humour and wisdom of the Book of Jonah lost in debate about the capacity of a whale's stomach. Such a procedure merely makes the Christian a champion of an outdated cosmology and a superstitious ritual neither of which were present in the creative symbolism of faith.

THE MYTHOLOGY OF MODERN MAN

While the misplaced apologetics of literalism have attempted to defend historical faith, modern man has been busy recovering mythology for himself. The collapse of the great religions in the west has thrown man back upon his own resources which produce a mythological outlook just as they did once in the ancient past.

It may seem strange to suggest that there is a recovery of mythology in modern Europe because there can be little doubt that most men would hardly recognize themselves as myth-makers. Equally, however, we must grant that the creators of the ancient myths were probably quite unaware of what they were doing. Modern man generally believes that he is merely facing and stating the facts but equally it would seem ancient man thought he was doing the same.

Mircea Eliade finds that the archetypal intuitions of man are never discarded but are repeated in numerous activities.[6] He points out that comics, films and plays constantly reiterate mythic themes. In view of the irrational emotions raised by sport at the present time, one must wonder whether athletic contests do not sometimes provide a substitute for the mythological drama of the cosmic battle in which the enemy must be overcome. The carrying off of a square of turf which marked the penalty spot on a football ground is certainly reminiscent of Naaman filling bags with Israelite soil to take back to Syria.[7]

Carlyle left the established church to find new symbols in nature. His century appears, in fact, to have rediscovered a crude nature mythology. The eighteenth and nineteenth centuries hypostatized nature first as a benevolent being and later as destructive carnality. The poet Wordsworth represented the new romantic feeling for nature and Tennyson the shock experienced on the rediscovery of nature 'red in tooth and claw'. Men had recovered an awareness of nature as both the benevolent deity who made the landscaped gardens of England possible and the black, devouring Kali who dripped with the blood of the slain. Once again the principle of creativity which was found exemplified by man at his best was opposed by the forces of destruction. The stage was set for a new myth in which an anthropomorphic deity confronted the theriomorphic monsters of the chaotic deep.

In the popular idea of evolution, which has little to do with scientific theory, the primal man of mythological thought is reborn as the creature who rises against tremendous odds from the primeval swamps and progresses steadily upwards towards a day in which he will rule the cosmos by his technological prowess. As with all myths it is produced mostly by imaginative selection of data and is designed to satisfy the emotional needs of man rather than his intellect. It constitutes an impressive unity and has sufficient connection with the facts to be confused with them. It can, therefore, be taught as fact to children and constitute their initiation into modern society. But it speaks with an authority which is independent of research, for in essence it is a recovery of an ancient mythological idea.[8]

In this modern nature mythology we can see that there has been an imaginative blending of a mythological idea with a historical and eschatological sense. In some developments of modern mythology it is possible to see how other mythic themes have been historicized.

The collapse and renewal of cultural symbolism has always been accompanied by the fall and rise of sacral society. Man has constantly embodied his myths in his social structures. To this rule modern man is no exception. We begin to suspect a kind of social mythology when we consider the potential totemic element in such ideas as the fatherland, Britannia and Uncle Sam and when we find political programmes conveyed more through parades and flags than by exposition. That such motifs may underlie these apparently peripheral phenomena becomes even more obvious when we note the way in which they often accompany processes which are more clearly mythological.

Marxist communism has frequently been seen to manifest a historicized and secularized mythology. It took its historical orientation from Judaism and secularized it even further, replacing the idea of a personal, living God of history with an impersonal and inevitable dialectic. In consequence it appears as a radical opponent of religion in the modern world. Yet there remain powerful mythological ideas within it. The golden age must be brought in by a final struggle between the forces of good and evil. Self-sacrifice is called for by the just man who alone can bring in the redeeming situation.

The twentieth century has also witnessed a deliberate attempt to create a folk mythology in the national socialism of Germany. The heritage of biblical, Roman and Greek culture was rejected and in its place an attempt made to find a distinctive and exclusive past in Indo-European mythology for the master race. It took to itself a saviour in the Führer, who was seen as a typological improvement on Christ and exalted the folk-spirit to divine status, reviving ancestor worship in the cult of heroes.[9]

Other manifestations of similar mythic ideas have been found throughout the world. Sometimes they have been transparent as in the cases cited or in the revival of folk mythologies in Japan and the emergent nations of Africa. In other cases they are disguised in nationalistic movements which like to think of themselves as secular and rational.

PROSPECTS FOR THE FUTURE

Modern man has retained a mythology of sorts, but it would hardly be a proper use of words to proclaim that he has achieved a mythological religion, for there is lacking an essential ingredient of religious perception. The common evolutionary myth has retained the Hebraic–Christian sense of history but it leaves man alone in his subjectivity. It is precisely this, as Sartre saw, which makes the difference between a religious and a non-religious appropriation of the universe. Sartre confessed that for himself history was a dialogue between man and an absent God. Religion has always maintained, however, that there is a personal dimension to nature and the Hebraic–Christian tradition that there is a God creative of historical contingency.

Faced with this situation a number of alternatives are open to modern man. He can with Sartre sadly regret the loss of the sacred other with whom he can communicate in the ongoing process of history. He may find the symbolism of the past to be without any power to elevate his spirit beyond the confines of his own finitude. In such a situation he can only cry out with anguish with Nietzsche's madman that the churches are merely mausoleums of the dead god.

Others have found that the symbolic language of a past age no longer speaks with authority but have wished to preserve something from the wreck. Bultmann argued that the mythological language of scripture was a hindrance to modern man and should be removed.[10] This demythologization was then to be followed by an existentialization based on the work of Martin Heidegger. This proposal, however, appears to have been based upon a misunderstanding of the nature of symbolic language. Bultmann's demythologization is only necessary because he has taken myth in a literal sense and so as descriptive cosmology or primitive science. The fundamental error is apparent in that he thought it possible to translate symbols into existentialist ideology. The symbols had clearly become for him signs and so he thought it possible to get rid of them by a process of de-allegorization.

It must be noted, however, that one cannot de-allegorize symbol systems because they are not made of signs. As Frankfort points out with regard to the anthromorphisms of Egypt, they cannot be understood if taken as allegories and we cannot take the meaning out of them and then discard them without misusing them. They had been arrived at intuitively and not intellectually and hence they were inseparable from that which they symbolized.[11] Bultmann has attempted with New Testament symbolism what Frankfort would not allow of Egyptian mythological symbolism. In translating the symbols into the language of Heidegger's philosophy, Bultmann certainly recovered for the twentieth century some of the importance and meaning of the New Testament message but, if it is remembered that symbols are multivalent, it will be appreciated that this process necessarily ends by destroying all but that meaning which has been abstracted. The symbols of the New Testament were not merely existential. They worked on that level because they also spoke of a reality in nature and in history.

Bultmann claimed that he intended to go back to the beginnings, to recover the original simplicity of the original faith. Others have also found the answer to the modern predicament by a return to the past. Such people, however, must be divided into two types.

The first type is found among the secularizers of modern theology. These people choose like Bultmann to go back to a point at which a new revelation had swept away the previous patterns of symbolic faith. Thus Dietrich Bonhoeffer, the father of much secularizing theology, confessed that he had been radically influenced by the Old Testament and betrays some uneasiness in handling the New in his last letters.[12] The reason for this is simply that the Old Testament reflects a smashing of icons and an absence of otherworldly symbolism which was concordant with his own loss of symbols. In a state of mind which finds knowledge of the transcendent difficult there is a natural affinity with any point in the past at which the symbol structure had collapsed. The appeal has the advantage of appearing to be a return to the pristine purity of the beginnings.

The second type is quite different. They wish to return to a point in the past when symbolic language flourished. Bultmann was much upset when his teacher, Heidegger, determined to go back to the mythological past for present guidance. Heidegger deliberately intended in his later writings to take a 'step backwards' behind the categories of science and the conceptualizing metaphysics in vogue after Plato to recover the primitive intuition which preceded them both. He wished to indulge in primal thinking, in the wordless insight which can only be hinted at in the symbols of the poets. He looked in particular to the gods and heroes of Hellenic mythology who for him gave voice to being poised over the abyss of nothingness. There he felt the secrets of the universe were disclosed, man's subjectivity safeguarded and the world's numinosity apparent.

The return to mythological voices is not, however, the prerogative of the philosopher alone. Others have abandoned the secondary language of metaphysics, science and technology to attempt a recovery of first-order language born out of immediate experience. Mircea Eliade exemplifies the historian of religions who finds that ancient man has something to teach the modern world, an ability to formulate the impingement of that which man calls the sacred on himself. Many artists have gone back to the inspiration offered by primitive symbolic art after the collapse of the humanistic idealism of the western world. In religion, many in the western world have taken themselves backwards by a move into the orient, particularly to Buddhism and Hinduism. In the emergent nations, the step backwards into indigenous mythological thought is not entirely the result of the desire to assert distinctive nationalism but is probably also the result of a hollowness in the symbolic structure given or imposed by the western world.

For those within a living religious tradition there is no need to go back at all. Intellectual difficulties may abound but cause little concern because experience of symbolic power makes them a peripheral concern. For such as these there is a rich store of symbolic language and ritual on which they can call in periods of religious strain. In a comparable period of intellectual difficulty and scepticism, the Tractarian movement in the Church of England during the nineteenth century answered the threat of religious dissolution by a reappropriation of the classic past and established itself as a direct continuation of that past by a participation in an apostolic succession. In the twentieth century many Lutherans have found their personal answer by a recovery of Luther's language and perspective. The danger inherent in this procedure is, of course, that it tends to create esoteric groups whose symbols cannot be understood by the uninitiated. When the church becomes a preserver of obscure symbols, it tends to appear as an institution doggedly maintaining irrelevancies.

Finally there are those who would attempt to preserve the old while moving forward and capturing the new. For such men there can be little spectacular glamour, for it involves the building up of a great synthesis out of the dialectic of history. It has to work on many fronts at the same time. First of all there must be the sound learning which retains the insight embedded in past symbols with all the sweat of literary and historical research. Secondly it involves a tenacious grappling with the problems of metaphysics in an age when many find it easier to dismiss them, for only in this way can there be any provision of an ontological basis for religious experience and language. Without ontology the words of the spirit have to speak only to itself. Finally, and most important, such learning, tenacity and breadth of vision must be combined with the kind of experience which brings old symbols into creative life and is open to the impingement of new symbolic formulations. There can be no new song until the angelic voices have first been heard to sing it in heaven. Only then can the theological task be given the depth out of which a new hymn of the universe may come.

NOTES

1 Hamilton, *The New Essence of Christianity*, Darton, Longman and Todd 1961, p. 53.
2 I Kings 8; Isa. 1; 3; 5; 29; Jer. 7.4; Micah 3.
3 Mark 8.16.
4 John 3.4.
5 John 4.11.
6 See M. Eliade, *Myth and Reality*, pp. 184 ff.; *Patterns of Comparative Religion*, pp. 431 f.
7 II Kings 5.17.
8 See C. S. Lewis, 'The Funeral of a Great Myth', *Christian Reflections*, Geoffrey Bles 1967.
9 See M. Eliade, *Myth and Reality*, pp. 183 f.
10 R. Bultmann, *Jesus Christ and Mythology*, SCM Press 1960.
11 H. Frankfort, *Ancient Egyptian Religion*, p. 28.
12 *Letters and Papers from Prison*, pp. 103 f., 108, 156, 185 f., 205; cf. Harvey Cox, *The Secular City*, SCM Press 1965.

Index